D1071207

Intimations of Difference

Judaic Traditions in Literature, Music, and Art
Ken Frieden, *Series Editor*

Intimations of Difference

Dvora Baron in the
Modern Hebrew Renaissance

Sheila E. Jelen

SYRACUSE UNIVERSITY PRESS

A part of chapter 4 of this book was previously published in *Prooftexts* 23, no. 2 (spring 2003): 182–209. Reprinted by permission. An excerpt from chapter 1, "All Writers Are Jews, All Jews Are Men: The Autobiographical Imperative," will also be published in *Hebrew, Gender, and Modernity: Critical Responses to Dvora Baron's Fiction* (College Park: University Press of Maryland, 2006).

The photographs of Baron and her family that have been published here were provided by Gnazim Archive in Ramat Gan, Israel. The Alter Kacyzne photographs, included in chapter 3 and featured on the book's cover, are from the archives of the YIVO Institute for Jewish Research, New York.

The paper used in this publication meets the minimum requirements of American National Standard for Information Sciences—Permanence of Paper for Printed Library Materials, ANSI Z-1984.∞™

For a listing of books published and distributed by Syracuse University Press, visit our Web site at SyracuseUniversityPress.syr.edu.

ISBN-13: 978-0-8156-3130-9
ISBN-10: 0-8156-3130-8

Library of Congress Cataloging-in-Publication Data
Jelen, Sheila E.
Intimations of difference : Dvora Baron in the modern Hebrew renaissance / Sheila E. Jelen.—1st ed.
p. cm.—(Judaic traditions in literature, music, and art)
Includes bibliographical references and index.
ISBN-13: 978-0-8156-3130-9 (hardcover : alk. paper)
ISBN-10: 0-8156-3130-8 (hardcover : alk. paper)
1. Baron, Devorah, 1887–1956—Criticism and interpretation. 2. Baron, Devorah, 1887–1956. 3. Authors, Israeli—Biography. I. Title.
PJ5053.B34Z75 2006
892.4'35—dc22   2006037304

In loving memory of
Mason Irving Himelhoch (1932–2004)
With gratitude

Sheila E. Jelen is assistant professor of English and Jewish studies at the University of Maryland, College Park. She has studied and taught Hebrew literature, modern Jewish literature, and the literature of the Holocaust and is author of a variety of essays and reviews that have appeared in publications such as *Tikkun, Prooftexts, Hebrew Studies, AJS Review,* and the *Jewish Quarterly Review.*

Contents

Illustrations

Acknowledgments

THIS BOOK COULD NOT have been written without the assistance—
intellectual, emotional, and practical—of numerous people in the
United States and Israel. It began as a seminar paper for Robert Alter, my
adviser and teacher at the University of California, Berkeley. That early
work blossomed and grew under the loving and rigorous scrutiny of
other teachers, such as Chana Kronfeld (also of the University of California, Berkeley) and Naomi Seidman of the Graduate Theological Union.
Chana's and Naomi's translations of Baron inspired me, early on, to pursue this topic, and rendered them particularly able close readers and critics of my work. Naomi also read an earlier version of this completed
manuscript and, as always, provided concise and brilliant comments. My
colleagues at Berkeley—Yael Chaver, Todd Hasak-Lowy, Matthew Hoff-
man, Shachar Pinsker, Miryam Segal, David Shneer, and Hamutal
Tsamir—all saw early versions of the nucleus of this book. Although we
are now scattered, the intellectual and personal bonds cultivated
through our common discourse sustain my work to this day. Shachar
Pinsker, in particular, shares my fascination with Baron, and together we
have collaborated on a collection of essays about her work and translations of her stories.

I am grateful to the Graduate Research Board at the University of
Maryland for funding me to do research in Israel during the summer of
2003. Dvora Stavi and Hedva Rokhel and all of the support staff at the
Gnazim Archive in Ramat Gan were particularly helpful to me as I
sought out Dvora Baron's correspondence and photographs that summer, and to the present day. While in Israel, I found a quiet, peaceful
place to work in the Holocaust Division at the Tel Aviv University library,

and I thank the staff there who allowed me in first thing every morning and locked up after me every afternoon.

Nurit Govrin of the Department of Hebrew Literature at Tel Aviv University, and Baron's official biographer, has been immeasurably helpful to me throughout my writing of this book. She has discussed my work freely, giving guidance where necessary, and has even opened her home to me. Her book on Baron, *The First Half: Dvora Baron, Her Life and Work,* has accompanied me on my own journey through Baron's work and has proved essential to my understanding of Baron's social and literary context. Without it, I could not have written my own book. Tova Cohen of Bar-Ilan University has also given generously of her time to me, reading parts of my work and discussing Baron through e-mail correspondence.

Much of this book was written when I was a fellow at the Center for Advanced Jewish Studies (CAJS) at the University of Pennsylvania. David Ruderman, the center's director; Sheila Allen, the center's administrator; and Judith Leifer and Seth Jerichower, the librarians with whom I had the most contact, facilitated my work tremendously. Other fellows who attended a presentation of my work and participated in ongoing intellectual dialogues with me—Kathryn Hellerstein, Nurit Gertz, Marc Kaplan, Alan Mintz, Anita Norich, Alan Rosen, Anita Shapira, and Deborah Starr—served throughout my writing at the CAJS as teachers and friends. I am especially grateful to Anita Norich, who guided me toward the study of modern Jewish literature in my undergraduate days at the University of Michigan, and Alan Mintz, who read a complete version of this book before publication, offering insightful and valuable comments on the direction I took.

The English Department at the University of Maryland and the Joseph and Rebecca Meyerhoff Center for Jewish Studies at the University of Maryland have supported the writing of this book, both through paid leaves and through financial assistance for editing. My English colleagues Adele Berlin and Theresa Coletti both read early versions of this manuscript and gave me much needed emotional and departmental support as the project progressed. My departmental chairs, Hayim Lapin and Charles Caramello, have both graciously bolstered my ego (as well as

my salary) and protected my time as a junior faculty member throughout the writing of this book. Eliyana Adler, Bernard Cooperman, Einat
Gonen, Max Grossman, Miriam Issacs, Yelena Luckert, Chip Mannekin,
Marsha Rozenblit, and Eric Zakim—my Jewish studies colleagues—have
all provided a comfortable and productive home for me at the Center for
Jewish Studies. Eliyana Adler, in particular, has engaged in many conversations with me about Dvora Baron, in addition to reading versions of
several chapters of this book in the course of their composition. She as a
historian of Jewish women's education in czarist Russia and I as a scholar
of modern Hebrew literature have come to Dvora Baron with different
expectations and different needs. Yet we have learned an immeasurable
amount from each other methodologically and are in the midst of a col-
laboration on the basis of our mutual interest in Baron.

Ken Frieden, the series editor of Judaic Traditions in Literature,
Music, and Art; Ellen Goodman, the assistant to the director at Syracuse
University Press; and John Fruehwirth, the press's managing editor, have
facilitated the process of bringing this book to light with much warmth
and skill. I am grateful to them for making me feel I can do it all over
again one day. Michele Alperin helped me at the very end of my submis-
sion process in an infinite variety of ways. Her skill as a copy editor is un-
surpassed.

My deepest gratitude goes to my family. My mother, Syma Ralston,
despite her distaste for nonfiction, has been editing this book, in all its
different manifestations, for years. My father, Henry Jelen, has always
supported all my endeavors with much pride and some mystification.
My brother and sister, Dov and Leana Jelen, have both given me uncon-
ditional love despite the great geographic and life distances between us.
Toby Ehrlich and Gary Bement, my stepparents, have graciously supported me and my work, alongside and independent of my parents. My
parents-in-law, Anna and Mason Himelhoch, stepped in, always at the
right moment, with child care to help me through the rough times when
I didn't think my work could get done, and demonstrated their love and
commitment to me as more than just a daughter-in-law, but as a real
daughter. Mason passed away unexpectedly in 2004, before he had the
opportunity to publish his own book—the subject of many conversa-

tions between us. It is to him that I dedicate this book. Renee Himelhoch, my sister-in-law, through her logistical genius and her selfless generosity, has enabled my family to spend time in Israel, and has run errands to bookstores throughout Jerusalem and Tel Aviv during my years of research and writing. Ilana Blumberg, my friend and near family member, despite a new marriage, new motherhood, and a new job, has taken the time, over the years, to read my drafts.

My husband, Seth Himelhoch, encouraged me to write about what I love when I was not sure in which direction to go. He has been a real helpmate and intellectual partner, despite his own demanding academic research and clinical schedule. Without him I would not have had the stamina or the will to balance my career with my family life. Finally, my children, Malka, Nava, and Akiva are my past, my present, and my future. I am grateful to them for everything they are and look forward to everything they will become.

A Critical Preface

"FRADEL" (1949) IS THE STORY of a young woman in an unnamed eastern European shtetl who struggles to maintain her dignity and sanity in the face of an unhappy marriage and an oblivious community. After countless disappointments and immeasurable grief, after the death of an infant son and her loss of faith in the potential for love from her husband, Fradel quietly and firmly demands a divorce; her husband, surprisingly, complies. At the story's conclusion, Fradel marries a playmate of her youth with whom she has long shared a mutual affection, and bears another son. The unhappy marriage that precedes the happy one and the dead son who precedes the live one represent the "false starts" or the alternative narratives that make "Fradel" far more than a typical fairy tale on a linear path toward a "happy ending." It is, rather, a story about the possibility of happy endings for a Jewish woman in a nineteenth-century shtetl within the confines of proscribed tradition. Fradel's redemption, after all, is not contingent on her escape from marriage altogether. Rather, it occurs in the form of another marriage and the grace of a son's birth. In fact, the critical event that precipitates Fradel's divorce is her punctilious observance of Jewish marital laws and her husband's apathy toward them. "Fradel" provides a purportedly ethnographic glimpse into an unforgiving world of traditional values even as it insists, in its (almost too) hastily executed happy ending, on its fictional identity.

When first reading Dvora Baron's work, I was powerfully drawn by the voice of "Fradel" 's narrator who asserts, about midway through the story:

> In that place, in those days, they did not believe in shielding the eyes of a child by throwing an elegant prayer shawl over life's nakedness. And so,

along with the song of sun-dazzled birds and the scent of dew-drunk plants, she also absorbed impressions of daily life, bits of local color, of heartache and heart joy, which in the course of time—when they had been refined and illuminated by the light of her intellect, and experience had bound them into life stories—became for her, in the solitary nights of her wandering, a source of pleasure and comfort.[1]

Here, "Fradel" became, for me, much more than the story of the protagonist for whom it was named. It became the story of its narrator, the child grown up who looked back at her life in a world inhabited by Fradels and found expression for them in her fiction. This grown-up child, this narrator of women's lives was, when I first encountered her, conflated with the figure of Dvora Baron, the story's author. In time, of course, I came to realize that "Fradel"'s figure of the narrator/returnee, of the innocent come face-to-face with the facts of life, is as much a fictional invention as is Fradel herself. As I read more and more of Baron's work and became exposed to her gallery of female protagonists (with a few men thrown in for good measure), I was not disturbed by the fact that other women writers of Hebrew from the same period had been excluded from the literary canon of the modern Hebrew renaissance. In essence, Baron's subject matter—the nineteenth-century eastern European Jewish shtetl from a female perspective, with brief forays into major European cities and the tumult of Jaffa-Tel Aviv during the period of the second aliyah—absolutely captured the nodal points of my own sense of modern Jewish history.[2] To me, raised within a Zionist milieu by children of Holocaust survivors born en route to the United States from the steppes of Siberia and the forests of Poland, Dvora Baron's stories were totally gratifying. I saw them as restoring the voices of my loving, but traumatized, grandmothers from within their native context. For the time being, I did not miss other women's voices; those created by Dvora Baron seemed authentic and sufficient.

I grew up seeking a "lost world," like the one depicted in Mark Zborowski and Elizabeth Herzog's *Life Is with People* or Abraham Joshua Heschel's *The Earth Is the Lord's.*[3] It was in my reading, as a young college student, stories like "Fradel" that I thought I finally found an "authentic" representation of the world I so longed to understand. Later, however, in revisiting this story, I found in "Fradel" the very heart of Baron's deft juggling of her sense of responsibility as the "authentic" voice of a lost culture and her sense of herself as, first and foremost, a literary artist. The tension I came to observe between these forces led me to ask why were there no other women writers in the modern Hebrew renaissance canon of prose fiction, and what impact did Baron's singularity have on her literary output? On the one hand, did Baron sense that if she did not represent women's lives as they had been in the shtetl, no one else would? On the other hand, did Baron believe that she must declare herself a Hebrew fiction writer like other fiction writers without drawing attention to her gender and all the potential "differences"—narratological, thematic, generic—her biographical identity would imply for her readership?

I have, over time, come to hear an explicit articulation of the complex relationship between an ethnographic impulse and a fictional one in the narrator's voice in "Fradel." What follows is the passage from "Fradel" that led me, inexorably, and passionately, to write this book. First, however, a brief note about the narrative and cultural context of "Fradel." The scene that follows (the catalyst for Fradel's divorce) takes place on the night of her husband's unexpected return from an extended business trip. Fradel's aunt Chana helps Fradel make a last-minute appeal to the community rabbi that Fradel be allowed to immerse herself in the *mikvah*—the ritual bath—so she can engage in sexual relations with her husband, as legislated by Orthodox Jewish law:

> The master's carriage was brought into the yard, and the practical and efficient Aunt Chana could be seen making her way among the curious and turning toward the community house.
>
> For the woman [Fradel], who had not purified herself according to Jewish law before her husband's arrival, was forbidden to him, and so the aunt had been sent by her to the rabbi on some matter regarding her ritual immersion, and the response came that she would be permitted to immerse. And then, after the visitor had eaten a little something and rested and gone off to take care of his business, she went out, a small package in hand, to the end of the alley, where the bathhouse stood open, one of its sections heated.
>
> About this commandment, and how the daughters of Israel in the shtetls fulfilled it, it's worth writing a special section.

They, these shy women, who concealed themselves within their kitchens, would make their way, when the time came, through the alleyways to the bathhouse before the eyes of the curious, each of whom knew them by name.

The kerchief was too small to obscure their flushed, shamed faces, and the ground beneath was stiff and unforgiving and so slippery that it was easy to trip.

And behind them, had they not left a house in disorder, a goat waiting to be milked, hungry children crying for their supper, and an unperturbed husband who paid them no mind? He was a moody man, who did not pamper his household or speak softly to them, and against him the heart swelled with rage. And indeed it was not the desire for a little love-making that propelled these women, but rather, the holy duty, the inheritance of their mothers, the commandment of life itself.

And these were the women who raised clear-eyed sons, weaned them and fed them on suffering. The sons were washed not with water but in their mother's tears, and they were sated, in the absence of bread, on the sorrow of her love, which they absorbed like nectar of the gods.

There were some among these sons who were overtaken and slaughtered by violent gentiles, but there were also some among them who went out at such times with an outstretched hand and were a child and savior to their brothers, or else, with the redeemers of their homeland, prepared themselves to work the soil and provide a place to settle for the rest of their nation, who were perched wherever they were, at the edge of an abyss.

And so Fradel, after she too had taken the tortuous road described above, and then come out again after her immersion, fingernails clipped and her hair dripping wet—and there was still some light left in the day— she turned to walk along the winding path through the gardens, whose owners had already gone inside by this hour.[4]

Here the narrator acts simultaneously as an ethnographer and as an omniscient teller of Fradel's fictional story. After a brief description of Aunt Chana's intercession on Fradel's behalf in order to ensure her ability to "welcome" her long-absent husband back from his journeys, the narrator digresses with a prolonged meditation on the institution of mikvah and the situation of women who observe the laws of family purity despite the provincial, prying eyes of their community. This meditation is prefaced by the juxtaposition of "daughters of Israel" and "shtetls" ("About this commandment, and how the daughters of Israel in the shtetls fulfilled it, it's worth writing a special section"). The narrator sheds light, as it were, onto the world of all women in all *shtetlakh* throughout all time.

Although purportedly an illustration of the cultural institution being described in general terms by an "ethnographic narrator," upon closer scrutiny Fradel is distinctly not one of the women with bleating goats and crying children and an indifferent husband waiting for her at home. She is, in fact, childless (because her child has just died), and her husband is a merchant (which is why he is away on a business trip), so they probably do not keep any livestock. Finally, when she returns home after having immersed herself in the ritual bath, she finds that her husband has not waited there—indifferently or otherwise—at all. He has left home to go on another business trip without having even seen his wife. Indeed, the discrepancy between the "ethnographic" description provided by the narrator and the facts of Fradel's life provides the narrative motivation for Fradel's decision to leave her marriage. She need not stay married to a man who cannot help her maintain the life of a "typical" woman in a "typical" shtetl. Rather, she may now demand a divorce. The purportedly ethnographic tangent we read here, then, functions as the turning point of the fictional story; Fradel comes to realize that no matter how hard she tries to make her marriage "normal"—despite the disappointments that effort entails—it never will be.

"Fradel" embodies the tension that can be found throughout Baron's mature work between the author's impulse to represent a world that had, by the middle of the twentieth century, disappeared and her impulse to write fiction with no obligation toward historical ethnographic memory. Furthermore, the strain felt in the above passage between the specific and the general—between "every" Jewish woman who went to the mikvah in the shtetl and a specific Jewish woman like Fradel—is felt throughout Baron's work as she develops characters in all their material specificity who came to be understood by much of the Hebrew critical community during the twentieth century as ethnographic descriptions. Ironically, simply in her attention to detail, Baron demonstrates her aesthetic acumen and fictional artistry, but because of her subject matter and her own personal identity as a woman, her work was viewed, in many ways, as artless. Baron's position as the only canonical woman writer of the modern Hebrew renaissance exacerbated this struggle—making her a spokeswoman for women whether she liked it or not, and also necessitating her declaration of a woman author's right not to be a spokeswoman, but simply to be a writer evaluated on genderless terms. In this book, I provide an overview of Baron's literary milieu and attempt to identify her place in it as reflected by the "intimations of difference" throughout her work. As in "Fradel," Baron's "fairy-tale" declaration of fiction is rendered "different" through her ethnographic foray into the institution of the mikvah. She moves back and forth between fiction and ethnography in vital ways that help us make sense not only of the gendered politics of the modern Hebrew renaissance but of the dynamics of the modern Hebrew renaissance as a whole. But before we embark on close readings and cultural overviews, let us take a brief look at Dvora Baron herself.

Dvora Baron was born on December 4, 1887, to Rabbi Shabtai Eliezer and Sarah Baron, the rabbi and *rebbetzin* of Ouzda, a small town on the outskirts of Minsk.[5] Baron had an older sister, Hayah Rivka; an older brother, Benjamin; and two younger sisters, Tziporah and Chana. Two other children—both boys—died in infancy.[6] Benjamin introduced her to the Hebrew literature of the Jewish Enlightenment (the *Haskalah*), and her father encouraged her to study traditional Jewish texts in their original Hebrew and Aramaic.[7] Baron is known to have been an extraordinarily sensitive and bright child, frequently present at the classes offered by her father to community boys and men in their family home, which also served as the community synagogue and house of study. Legend has it that Baron was encouraged, although sitting apart from the men, to ask questions about the texts under discussion.

Baron's first Hebrew stories were published in April 1902 when she was fifteen years old, and her first Yiddish stories appeared two years later, in February 1904.[8] From 1903 until 1910 when she immigrated to Palestine, Baron moved among smaller and larger cities in the Pale of Settlement, including Minsk, Kovno, Mariampol, and Vilna, teaching, studying, and writing. Like many of the Hebrew writers of her period, she studied for entrance exams (in Mariampol) and became one of the few Jews who defied the quota placed on Jewish participation in secular establishments of higher learning. Unlike many of her colleagues, she passed her matriculation exams and was "officially" certified as a teacher. Baron's beloved father—the guiding spirit behind her commitment to the Hebrew language and the force behind her successful acquisition of the traditional textual knowledge that enabled her to become a Hebrew writer—died of tuberculosis in 1908.

When Baron emigrated, alone, to Palestine in December 1910, after having broken off her engagement to another young writer, Moshe Ben-Eliezer, she was appointed the literary editor of the important labor Zionist organ *ha-Poel ha-Tsair* (The Young Laborer) newspaper, and married its founder and chief editor, Yosef Aharonovitch.[9] Tziporah, Baron's only child, was born in January 1914. During World War I, in May 1915, Baron and her family were exiled to Alexandria, Egypt, as alien residents of Palestine. In 1919 they returned to Palestine, and shortly thereafter Baron's brother Benjamin, an army doctor, died in Russia during a typhus epidemic. Baron was, apparently, devastated by this loss since it was Benjamin who had fostered her development as a writer during her itinerant years; he convinced Baron's parents that it would be safe for her to leave home at the young age of sixteen, and the two lived together. Benjamin was Baron's protector and her mentor as well, by her account, as her best friend. Several years after Benjamin's death, in 1923, Baron and her husband left their editorial positions at *ha-Poel ha-Tsair,* and Baron began a thirty-three-year self-incarceration in her Tel Aviv apartment. Cared for by her epileptic daughter, Tziporah, throughout those years, Baron did not even leave her apartment to attend her husband's funeral in 1937. Word that her entire family remaining in Europe had been wiped out during the Holocaust reached her during those years. The murdered included her sister Chana and her mother.[10]

Although Baron tried as early as 1908 to have her work published in book form, she did not successfully do so until 1927 with the publication of her first collection, *Sipurim* (Stories). Baron's renowned Hebrew

1. Dvora Baron. *Courtesy of Gnazim Archive, Ramat Gan, Israel.*

translation of Flaubert's *Madame Bovary* appeared in 1932; until 1991, Baron's was the only unabridged translation of the novel available in Hebrew. In 1934 Baron won the prestigious Bialik Prize for her volume of short stories *Ketanot* (Trifles) (1933). She won a second prestigious Hebrew literary award, the Rupin, for her novella *le-'Et 'Ata* (For the Time Being), which was published in 1943 and treated the subject of the exile of foreign nationals from the Jewish settlements in Palestine during World War I. In 1951, Baron's most comprehensive collection of stories, titled *Parshiyot* (Tales), received broad recognition and multiple honors, including the Brenner Hebrew literary prize. Baron died in Tel Aviv in 1956.[11]

Introduction

Intimations and Imperatives—
A Biography Through the Looking Glass

THE NARRATOR OF DVORA BARON'S 1927 story "ha-Yom ha-Rishon" (The First Day) recounts the first day of her life and the disappointment of her paternal grandmother over the birth of yet another girl to the family. "My paternal grandmother, the rebbetzin of Tokhanovka, who was now visiting our house, was dissatisfied with my entry into the light of this world. Girls, she said, she already had enough of from her daughter-in-law the rebbetzin of Khmilovka and also from the other daughter-in-law, the rebbetzin of Borisovka, and she had reached her limit, she said, with these girls." Then she offers an authorial aside that purportedly describes how she feels about her grandmother's words: "It's embarrassing to relate, but the events should be written simply, exactly as they happened."[1] When an author explicitly gestures, as does Baron here, to the truth or transparency of a particular narrative, the careful reader is alerted to the inherently tenuous nature of such a claim. To what extent, then, is it appropriate to read Baron's work as an account of her life "exactly as [it] happened," and to what extent is it dangerous and blinding to read her work for hints of her biography?

On the one hand, Baron tantalizes her readers with "fictional" details that intimate biographical connections. Baron, the daughter of a rabbi, designates the narrator and main protagonist of many of her later stories a rabbi's daughter as well. She alludes to her siblings by using their names for characters that people her fiction. The spirit of Baron's sister Chana, an ardent Yiddishist killed in the Holocaust, seems to hover over Baron's

2. Chana Baron, Dvora's sister. *Courtesy of Gnazim Archive, Ramat Gan, Israel.*

works because Baron frequently uses the name for the narrator through-out her later stories. For that matter, Baron's brother Benjamin makes cameo appearances as an older brother and teacher—a simultaneously magnanimous and threatening figure. Baron, in many ways, compels critics to read her work biographically through many of her narrative choices, while at other times she entraps critics who do so. In a comical reproach to Yehudit Harari who included an essay on Dvora Baron in her 1959 lexicon of important women in the modern history of the Jewish people, Baron's daughter, Tziporah Aharonovitch, attempts to correct Harari's misapprehension, based on the birth order depicted in the family in "The First Day," that Baron was the second of two daughters and that her grandmother was devastated that she was a girl. Rather, Aharonovitch informs Harari, Baron was the third child born to a family that already included a boy. "It is important, dear woman," she scolds, "not to rely on fictional belletristic material for biographical information."[2]

Whereas biographical readings of fictional works can obscure their fictional artistry, it is equally blinding to insist that biographies and autobiographies are only those works that frame themselves as such. Other works declare themselves biographical, although not in strictly conventional, generic terms. Indeed, James Olney, in reflecting on what led him to the study of autobiography, says that in reading autobiography and fiction side by side as a student, "what I came to feel was frequently the case was that works in the one group were works of art that presented themselves as autobiographies [that is, Montaigne] while works in the other group were autobiographies that presented themselves as works of art [as in Joyce]."[3] Olney, trained to believe that autobiographies and "works of art" were mutually exclusive, wanted to eliminate the boundaries between them. Many feminist critics from the 1970s and 1980s agreed; they observed, in a positive vein, that modern biographers (and autobiographers) were attempting to reinstate the self in aesthetic culture, to build, in fact, an aesthetic culture around the self. Although this view contradicts more current feminist theory, which censures the impulse to render biographical (and thus, in their opinion, to trivialize) women's literature, it flows out of humanist trends that make the human character, male or female, a primary aesthetic concern. Later feminists were reacting to the fact that a "human being" had come to be identified exclusively as a male.

Feminist literary critics Celeste Schenck and Nancy K. Miller, attempting to create room for women in the culture of the universal human, sought a way, in the 1980s, to read women's biography and autobiography into women's works that do not explicitly declare themselves as such. Schenck, in reading women's poetry as a form of autobiography argues, like Olney, against the rigid institution of generic boundaries in considering what constitutes autobiography: "The history of genre, seemingly, has not only failed to address its own politics adequately; it also has been blind to its own gender inflection." The word "genre," she reminds us, was identified by Jacques Derrida as including, and even connoting, "gender." She goes on to outline the study of "gender generics" that first focused, in the 1980s, on the ways in which women's literature was pushed into noncanonical genres (such as the poetic epithalamium or the fictional gothic). Miller, however, warns against the wholesale classification of any literature written by women as autobiographical in her rejection of what she calls "biographical hermeneutics."[4] She recommends, instead, that critics engage in a "double reading" of autobiography with fiction. Modeling this literary practice, Miller "double reads" the work of Simone de Beauvoir, Daniel Stern (Marie d'Agoult), and George Sand (Amandine-Aurore-Lucile Dupin Dudevant), situating explicitly autobiographical texts alongside explicitly fictional texts as commentaries on one another.

Unlike the authors analyzed by Miller, Baron has no texts that she explicitly designates as autobiographical. At the same time, before rejecting the possibility of reading Baron's texts autobiographically, one must take into account Baron's frequent use of a first-person narrator who thematizes her own process of textual acquisition and literary birth, alongside the autobiographically identifiable "traces" of the father/rabbi, teacher/ brother, narrator/sister in Baron's stories. If we accept that Baron is leading us, obliquely, toward her biography, the issue becomes how to read Baron's biographical clues without falling into the trap of reading her work as autobiography. Although contemporary critical discourse has demonstrated the ways in which autobiography and fiction need not be mutually exclusive, in the case of Baron, overdetermined biographical readings have, to this day, been used to avoid studying her work seriously within the poetic paradigms both of her own literary generation and of the literary movement—modernism—with which she, along with her peers, strove to affiliate.

In this study I read Baron's fiction as a literary biography, not a life autobiography. I distinguish between the two here in order to focus on Baron's oblique presentation of herself in her fiction, through her mastery, her critique, and in some cases her rejection of the norms and assumptions of the literature of the modern Hebrew renaissance. Her work is distinctly not autobiographical insofar as it is not an articulation of her life story, or any variation of it. Rather, it is literarily biographical—a record of Baron's evolution as a writer and her position within the prose canon of the modern Hebrew renaissance. Biography, by this definition, is an account of a literary genesis, whereas autobiography is an account of one's life, inclusive of literary development, but not limited to it. Virginia Woolf, in *A Room of One's Own*, says that women are "looking glasses reflecting the figure of man at twice its natural size." [5] Dvora Baron's literary biography is a sort of looking glass in the same vein, reflecting the literary culture of the modern Hebrew renaissance—its assumptions, its exclusions, its strengths, and its weaknesses—at twice its natural size. Thus, reading Baron's work as literary biography entails obtaining a deeper understanding not just of her own literary development but of the contours of her literary milieu.

Dvora Baron, arguably "the founding mother of Hebrew women's literature," was the only woman to achieve recognition in the modern Hebrew renaissance. [6] Concentrated in Odessa, Warsaw, and Jaffa at the turn of the twentieth century, with satellites in Berlin and New York City, the modern Hebrew renaissance was a movement of primarily male writers who rose through the traditional Jewish educational system in eastern Europe. Under the influence of the Haskalah and modern European nationalistic movements, these writers fought to establish a Hebrew secular culture when Hebrew had until then, with few exceptions, been forcibly reserved for the study of sacred texts within a religious and social hierarchy. I have called this exploration of Baron's literary corpus *Intimations of Difference: Dvora Baron in the Modern Hebrew Renaissance* because I trace here the "intimations" of difference—not the explicit declarations or the unidentifiable sublimations—that facilitated Baron's entrance into the canon of the modern Hebrew renaissance. Baron's difference from her peers—as a rabbi's daughter in the company of rabbis' sons, as a writer of the shtetl in the company of writers of the new *Yishuv*, as a physical isolate in Tel Aviv amid the foment and communality of nationalist Zionism—was not significant enough to disqualify her from inclusion in the canon of the modern Hebrew renaissance. Rather, her differences were, simultaneously, variations upon and revisions of the very imperatives that qualified writers for inclusion in the canon of the modern Hebrew renaissance. She was similar enough to her peers to warrant a place in their canon, but different enough to be considered a valuable addition to that canon.

In part, Baron needed to write differently in order for her peers to accept her as a woman in their midst. Why would a woman write "like a man"? If she did, as we will see, she would automatically be suspected of not writing in "her own voice" or even of having someone else (her brother, for example) write for her. At the same time, Baron's writing could not be so different that it did not resonate at all with the themes and tropes of the literary movement in which she participated. Thus, her differences were intimated both from without and from within—she was expected to be somewhat different because of her biographical gender, and in response she presented many common themes and rhetorical gestures of her generation, with a twist. When carefully explored, these differences are the key to understanding Baron's successful critique of her literary cohort. Throughout this study, I focus on loci of difference that also can be identified as loci of sameness—those moments when Baron's work resembles the work of her peers yet, when carefully read, reflects the differences that were imposed upon her but that also empowered her to innovate and criticize. These loci are approached here, "anecdotally," through close readings.

This study is an exercise in the power of textual anecdotes. When "new critics" challenged classic historical criticism, positing the literary work as the only relevant object for literary scrutiny and proposing that formalist readings replace authorially oriented historical ones, they were responding to the tendency, in classical historical literary criticism, to overlook the literary text, or at the very least to avoid close readings in favor of a more "humanistic" scrutiny of the context of literary production. "New Historical" criticism responded, in kind, by advocating a variety of historical criticism that is oriented toward close literary readings. Through an "anecdotal" approach to the literary text, New Historical critics argued that broad cultural lessons could be drawn without compromising close textual readings. Carefully selected anecdotes, or passages in literary texts, were to be used in the production of "thick descriptions," an anthropological term used by New Historicists to denote a culturally broad, yet literarily sound, interpretive practice.[7] The anecdotal approach is both a rehabilitation of close literary readings within the contemporary literary climate and an assertion of the necessity for historical contextualization and cultural extrapolation. Although I do not employ a strictly New Historical methodology here, I draw upon Baron's stories as textual anecdotes, or keys to the culture of the modern Hebrew renaissance. How did Baron view her own singularity within that culture and what does this teach us about the movement's contours, its imperatives and assumptions, its successes and failures?

The modern Hebrew renaissance was a period of intense cultural change, linguistic and social revolution, and literary innovation. It began in 1886, with the establishment of the first three daily Hebrew newspapers in eastern Europe (*ha-Yom* [The Day], *ha-Melitz* [The Advocate], and *ha-Tzfirah* [The Siren]), and with the publication of the first of a series of stories by S. J. Abramowitz (1835–1917), otherwise known as Mendele Mokher Sforim, the "grandfather" of both modern Yiddish and modern Hebrew literature. It drew to a close in approximately 1921 with the murder of Yosef Haim Brenner (1881–1921), after his participation, from 1909 to 1920, in the successful creation of a Hebrew literary establishment in Palestine.[8] Y. H. Brenner was a rising star of the modern Hebrew renaissance, and a strong supporter and editorial colleague of Dvora Baron. His death did not catalyze the end of the modern Hebrew renaissance, it simply marked it; it was at that political and historical juncture in modern Jewish experience that Hebrew writers no longer struggled to "revive" Hebrew as much as they struggled to map out future literary directions.

Of course, no literary movement can begin or end in a single year. Dvora Baron, for example, whose first story was published in Europe in 1902, began publishing her canonical collections only in 1927, seventeen years after she emigrated to Palestine. By bracketing the modern Hebrew renaissance between the figures of Abramowitz and Brenner, and between the years 1886 and 1921, I do not exclude writers who wrote beyond those temporal parameters. Rather, I accentuate the stylistic waves in the culture of the modern Hebrew renaissance at their moments of inception and mark the major cultural movements that accompanied, defined, and, finally, were reflected in those waves: the end of the Haskalah, the mass dissolution of traditional Jewish society in Europe, the gathering strength of political Zionism, and the birth of Hebrew modernism.

Otherwise known as the *tehiyah,* or the "revival," the modern Hebrew renaissance spanned eastern and western Europe, the United States, and Palestine and has become inexorably linked in the popular as well as the scholarly imagination with the rise of Zionism and its commitment, along with other nineteenth- and twentieth-century nationalist movements, to the naming of a "primordial" language—in this case Hebrew—as the essential expression of national character.[9] *Tehiyat ha-am,* the revival of the Jewish nation, was linked to *tehiyat ha-lashon,* the revival of the Hebrew language, in the earliest pages of the first Hebrew periodical, *ha-Measef* (The Gatherer), published in Germany from 1783 to 1811.[10] Early well-known Haskalah activists, or *maskilim,* were vocal supporters of the revival of the Hebrew language as part of the rehabilitation of the Jewish nation. Major Jewish maskilim such as Naftali Hertz Weisel, Isaac Satanov, Yoel Brill, Haim Kaslin, Solomon Pappenheim, and Yehudah Leib Ben Zeev all published Hebrew grammar books and articles on the revival of Hebrew, advocating it as integral to the Haskalah as a whole.[11]

Although the term "revival" implies the bringing back to life of something that has died, the Hebrew language was very much alive within a scholarly religious context at the turn of the twentieth century; it was "dead" only within a secular spoken one. Even in Palestine at the turn of the twentieth century, despite the well-known campaign of Eliezer Ben Yehudah (1858–1922), Hebrew was still not the language of daily life for a significant majority of the Jewish population.[12] Gershom Scholem (1897–1982), the first modern scholar of Jewish mysticism, tells of his reception at Chaim Nachman Bialik's house in Tel Aviv on Friday nights during the last few years of Bialik's life. When Scholem arrived, Bialik (1873–1934), the first Hebrew national poet, would say, in Yiddish, "Der yeke is gekumen, m'darf reydn loshn koydesh" (The *yeke* [German Jew] has come, we've got to speak the holy tongue). Although

Russian-born Bialik was clearly poking fun at his German-born colleague as much for his national origins and all its stereotypical behavioral implications as for his earnest devotion to Hebrew, Bialik also betrays his own level of discomfort with Hebrew as the language of casual, social discourse. "Yiddish speaks itself," Bialik said. "Hebrew must be spoken."[13] Most, if not all, of the writers of the modern Hebrew renaissance were multilingual. Hebrew, in fact, was the least comfortable of their literary choices, whereas Yiddish, Russian, Polish, French, or German, among others, were far more natural and perhaps more productive options. But the thrill of rendering something so inappropriate for secular usage into a secular language, of "reviving" the dead, even at the expense of the "living" (namely, Yiddish's banishment from many Zionist circles), far outweighed the pragmatic concerns of finding a sustainable readership and forging a readable modern idiom in the language of legislation and myth.

Y. H. Brenner, U. N. Gnessin (1881–1913), and M. Y. Berdischevsky (1865–1921), three major writers of the modern Hebrew renaissance, in their published correspondence with one another, use the term "revival" with obvious despair and even a hint of sarcasm. They lament the state of Hebrew literature, just as their Haskalah predecessor poet Y. L. Gordon (1860–1927) did, in his most famous poem, "For Whom Do I Toil?" in which he questions the wisdom of creating a modern secular literature with barely any readership.[14] Scholarly accounts of popular and elite attitudes toward the potential for a successful revival of Hebrew language and letters abound with anecdotes about people who have, in retrospect, been viewed as the founding fathers of the modern Hebrew renaissance, but who, in their own daily discourse, challenged its possibility. Peretz Smolenskin (1842–1885), a novelist during the Haskalah, called Hebrew "a dusty language" *(sfat efer)* instead of "the language of the Hebrews" *(sfat ever)*. An anonymous writer from a Russian Jewish newspaper said that Hebrew was a "dead language for the living or a living language for the dead," but not a living language for the living.[15] Finally, major Hebrew writers from the period of the modern Hebrew renaissance who expressed reservations over the possibility of Hebrew speech included the well-known Zionist ideologue Ahad ha-Am (Asher Ginsburg,

1856–1927), the Hebrew writer and critic David Frishmann (1865–1922), and the poet laureate of Zionist nationalism, Chaim Nachman Bialik.[16]

The literary culture of the modern Hebrew renaissance was fraught with a simultaneous sense of its own importance and its own irrelevance, its own teleological resonances and its own pointlessness. Its major players were men who had escaped the shtetl and the yeshiva (an institution of higher Jewish learning within a religious context) yet created a literature out of the texts valorized in the shtetl and the yeshiva. In fact, the poetic standards for the literature of the modern Hebrew renaissance were determined by an allegiance to the voices and the assumptions of the world left behind; only those who could manipulate rabbinic and biblical texts in particular ways, twisting them to suit the demands first of realist, then of modernist, prose, were considered viable stylists. In a similar vein, only those writers who told the story of an ambivalent break from tradition were considered worthy of canonization within the literature of the modern Hebrew renaissance by early twentieth-century critics such as Joseph Klausner (1874–1958) or Fishel Lahover (1883–1947) and mid-twentieth-century critics such as Dan Miron and Gershon Shaked.[17] Stylistic and thematic deviance was rare, and almost undocumented.

The modern Hebrew renaissance, both because of its belated position after the demise of the Haskalah and because of its genesis in the houses of study, in the homes of rabbis, and most important in the hearts and minds of people who were unwilling to continue on the assimilationist path of modern Jewish experience in Europe, was a movement of continuity, not of rupture; it was a movement that depended on young men, disillusioned with rabbinic systems of knowledge, yet unwilling to break from the wealth of its language, its imagery, its discursive breadth, and its history. Even so, the history of the modern Hebrew renaissance is generally told as a tale of rupture, of apostasy, of departures from the traditional Jewish home and the yeshiva.[18] This narrative of fissure has long impeded the ability of critics to discern the traditionalism inherent in the movement. Dvora Baron was the only writer acknowledged in the canon of the modern Hebrew renaissance who did not emerge from a yeshiva and who did not, as part of her literary debut, tell the tragic story of her break from tradition and her inability to remove herself from the centripetal force of her overbearing teachers, parents, and an unforgiving God. Rather, Baron tells a different story in her work—the story of a woman's emergence into modernity despite the continuing monopoly of tradition.

In the third chapter of his 1596 *Brantshpigl* (Burning Mirror), an early work of ethical literature in Yiddish, Moses Ben Henoch Yerushalmi Altshuler (1546–1633) explains that his book "was written in Yiddish for women and for men who are like women."[19] In other words, Yiddish ethical literature and other religious works were viewed by Altshuler as being appropriate only for those Jews, like women, who could not learn Jewish texts in Hebrew and Aramaic. Those Jews, to Altshuler's mind, who must resort to Yiddish are "different" from the gold standard of Jewish intellectual acumen; they are, in stronger terms, to be understood as "deficient."

This same deficiency, or "difference" on the part of women and "men who are like women" in traditional Jewish society, was seen in the nineteenth century by eastern European maskilim such as Yehudah Leib Gordon (1830–1892) as advantageous. Because women were not inducted into the culture of rabbinic study, Gordon argued, their approach to the Hebrew language would be free of the heavy polemics typical of the Talmud and the florid pastiche style typical of Haskalah writers translating their scholarly expertise into a modern idiom. Gordon wrote, in 1881, to a female correspondent, Mrs. Shana Wolf of Grodno:

All the letters in Hebrew, authored by women, that I have had the opportunity to read, were far more stylistically and lexically lucid than the letters written by men. Women write with a bird's touch, while men write with the touch of iron and lead. Women's writings are rendered in a simple style and approximate the spirit of the Hebrew language. They do not contain the bombastic rhetoric [*melitsah*] that assaults the civilized person. . . . The reason for this is that the brains of girls have not been spoiled in their youth in the deadly cheder, and their linear intellects have not been rendered crooked by all the homiletics and polemics of traditional study. Because of this they have maintained a sense of style and their writing spirit has not been destroyed.[20]

In the sixteenth-century formulation by Rabbi Altshuler, we encounter an affirmation of the intellectual poverty of certain "men who are *like* women." In the formulation by Y. L. Gordon during the nineteenth century, this analogy is broken down, and we see a valorization of "women who are *not like* men." What happens, though, when women are identified as being "like men" or writing "like men" and the authenticity of their texts is called into question? In light of this dilemma, Gordon expresses concern, elsewhere, over the authenticity of a particular letter he received from a young woman because of its rabbinic content: "The young woman is indeed enlightened and knows the Hebrew language, but there is a tutor in their house and he must edit her letters for her . . . it seems to me that her letters have been tampered with because she uses rabbinic language that a girl who has not learned Talmud cannot possibly know."[21] Gordon here dismisses outright the possibility that, first, a woman can know rabbinic language or the Talmud and that, second, she could have written Hebrew prose based on an acquaintance with either one.

The novelty of Baron's emergence as a woman writer of Hebrew from a rigidly defined educational system in which even the most educated women did not have Hebrew proficiency seems to be the one biographical consideration without which her work cannot be given a fair reading. Up to the period of the Haskalah, and in many locales affected by it, Jewish girls of all social classes in eastern Europe were taught, by and large, to read prayer-book Hebrew and were able to read and write in Yiddish. They were able to pray, or at least to follow prayers in synagogue, and to read the wide range of Yiddish devotional, homiletic, and ethical literature written for "women and for men who are like women." They were also sufficiently literate in the language of the land in which they resided to navigate the marketplace and to do bookkeeping in a shop or at home. In general, however, girls were not taught, at least in a communal setting, the Hebrew and Aramaic linguistic rudiments necessary to pursue an in-depth study of the Bible or the Talmud.

Mastery of traditional Jewish sources was the only key to social advancement in Jewish society aside from financial success. Even those individuals who achieved social mobility through monetary wealth were considered "lesser" than those who had achieved status as accomplished scholars.[22] To this day, the fact that women are not members of the scholarly religious elite prevents them from legislating away some of the more ugly and difficult aspects of Jewish law that affect women in particular.[23] Shaul Stampfer has demonstrated, in his study on gender differentiation in eastern European Jewish education, that most eastern European women were not technically "illiterate" because they were proficient in Yiddish and in the native tongue of their country of origin as well as being able, generally, to follow the Hebrew prayer book. However, because they were institutionally barred from mastery of traditional authoritative texts such as the Talmud, they were rendered functionally illiterate within the Jewish community.[24] Although there exist literary, historical, and autobiographical accounts of women formally studying (and teaching) the Hebrew language either in tutorials, in mixed gender heders (religious schools), or in modern Jewish schools, the social role and recognition of girls' proficiency in Hebrew or Hebrew textual culture or both were severely circumscribed.[25]

The well-documented embourgeoisement of upper-class Jews all over Europe, but particularly in western Europe throughout the eighteenth and nineteenth centuries, created several generations of women who were accomplished readers and critics of European literature, musicians, and benefactresses of literary and cultural salons.[26] The sign of social success for women in upper-crust Jewish society was a form of cultural and linguistic assimilation, whereas for men it remained Talmudic erudition. Marriage between women trained to participate in the highest of European culture and men trained to spend their lives swaying over the Talmud and punctiliously observing Jewish law became a virtual impossibility.

In the testimonies provided by maskilim in their autobiographies, it is apparent that as men began to pursue enlightenment there was a mismatch of conjugal partners in the lower classes as well.[27] The boys who excelled in Jewish studies but broke out of that world in order to agitate for Jewish modernization were often married off before they had their falling out with Jewish tradition. The women (or girls) that they married, not having been educated in classical texts, could not participate in the common trajectory of the generation of maskilim who used their proficiency in classical texts both to read and (in some cases) to produce modern Haskalah-oriented Hebrew literature. Mired within the parameters of provincial traditionalism by their limited intellectual training, young lower-class women were an uneasy match for their adolescent husbands, newly converted to the promise and the possibility of Jewish enlightenment.[28]

One outstanding feature of the discourse of the Haskalah was its rhetoric of women's liberation.[29] This rhetoric, however, was paradoxical. Because it was a reaction against assimilation and conversion in the upper classes, and a move to preserve the integrity of the Jewish family in the lower classes, it was fundamentally a conservative movement.[30] Women were to be taught Hebrew as opposed to (or in addition to) Russian, French, or German in order to make them more suitable partners for traditionally educated husbands. They were to be encouraged to participate in the cultural life of the Haskalah as opposed to the European Enlightenment not for their own sakes, but in order to assign a new face to Jewish life and to maintain coherence between the sexes in the Jewish community. The actual implementation of that objective, because its goals were reactionary, was somewhat random and inconsistent. Ideology and anxiety made the topic of women's education in Jewish society far more contested than it would seem on the basis of the Haskalah rhetoric of women's liberation.[31]

Y. L. Gordon, as we saw earlier, even articulated the necessity to capitalize on the ignorance of Jewish women. They were not, to his mind, jaded by the vagaries and involutions of rabbinic thought and could thus be better receptacles for a more expansive, enlightened way of thinking. In educating women, he envisioned skipping the basic traditionalist components; yet in doing so, he was thereby depriving them, as had his forebears, of the tools to participate fully in a modernization that was predicated on mastery of the very traditions that were being subverted. It became increasingly clear, however, as a generation of yeshiva dropouts came to dominate not only the literature but also the poetics of the modern Hebrew renaissance, that anyone without the textual basis to subvert the traditional texts could not participate in the creation of a modern Hebrew secular literature. In the absence of a living, speaking Hebrew culture, only those individuals who were the "elite of the elite" could "use the system against itself."[32]

The Yiddish and Hebrew writer S. J. Abramowitz, who has been described as one of a "small minority of writers committed to advancing Jewish women's education as a goal in and of itself," has also been described as "not liking to hear Hebrew spoken in general, and not liking to hear women speak it in particular."[33] An anecdote describing Abramowitz walking out of a lecture delivered by a woman in Hebrew at a meeting of the Hibat Zion, or "Lovers of Zion" movement, illustrates his dislike of women speaking, teaching, or using Hebrew in public.[34] Abramowitz, ironically, advocated modern, progressive approaches to educating Jews of both genders.[35] His appreciation for women's involvement in the culture of the modern Hebrew renaissance, like Gordon's, appears to have been highly selective.

As evidenced by this suspicious reception of women in a Hebrew linguistic milieu, women writers of Hebrew during the Haskalah were valorized primarily as a form of reproach to the men who were not choosing to write in Hebrew. The Haskalah activist and editor Abraham Baer Gottlober wrote an editorial in his newspaper, *Morning Light*, about his correspondence with a young woman, Sarah Navinsky:

> The writer of these lines is a virginal young woman, beautiful and graceful who is not yet even eighteen years old. . . . This enlightened young woman knows Russian, Polish, German, French and Italian and began learning Hebrew about two years ago. . . . The young Jewish men who turn their backs on the language of their fathers should see her and be ashamed, and the Enlightened of our generation should hold her up as a model for them and they should grant them the "fruits of her labor and praise her deeds at the gates."[36]

By concluding his remarks in the traditional language of the "woman of valor" drawn from Proverbs 21, Gottlober situates Sarah Navinsky's Hebrew literary accomplishment only in relationship to the men who may draw lessons from it. If there are no men "praising her deeds at the gate," her deeds may as well have not taken place. In a separate editorial introducing another letter by Navinsky to his readership, Gottlober explicitly states the following: "It is very wonderful, to my mind, to see women associating themselves with the Hebrew literary establishment even as their male contemporaries have discarded, as they would a divorced wife, their Hebrew writing compatriots. This honorable woman should serve as a model and chastisement for them."[37] The rhetoric in Gottlober's earlier statement, derived from the biblical book of Proverbs, of a husband praising his wife at the gates, and in this allusion to a husband divorcing the Hebrew literary establishment as he would a wife who has fallen out of favor, reveals the attitude toward women's writing during the period of the Haskalah. There were virtually no women being published in the Hebrew-language press before the 1860s; when occasional letters and essays began to appear, they were most often framed by the editor as relevant only insofar as they galvanized men to write in Hebrew.

As the Haskalah drew to a close in the latter part of the nineteenth century and the modern Hebrew renaissance focused its energies on political Zionism and the secular revival of the Hebrew language, its champions found themselves with a serious problem on their hands:[38] they had to reinterest their adherents in Hebrew. Much of the sensibility of the Haskalah period, expressed in the attitude toward woman writers in the pages of Gottlober's newspaper, *Morning Light*, still dominated the modern Hebrew literary scene. Women writers were still such a rarity that they were easily mobilized as objects of astonishment and awe simply in order to shame the male population into following suit. This position was the same one in which Baron found herself when she emerged at the turn of the twentieth century into the post-Haskalah modern Hebrew renaissance.

Baron's reputation preceded her and motivated a surprisingly enthusiastic reception of her initial stories. As pointed out by Baruch Ben-Yehudah, a young acquaintance of Baron in eastern Europe: "I don't remember when we first heard about her, but I do remember our initial conversations about her—a female student in the local high school, the daughter of a Rabbi from one of the Lithuanian shtetls and a Hebrew [woman] writer [*soferet*]. The mystique of a Hebrew writer in the guise of a high-school girl cloaked her instantaneously in an aura of honor and admiration."[39] Similarly, in a letter to Baron (addressing her, strangely, in the third person) dated December 8, 1908, from an admirer named Leib Fink, we read:

> I was especially surprised by her careful Hebrew style, filled with Talmudic allusions. At first I was surprised and I thought, "How did she acquire all this knowledge and in such a logical clear way, that no other girl seems to have acquired? And also, how does she even know Hebrew?" I realized over time that because she was the daughter of a rabbi, she received a unique national and religious education and enriched her ability not just to represent the lives of women, but also the lives of men at home, in the street, and in the house of study.[40]

The simple biographical fact of Baron's emergence as a Hebrew author was undoubtedly the source of her seemingly instant, and perhaps undeserved, popularity early in her career. It certainly was not the unique or outstanding nature of her literary works or the powerful resonance of her literary voice. Dvora Baron's gender, with rare exception, preceded and continues to precede assessments of her place in the genesis of modern Hebrew literature; her identity as a Hebrew writer has consistently been preempted by a nod toward her being a Hebrew woman writer.

This focus is due, in part, to the lack of a gender-neutral term for authorship in Hebrew;[41] the Hebrew term for a woman writer, *soferet,* is distinct from the male *sofer.* When encountering a soferet during the period of the modern Hebrew renaissance, readers and critics felt (and continue to feel) pressed to define the term further, as one would a rare or singularly occurring word in the Bible. From the time Dvora Baron's Hebrew fiction was first published, she was called by many names, all meant in some way to explain her unusual identity as a soferet. She was referred to by many of her readers, critics, and peers as "the rabbi's daughter."[42] After her emigration to Palestine in 1910, despite her own prodigious contributions as literary editor of *The Young Laborer* to the fledgling Hebrew literary establishment in Palestine, she was known as "the editor's wife." [43] Yeshurun Keshet (Yaakov Kapolovich), an early Israeli literary critic, called her "the poetess of modest women in the Lithuanian shtetl of the last generation." The cultural critic and first "first lady" of the State of Israel, Rachel Katznelson-Shazar, called her *"the great Hebrew woman writer."* Contemporary critics such as Naomi Seidman and Chana Kronfeld have called Baron, simply, "the *first* modern Hebrew woman writer." [44]

Women, in fact, were writing in Hebrew, during the modern period, long before Baron. Rachel Morpurgo (1790–1871) wrote Hebrew poetry in Triest, Italy, during the period of the Haskalah. [45] Chava Shapirah (1879–1943) published her first story in 1901 in the Cracow-based Hebrew journal *ha-Dor,* more than a year before Baron's first stories were published. [46] Nechama Puchechevsky (1869–1934) wrote Hebrew short stories contemporaneously with Dvora Baron and is best known for two collections of short stories, published in 1911 and 1930. [47] Sarah Feige Meinkin Foner (1854–1936) wrote two novels and a memoir, published between 1881 and 1903. [48] Hemda Ben Yehudah (1873–1951), the second wife of Eliezer Ben Yehudah, wrote short stories and essays throughout the period of the first aliyah (1881–1903), the first mass settlement of Jews in Palestine during modernity. [49]

Although our subject here is the prose fiction of the modern Hebrew renaissance, it is important to acknowledge the handful of women who, albeit belatedly and in a qualified manner, were recognized within the arena of modern Hebrew and Israeli poetry. Rachel Bluwstein (1890–1931) has come to be regarded as an Israeli folk hero because of her early, tragic death and what has been construed as her potent Zionist and poignantly personal poetic voice. Esther Raab (1899–1981), known as the first modern Hebrew poet to be born in Palestine, has been acknowledged only recently as an outstanding (and subversive) landscape poet. Finally, Yocheved Bat Miriam (1901–1980) has come, in the past several years, to represent a distinctly female and feminist voice in the Hebrew milieu of European-born poets who emigrated to Palestine midway through their careers.

In addition to those women writing poetry and fiction throughout the nineteenth century and into the twentieth, various women are known to have been active in Hebrew journalism and literary criticism. Toybe Segal published an important feminist essay in six installments in the journal *ha-Ivri* (The Hebrew) in Lvov, Galicia, titled "The Question of Women" in 1879; Miriam Varnikovsky published another piece on women in 1901 titled "In the Path of Righteous Women" in the Vienna- and Cracow-based journal *ha-Magid ha-Hadash* (The New Preacher).[50] Finally, Devorah ha-Efrati corresponded with the major Haskalah novelist Avraham Mapu (1808–1967), and Miriam Markel Mosesohn (1837–1920) corresponded with the major poet Y. L. Gordon.[51] Both women can be considered among the first modern Hebrew literary critics because their letters were formulated in response to their correspondents' literary works.[52]

If Dvora Baron was neither the first nor the only woman writer of Hebrew at the turn of the twentieth century, what makes her distinctive and singular, not only among male writers but among women writers as well? The simple answer is that Baron's was the only woman's literary corpus acknowledged within the prose literature of the modern Hebrew renaissance. The more complex answer is that Baron negotiated the stylistic, thematic, and ideological "imperatives" of the modern Hebrew renaissance in ways that "intimated" her differences. She was guaranteed a place in the literary canon of the modern Hebrew renaissance because she was perceptibly different enough from her peers to justify her presence in it as a woman writer, but similar enough to be recognizable; Baron's "intimations of difference" allied her work with the stylistic and thematic imperatives of her generation even while maintaining her independence. Baron became, I argue throughout this work, one of the most sensitive critics of the literature of the modern Hebrew renaissance because of her "intimations of difference." From within the movement itself, she subtly yet forcefully illuminated the strengths and weaknesses of particular stylistic, thematic, and intellectual stances that were forged in relation to Jewish literary history, contemporary Jewish modernization, and broader European literary movements such as realism and modernism.

I began my discussion of "imperatives" with an overview, in this Introduction, of the "biographical imperative," the imperative to read

Baron's work biographically because of the biographically identifiable details scattered throughout, that has long governed readings of Baron's fiction. Awe over the emergence of a woman writer of Hebrew from a segregated Jewish educational culture has consistently preempted serious literary considerations of Baron's work. At the same time, Baron herself plants the seeds of "biographical" readings throughout her corpus: an older brother, seemingly modeled upon her own brother; a rabbinic father, similar to her own father; and a rabbi's daughter, akin to Baron herself, are omnipresent in Baron's work. Given Baron's singular canonization as a woman in a cohort of men, it is limiting to insist upon her stories' wholly fictional qualities. An understanding of her literary biography, I have argued, and of her emergence as a female child both of the Haskalah and of Jewish tradition, is in order when analyzing Baron's work.

The next imperative, discussed in Chapter 1, is the "autobiographical imperative." Hebrew fiction of the modern Hebrew renaissance was often regarded as a direct extension of Haskalah autobiographies. As a result, much of the fiction of the modern Hebrew renaissance was read as a monolithic or collective autobiography of a generation of former yeshiva students. The "types" that evolved in these pseudoautobiographical works—the sexually ineffectual young writer with writer's block, for example—were all men. In her simultaneous adoption and subversion of the autobiographical imperatives of the canon, Baron's difference is "intimated." Her unique position as someone who did and did not share the collective biography of her generation becomes apparent.

In the second chapter, I present Baron's formulation of an alternative voice of modernist "uprootedness" *(tlishut)*. Tlishut, the state of uprootedness, or the literary *talush*, the uprooted, was the Hebrew equivalent of "modernist man" in a state of exile, existential despair, and artistic isolation. Indeed, the talush was so popular in the Hebrew literature of the turn of the twentieth century that it became "imperative" to write in his voice. Baron's narratives feature an "uprooted" narrator who is caught between the present and the past, the shtetl and Palestine, the male culture of Hebrew and the female culture of Yiddish. As such, she does not write the classic talush texts of her peers, but taps into (and rejects) a talush sensibility.

The third chapter presents the "mimetic imperative" of the modern Hebrew renaissance, the imperative to create a realist literature that represented "things as they are." This imperative was drawn from contemporaneous Russian positivist approaches to a literature engagé—a literature on the barricades of social awareness and social change. Baron challenges a variety of the assumptions implicit in this mimetic imperative through a complex invocation of the discourse of photography throughout her corpus.

In Chapter 4, I look at a subset of the mimetic imperative—the "vernacular imperative." The vernacular imperative reflected Hebrew renaissance writers' attempts to turn an ancient, ungainly language into a fluent literary vernacular. I argue here that Baron's identity as a woman enabled her to contribute to this discourse in significant ways. Indeed, because she encountered primary Jewish texts orally (and aurally) in the absence of more formalized, school-based training, she outshone her peers in successfully strategizing the creation of a "speakerly" Hebrew literature—a literature made out of wholly literary materials but with a distinctly vernacular flavor.

The "intertextual" building blocks of a Hebrew vernacular literature in the absence of a Hebrew vernacular speech are the basis of the final imperative to be discussed, in Chapter 5 of this study—the "intertextual imperative." Hebrew writers were pressed to find very subtle intertextual strategies to communicate orality without making their literature sound facetious or stilted. In her treatment of the intertextual imperative, Baron challenges her own decision to weave her fiction's rhetorical fabric from the Hebrew texts of Jewish tradition as opposed to the more naturally "vernacular" Yiddish texts that could have served as models for a vernacular Hebrew idiom. Baron's treatment of intertextuality in the context of the language wars between Yiddish and Hebrew—between the purportedly "female" language of intellectual impoverishment and the purportedly "male" language of scholarship and legal empowerment—allows us to explore her own distinct position as a modern Jewish woman writer who chose Hebrew over Yiddish early on in her career.

Intimations of Difference

1

All Writers Are Jews, All Jews Are Men

The Autobiographical Imperative

For two years he has frequented the study halls of the local university and he is still completely isolated, without a single acquaintance in this Christian land. He is poor and lives in the way of the Torah . . . day and night he studies human life from a scientific perspective, but life itself touches him as if only from a distance. His thoughts and rarefied logic swallow up his desire to live. He sits like a monk in the bustling city, with no practical needs.—M. Y. Berdischevsky, *A Raven Flies* (1900)

Here I am, lying prone on my large sofa, with my eyes wide open. My head is totally sunken into my pillow. Fluttering and stumbling within my empty brain is one persistent thought: Who cares?—Dvora Baron, "Exams" (1910)

SIMON HALKIN WAS THE FIRST CRITIC to assign a unifying Hebrew name, talush, literally translated as "uprooted," to the socially estranged, sexually frustrated, and self-deprecating protagonists of the prose fiction of the modern Hebrew renaissance.[1] He called the Hebrew literature of the period, "sifrut ha-tehiyah veha-temiyhah" (the literature of revival and perplexity), as a means of acknowledging the ever present "uprooted" figure at its center.[2]

More than just an alienated young protagonist conceived in keeping with the eighteenth- and nineteenth-century literary movement toward introversion, the talush is an alienated young *male* Jewish protagonist ei-

ther in Europe or in Palestine at the turn of the twentieth century, traversing various worlds and successfully settling in none..A would-be
writer who often laments, paradoxically in writing, his inability to write,
the talush is a scholar of traditional Jewish texts who has exchanged his
Jewish religious library for a secular one, losing his taste for all scholarship in the process. He is a lonely mama's boy in search of female com-
panionship who always desires the woman he cannot have and ruins the
life of the woman he can have but does not desire. The talush is often an
"extern," a student-at-large attempting (largely unsuccessfully because
of Jewish quotas) to matriculate at a university. Or he is a pioneer realiz-
ing that he is not suited for physical labor or the life of the soil after he has
emigrated to Palestine to join an agricultural collective.[3] Distinguished
by an inability to return to the traditional Jewish world he left behind
and to fit into the secular European world he seeks to break into, the
talush is literally "uprooted" from any collective identification.

Modern Hebrew renaissance authors, in their fashioning of the
talush, were attempting to reclaim the "Jew" as an emblem of ambivalence and ambiguity from European culture. Dvora Baron's particular
reaction to the talush's exclusive masculinity within a Jewish context, his
"femininity" within a European cultural context, and his generational
"exemplarity" within the context of the modern Hebrew renaissance will
be the subject of this chapter.

Zygmunt Bauman provides an excellent introduction to the place of
the "Jew" in modern European discourse in his argument that, with the
advent of modernity in Europe,

> in the mobile world, the Jews were the most mobile of all; in the world of
> boundary breaking, they broke most boundaries; in the world of melting
> solids they made everything, including themselves, into a formless
> plasma in which any form could be born, only to dissolve again. As the
> eponymous ghetto dwellers, the Jews were walking reminders of the still
> fresh and vivid memories of a stable, transparent caste society; among the
> first to be released from special laws and statutes, they were walking
> alarms alerting society to the arrival of the strange new world of the free
> for all.

Jews, in other words, were not just a representation of otherness, but were "ambivalence incarnate"; Jews were the "epitome of incongruity." [4]

Daniel Boyarin and Jonathan Boyarin trace this modern European attitude toward the Jew back to Paul's doctrine of allegorical as opposed to literal genealogies. They explain that in his statement "There is neither Greek nor Jew," Paul initiated a rhetoric of sameness that "deprived difference of the right to be different." [5] Herein, according to them, lies the locus of Christianity's break from Judaism. The Jew was construed as particularly irrelevant in light of the push toward universalism and then threatening to that universalism as a metonymy for difference. The Jew came to be rendered in the abstract as "notional" or "mythical." [6]

Modernist and postmodernist thinkers and writers have picked up on what is, to Boyarin and Boyarin, a millennial strain in thinking about Jewish difference within Christian culture and, in Bauman's reading, a product of the dawn of modernity in Europe. In his overview of postmodern French philosophers' appropriation of the Jew, Max Silverman has summed up various positions: "According to Jean Luc Nancy the Jew is the allegorical marker of the interruption of myth and community; or, as Lyotard says more recently, the Jew is the challenge to the blind narcissism of the community, even the Jewish community. Ultimately these Jews are the marker of the unnameable, a reminder of what is forgotten or what is lacking in all representation, what cannot be spoken or named, since all representation is a form of forgetting." [7] Silverman concludes by asking, "Are there alternative paths available in our postmodern landscape which neither allegorize nor essentialize the Jew?" Gillian Rose has called the postmodern attitude toward the Jew "the tyranny of the allegorizing of the Jew" and has described "a need to transform the trope of the Jew or the signifier Jew from a site for figures to a site for negotiation beyond the dichotomies of sameness and difference, universalism and particularism, reason and anti-reason, essentialism and relativism. It would imply defetishizing the Jew, conceiving of the Jew neither simply as an open ended signifier nor as an unproblematic signified, but as a real hybrid between the two." [8]

The concern expressed by Rose, Silverman, and Boyarin and Boyarin about the "universalization" of Jews "out of existence" by creating a category of "the Jew" is complicated and ramified by the discourse of "the Jew" in fin-de-siècle western Europe wherein the abstract "Jew" became concretely feminized.[9] In 1869 Rabbi Adolf Jellinek, a distinguished Viennese rabbi, declared in his book *The Jewish Tribe* that Jews' imitative abilities, which they share with women, guarantee that they will manage to adopt Western culture. Women and Jews, he argued, share a "quick and lively intellect, but are unsystematic, incoherent and digressive, receptive rather than original, and hence good at imitating others."[10] Otto Weininger, the Jewish author of the notorious book *Sex and Character* (1903), wrote a vituperative pastiche of misogynist and anti-Semitic statements about the stupidity and insensitivity of women in general and about the feminine nature of Jewish men in particular. Maximilian Harden, a Viennese Jewish journalist, claimed that, "just as Jews, though nominally in an inferior position, dominate the gentile world and take revenge for their mistreatment, so women can use marriage to dominate men and thus compensate for their nominal subjection." The psychoanalyst Otto Rank argued in "The Essence of Judaism" (1905) that "Jews are, so to speak, women among the nations and must join themselves to the masculine life source if they are to be productive."[11]

If Jewish men were viewed as women in order to rationalize the sense that Jews inverted all normative categories of identity, then how were women viewed within the Jewish community? To what extent would the voice of a woman, or even a discussion about "real" women in the context of the Jews as "feminized," upset the delicate balance of the "abstract" Jew as a "virtual" woman? Daniel Boyarin, a vocal proponent of the notion of the Jewish man as symbolically female in modern Europe, furnishes a fascinating example of how modern cultural criticism, in explicating the reduction of the "real" Jew to symbols and projections, continues to overlook those individuals who are even further abstracted and essentialized.

In *Heidegger and "the jews,"* Lyotard says, "what is most real about real jews is that Europe, in any case, does not know what to do with them: Christians demand their conversion, monarchs expel them; republics assimilate them; Nazis exterminate them." Boyarin and Boyarin respond in the following way: "Let us pause at the first here and test a paraphrase.

How would it work if a man or a woman said, 'What is most real about real women is that men continually try to dominate them'? The condescension of Lyotard's statement immediately becomes evident." Although Boyarin and Boyarin are correct in suggesting that the patent absurdity of the latter statement furnishes a wonderful illustration of the patent absurdity of the former, they themselves fall into the trap of designating some other "other" as an illustrative metonymy for the "others" under discussion. Whereas in the case of the modernist writer "the Jew" is a stand-in for the poet-in-exile and in the case of postmodern thinkers "the jew" is a stand-in for the "site on which unruly desire and ambivalence can, supposedly, be transformed into a coherent and univocal discourse," in this case, just as in the discourse of the fin de siècle on "the Jew," women become a stand-in for "the jew." [12] Two questions arise out of this assumption. First, where are "real" women—nonmetonymic, nonsymbolic, nonallegorized—in all this discussion? More important, where is the Jewish woman?

The writers of the modern Hebrew renaissance who crafted the talush, and the critics of that literature who embraced him as an exemplum of a historical and cultural generation, were perhaps responding to the figure of "the Jew" within European culture by figuring their own intrinsic variation on "the Jew." The talush was the Jews' "Jew." But as such, the female equivalent of the talush, a tlushah or acknowledgment of the female signifier buried deep beneath the monolithic maleness of the network of discourses on perceptions of the "Jew" in European culture, was completely absent. Brenner, for example, in his 1909 essay "Musings of an Author" presents his notion of the "Dmut Diyokno shel ha-Tsair ha-Boded" (portrait of the young lonely man) in modern Hebrew literature. He opens this essay in defense of the narrative quality of his work because his modernist aesthetic of interiority and fragmentation was called into question by many of his contemporary writers and critics. "If our mirror is not illuminating," he counters, "if it is broken, shattered, miniature, what can we do? We must look at our face even in miniature." [13] The imperative of looking at "our face" in the mirror of the talush texts reflects his approach to the talush as a generationally representative figure that must yet be stylized in the most idiosyncratic, individualized way possible. The "young lonely men" that Brenner identifies in his own work and in the work of others surround themselves with female figures; they even idealize or demonize women as part of the standard characterization of the male talush as sexually frustrated and erotically stunted. But stylistic figuration of a female tlushah through interiority and psychological realism is virtually never attempted. This fact can be attributed to the nationalist, literary, and autobiographical dimensions consistently granted the talush both by his creators and by his critics.

The talush-centered prose of the modern Hebrew renaissance tells the story of young men going through the cultural shifts and emotional disruptions that were documented about a century earlier in the autobiographies of their Haskalah predecessors. This generation, born, as it were, on the deathbed of the Haskalah in the 1880s, belatedly underwent its own "apostasy" and its own escape from the yeshiva and the shtetl. Like their Haskalah predecessors, these writers were discovering a secular Jewish literature within the context of traditional upbringings and educations. They were clandestinely reading and writing modern Hebrew in the garb of pious Jews, living at home with their pious families, and finally breaking violently, traumatically, and often unsuccessfully into the secular world of universities, publishing houses, and romantic love. To what extent then, Baron seems to be asking in her development of a classic talush alongside an ostensibly female tlushah in her Sender Ziv trilogy (1910–1919), does the literature of tlishut, or uprootedness, endemic to her generation exemplify the continuation of a traditional line of male scholarship and gender exclusivity? In other words, how are we to understand Hebrew renaissance writers' sense that they were enacting a radical break—stylistically, psychologically, linguistically—from the Hebrew Haskalah literature that came before them? Furthermore, how did the sense of self-made literary acumen, of a departure from the traditional norms that had dominated Jewish literary expression for millennia, really assert itself when held under the magnifying glass of a modern Hebrew woman writer?

Dan Miron, in his investigation of the group of women poets who distinguished themselves in Hebrew in Palestine in the 1920s, points to the requisite poetics of modern Hebrew renaissance poetry.[14] A rich allusive network demonstrating engagement with traditional rabbinic texts and the revision of classical biblical tropes were necessary criteria for inclusion in the canon of modern Hebrew renaissance poetry. The women writers (as well as various men) who produced a minimalist poetry not redolent of the kind of maximalist intertextual self-consciousness typical of those poets who become secular writers in a yeshiva atmosphere were considered "scribblers" who could never quite make their voices heard among the giants of their generation (Chaim Nachman Bialik or Saul Tschernikhovsky (1875–1943), for example).[15] It is clear that though the modern Hebrew poets viewed themselves as trailblazers for an entirely new poetic, an entirely new literary culture for modern Jews, they were, in effect, simply continuing an ancient scholarly tradition that had excluded women or other intellectual "undesirables" from the house of study and thus the ranks of legal and social power. Modern Hebrew literature, by this account, was simply a continuation of traditional Hebrew literature in that it was reserved for and transmitted by the privileged few.

Baron's treatment of the talush brings into further relief the pragmatic ramifications of the modern Hebrew literary establishment's being not much more than the sum of its traditionalist parts. Engagement in secular studies and abdication of religious practice, although considered the most rebellious and taboo of activities on the part of a Jewish male, were not enough to break the talush from his past psychologically. In Berdischevsky's *A Raven Flies*, the narrator muses that "just the books switched, the reader did not; just the thoughts changed their form. The thinker and dreamer did not stop being that which he once was."[16] The talush never achieves true secular integration because he remains the metonymy of the People of the Book, a *"ben sefer."* By using externship as his means of breaking with the traditional community, he has chosen to continue to associate himself with his textual past. He is a secular Jewish parody of Bialik's religious *Matmid,* adding new meaning to the phrase "the eternal student" *(ha-student ha-nitshi).*[17]

In all three stories of her Sender Ziv trilogy ("Exams" [1909], "Choco-late" [1912], and "The End of Sender Ziv" [1919]), Baron thematizes the situation of her protagonist, Sender Ziv, vis-à-vis the textual cultures be-tween which he hovers. In one particularly poignant instance, he sits in the house of his widowed landlady, hunched over a book, swaying back and forth like a Talmud student to heighten his concentration, while the chil-dren in the house cry from hunger and cold. Ziv is figured here as a surro-gate father to this fatherless family. But he can do no better than the stereotypical Jewish scholar, preoccupied with texts to the point of obliv-ion as his wife and children suffer from poverty. In another instance, Sender Ziv receives a letter, mentioned both in "Chocolate" and in "The End of Sender Ziv," from his sister telling him that she and his mother can-not afford to buy a tombstone for his father's grave and asking him when he plans to return in order to contribute financially to their household. Ziv is cast in the role of the only male in a household of women, shirking his responsibilities to them in order to pursue his studies, like the classical Torah scholar who will pursue God at any cost. Relentless study leads only to the constant scramble of the scholar's support structure (that is, his wife and children) to make do with less and less on a daily basis.

In Baron's "Exams" confusion over the choice of one textual lifestyle, or one textual corpus, over another becomes fully realized in a lyrical passage in which the narrator muses on the material that he should be studying for his exams: "Who is this rising out of the desert supported by her lover? Her hair is like a flock of sheep, her teeth are like a flock rising up from its bath. . . . [W]ho are you my beloved, my beauty, tell me. . . . Do you not recognize me? Woe is me, here I am Tatyana, Pushkin's girl, Yevgeni Oneigin's lover. Ask the students in the last class at the gymna-sium and they'll tell you about my unrequited love." [18] The beloved of the Song of Songs intersects with Pushkin's romantic heroine in this passage. Later in the same passage, Lermontov and Byron are juxtaposed with Rabba, the laws of gravity with Alexander Macedon, crying babies with the landlord's ugly daughter in a wedding dress. A sustained chain of metonymic associations takes Sender Ziv from the Song of Songs to Pushkin, from rabbinics to romantic poetry, and finally from ancient world history to contemporary domestic anxiety. The mixture of primary texts within Ziv's mind and his reduction of all of it to the mundane details of daily life point to the paradoxical seamlessness of his transition from the traditional Jewish scholarly world he has escaped and the modern European intellectual world he has chosen. At the same time, the situation of the traditional Jewish scholar in a domestic quagmire is intimated in the figure of the talush studying his new holy texts not in his wife's kitchen, but in a non-Jewish landlady's who, like a wife in her own way, is waiting for his room-and-board payment.

The intertextuality of Baron's "The End of Sender Ziv," "Exams," and "Chocolate," effected through the consistent presence of the externtalush Sender Ziv, is a gesture on Baron's part toward the unity of the talush figure as it was regarded in the work of her contemporaries. Sender Ziv displays all the characteristics seen in the work of Baron's Hebrew literary peers. He is painfully shy, effeminate, and sickly and engages in Brenner-style *"nakranut,"* defined by Yirmiyahu Feierman, the talush in Brenner's *In Winter* (1903), as solipsistic, pointless, excessive introspection. The nature of the subjectivity, the nakranut of the narrator of "Exams," is challenged by Baron as she develops a parodic version of a man thinking, for the length of three pages, "lo ikhpat li" (I don't care).[19] He also spends more time thinking about the prospect of failing his exams than he spends studying for them.

Despite their seeming regression back into the world of the yeshiva, stylistically writers of the modern Hebrew renaissance were writing at a particular juncture in European literary history that enabled them to translate autobiographical sensibilities into fictional form. They were, in effect, moving from the ethos and the poetics of the early nineteenth century directly into early-twentieth-century European modernism. Russian symbolism had its peak at the end of the nineteenth century, and although prose modernism was somewhat slower to develop, the writers of the modern Hebrew renaissance were brilliantly situated to try their hands (and pens) at the newest, avant-garde narrative styles. The renegotiation of realist and mimetic conventions to represent consciousness in idiosyncratic new ways coupled with the autobiographical conventions of Haskalah literature marked a distinct movement in Hebrew prose not only "inward" toward psychological representation and "backward" toward Enlightenment autobiography but "outward" as well into the modernist fold of the European literati.

Shmuel Wersses, in a descriptive essay titled "Portrait of the Maskil as a Young Man" about the autobiographical literature of the Haskalah, points to common thematic elements that populated those texts: "The struggles and doubts of young men trying to realize the Haskalah's ideals are reflected in the biographical, autobiographical, and memoir-style compositions and epistolary literature of the period, and also in fictional form, in stories, novels, satire, and epic poetry. Certain motifs are repeated again and again in different contexts." [20]

As in the autobiographical literature of the Haskalah, during the period of the modern Hebrew renaissance, the universe of Hebrew belles letters was so small that a closed system between readers and writers guaranteed a certain incestuous identification between writers, between readers and writers, and between readers of this literature. Whereas today we may read overt similarities of theme or style or both as a gesture toward a certain convention or genre, during the modern Hebrew renaissance these similarities served to reinforce a predilection toward identification of those works with the biography of the generation reading them, and of necessity with the generation writing them. The need for readers to understand modern Hebrew renaissance literature autobiographically despite the works' explicit fictionality (through their adoption of contemporary European literary conventions of psychological realism) reflected a need for a generation to read about its own process of modernization, migration, and disillusion. These narratives came to be read not merely as the autobiographies of individuals or of a literary generation but as the autobiography of an entire generation.

Georges Gusdorf, one of the earliest theoreticians of autobiography, describes the genre as a "concern peculiar to Western man." He says that "throughout most of human history, the individual does not oppose himself to all others; he does not feel himself to exist outside of others and still less against others. . . . The important unit is never the isolated being." [21] Although Gusdorf limits his definitions of autobiography to those works that declare themselves as autobiography, his point is well taken in the context of Hebrew literary culture at the turn of the twenti-

3. Dvora Baron as a student. *Courtesy of Gnazim Archive, Ramat Gan, Israel.*

eth century. Literary expression in Hebrew until the modern period, with the exception of the medieval Hebrew poets in Spain, was discursive rather than self-declarative. Though individual speakers are acknowledged and identified throughout the rabbinic corpus (the Talmud and Midrash), it is done in order to allow for the historicization of the text as well as to facilitate legislation. Certain generations of rabbis are always deferred to in legal rulings, as are certain individuals. Thus, the necessity of "attributing" rabbinic statements to their rightful owners, a critical value in the culture of rabbinic literature, does not grow out of a culture that prioritizes the individual voices of authorship or literary inspiration. Individual voices in rabbinic literature are, rather, only the pragmatic tools for legal discourse.

According to traditional views of the Bible, God is said to be the omniscient author of the five books of Moses. Alternative authors, such as those traditionally held to be responsible for the composition of the books of Jeremiah, Isaiah, Psalms, Samuel, Ecclesiastes, and Kings, are seen as having written their books through divine inspiration, as authorial extensions of God. The figure of King David, warrior and poet, musician and lover, is the closest the ancient biblical tradition comes to attributing creative authorship within the modern romantically conceived purview of "individual talent." Even so, midrashic traditions try severely to circumscribe the scope of David's independent inspiration and individual literary skill, in deference to the fundamental principle of the entire Bible having been revealed at Sinai, either through direct divine dictation to Moses or through divine inspiration.

When Haskalah personalities began writing their autobiographies, they were, as described by Gusdorf, looking in the mirror as if for the first time. "The primitive," says Gusdorf, "who has not been forewarned is frightened of his reflection in the mirror, just as he is terrified by a photographic or motion picture image." [22] Regardless of Gusdorf's problematic use of the term "primitive," he uses a metaphor that recurs again and again, both in the discourse of the modern Hebrew renaissance and in the work of Baron. The mirror and the photographic image are particularly poignant metaphors for describing the reflexive nature of modern autobiographical expressions, or modern fictional expressions of the self that are predicated on autobiographical models. As if for the first time, modern Hebrew Haskalah writers were trying to write about the world in a way that empowered the self. The "speaker" of texts—their authors, their narrators—needed to be acknowledged because they had never before declared themselves as artists. The fear, though, and the shock of that initial declaration of the self, that initial witnessing of the experience of the self, whether in autobiography or in fiction modeled upon the psychological rhythms of autobiography, governed the Hebrew renaissance. Fear, shock, and in some cases the elation of that initial self-revelation can lead to a certain entrenchment in the "self" and fear of the "other."

Carolyn Heilbrun, in her analysis of Gusdorf's rhetoric about "each man" discovering his singularity at a certain, relatively late, point in Western history, argues that Gusdorf includes, in truth, only men. She says: "In earlier times, Gusdorf points out, in those periods and places where the 'singularity of each individual life' had not yet evolved, there was no autobiography. Inadvertently he thus describes women's existence as it continued down to the day before yesterday, certainly until long after the period in which men found their 'singularity.' " [23] In modern Hebrew literary culture where women's arrival was also belated, where did Baron's fiction fit in? One of the major concerns that contemporary critics express about the place of Baron's work in the canon of the modern Hebrew renaissance is the overeagerness to read her work autobiographically. Autobiographical reception of her work, on the one hand, would affiliate her quite strongly with her peers, because their works, as we have discussed, were understood almost in strictly autobiographical terms. On the other hand, the "autobiography" expressed in Baron's work was not, by and large, identifiable with others produced in her generation, and therefore its autobiographical overtones were not included in a closed system of resemblances such as the one described by Wersses. With the exception of several early stories dealing specifically with the culture of Jewish "external" students in eastern Europe that we will examine below, Baron's "autobiographical" works were understood to be totally idiosyncratic, totally female, and totally divorced from the ethos of her generation. Autobiographical readings of Baron's work, therefore, served to obscure her literary affiliations with her own Hebrew peers as well as with larger European movements. Because Baron's stories were thematically different from those of her peers, her supposedly autobiographical overtones were, with few exceptions, viewed not as the expression of a generation undergoing modernization, migration, and cultural transition; rather, they were seen as the isolated autobiographical expression of a woman.

The talush was irremediably gendered. Simply put, he had to be male because he was seen as the collective expression of a generation of yeshiva students struggling to become modern. Women, barred from yeshivas, could not share the biography of the talush. Most important, the talush had to be male because all the ideologies that formed him— the notion of the premodern and Christian "Jew," the fin-de-siècle feminized "Jew," and the modernist "Jew"—were all male. Even when viewed as "feminized," he was never actually female. So, on the one hand, women were implied in his identity; on the other, real women never had to be invoked or acknowledged because they were free-floating signifiers of Jewish otherness.

A critical question that has never been asked about the talush is whether he need necessarily be figured as male. The term tlushah, the feminine inflection of talush, is not to be found anywhere in the critical or primary literature. In many classic talush texts, notably in Brenner's *In Winter* (1903) and in Berdischevsky's *A Raven Flies* (1900), the talush exists alongside a female counterpart. Critics have read these women as mere projections of the male talush or as the object of his desire, but never as a talush (or a tlushah) in her own right.

In her study of Jewish women writers in czarist Russia, Carole Balin reflects on the reluctance of the Jewish intelligentsia to employ the feminine noun "maskilah" to describe women active in the Haskalah and to parallel the term "maskil" broadly used for male Haskalah activists.

> The connections forged between *maskilim* and female Hebraists neither elevated any single woman writer of Hebrew to the vanguard of the *Haskalah* nor defined her as a *maskilah*. In fact, the designations used by the *maskilim* for a woman writing in Hebrew may be revealing. As in other patriarchal structures, masculinity was conflated with the universal and the unmarked, while femininity attracted ambivalence and attention as the 'other.' A woman writing in Hebrew received the appellation *almah maskilah* (enlightened maiden), *bat maskelet* (enlightened daughter), or *ishah maskelet* (enlightened woman). That is, an adjectival form (*maskelet*) was employed rather than the corresponding feminine noun for *maskil*—*maskilah*.[24]

Balin's observation about the total absence of a maskilah in the discourse of the Haskalah illuminates the absence of a tlushah or a female talush in the literary discourse of the modern Hebrew renaissance. The difference between a tlushah and a woman who is simply forlorn is the difference between a social and literary "type" and a state of being. In naming a woman a maskilah or a tlushah, one must commit to acknowledging a movement, or a trend. But women were viewed as marginal to the turmoil of Jewish modernization during the period of the Enlightenment and renaissance. Even, as we have discussed, when women were linked to a trend in Jewish secularization during the Enlightenment, their active pursuit of non-Jewish partners and education was viewed as a symptom, but not a statement. No one gave women abandoning the world of traditional practice and intellectual restriction and embarking on a path of secularization a distinct and unifying name. But what's in a name? What are the advantages and disadvantages of distinguishing female counterparts or equivalents to male "types," either literary or social? Is the lack of a maskilah or tlushah a form of concession to the compulsory male universal? Or perhaps implicit in the absence of female grammatical equivalents to these central types in European Jewish modernity we can detect a form of resistance to the reductive notion that male types must necessarily have corresponding female ones.

As a woman writer writing about a literary "type" who was nearly always inflected as male, as autobiographical, and as generational, Baron shifted the talush's center of gravity. In her trilogy "Exams," "Chocolate," and "The End of Sender Ziv," Baron creates a pastiche of talush figures and struggles with the possibility of a fully subjective, psychologically realized female talush, the tlushah. Stylistically and ideologically, Baron experiments with the modernist conventions established by the recognized talush writers—most notably M. Y. Berdischevsky and Y. H. Brenner. In the course of Baron's three-story cycle, Sender Ziv lives with a series of widowed landladies, is revolted by the daughter of one, and is in love with the daughter of another. He cannot pass his exams, cannot write, cannot study any longer, and is desperately trying to learn Russian. As in Berdischevsky's *A Raven Flies,* he follows the woman with whom he is obsessed across a body of water to a resort town, only to be rebuffed. As in Brenner's story *In Winter,* he has a female compatriot in "uprootedness," another extern who is in love with him, but whom he does not recognize as a potential lover. The other women in Baron's trilogy are either remote and unattainable love objects or hideous representations of the life that awaits the talush if he does not pass his exams. The only featured female protagonist can be found in the final story of the trilogy, "The End of Sender Ziv." She is named Rachel, reminiscent of Rachel in Berdischevsky's *A Raven Flies* and of Rahil in Brenner's *In Winter*. Berdischevsky's Rachel—also an extern—is in love with the male protagonist, the talush, but is rebuffed by him. Brenner's Rahil is an assimilated, upper-class young Jewish woman with whom his protagonist is in love, but she is unattainable. Baron's "Sender Ziv" trilogy offers an alternative to the exclusively male talush text while gently satirizing its overdetermined modernist conventions of psychological interiority and prodding its authors into a realization of the possible consequences of its gender exclusivity.

I will quote the beginning of the first story in Baron's talush trilogy, "Exams," in full to provide a general sense of the talush "type" as well as to furnish an introduction to the tone and content of Baron's trilogy:

Here I am, lying prone on my large sofa, with my eyes wide open. My head is totally sunken into my pillow. Fluttering and stumbling within my empty brain is one persistent thought: Who cares?

On the bottom floor of the house a clock strikes the hour slowly and stolidly—as if worried about making a mistake. It counts, precisely, hour after hour, twelve o'clock. And I wait until the echo of the final chord dies in the air, and then I go back to thinking: Who cares?

And I am certain that downstairs on the bottom floor, near the table, the shopkeeper sits—the mistress of the house—and counts small change. Her eyes are crusty, her kerchief is flung down around her shoulders, and her thin fingers, stained from salty brine, handles the small copper coins and combines them into rubles. Her narrow forehead is marked by two deep wrinkles and she thinks about the fact that up here, in my apartment, she should whitewash the filthy walls. The sofa (on which I am currently lying), she recalls, is punctured and losing its stuffing and if only I wanted, if I just said the word, they would decorate the whole room with nice furniture and hang pictures, curtains—just one word.

Opposite her, poking out from a pile of pillows and comforters in the bed, her spinster daughter's face darkens. Two rotten rows of teeth peep out of her gaping mouth—her breath smells. She hugs the thick, cold blanket to her chest with bare arms.

Tomorrow, when I go downstairs to get a spoonful of sugar for my coffee, the mistress of the house, the girl's mother, will lightheartedly call through her daughter's door: "Henya, Henya, come sweeten his life, ha, ha. . ."

And here, opposite my sofa there is a sliver of light from the room next door. There, skinny young men deliberate, their heads sunken into their books as they learn. A small light burns there—a naked bulb that throws weird disembodied shadows—people whose limbs are twisted and convulsing—onto the ceiling.

Ay-ay-ay, Ay-ay-ay . . .

Husky voices, saturated with sorrow, despair. They all join together into a single, heart-breaking melody. They just arrived today. The sons of small towns and villages—strange clothes on their backs, strange accents on their tongues, and their melody—like the sound of a single string—wistful and piercing:

Ay-ay-ay, Ay-ay-ay . . .

Why are they standing there?

In the corner of my room stands a rickety bed on broken legs. I turn my face to it: "Tell me please, Ziv, Why are they standing there?"

The bed opposite me creaks and my neighbor, Ziv, his body curled up under his blanket and his eyes squeezed shut says: "Strange! In the whole of God's world there are many cities, and in each city there are many gymnasiums—and to be tested, they all come to ours." [25]

The subjective voice that carries the narrative and the named "subject" of the story—Sender Ziv—are two different people. Baron will not allow for a homodiegetic narrator—a narrator who is fully embodied and named as a character in the story. This concession is to the fact that the talush was generally received as a male, purportedly autobiographical, voice. The talush as an autobiographical metonymy of modern Jewish experience was often figured as a writer. At the same time, part of what made him a talush was his inability to write. In Baron's "The End of Sender Ziv," this paradox is cracked wide open, as a woman writer who comes increasingly to identify with the narrator of the story writes the story of a talush, emphasizing his modernist fictionality and not his autobiographical identity. Is she a "tlushah" or isn't she?

The two main protagonists in the "The End of Sender Ziv" are Sender Ziv and Rachel, both externs. Sender Ziv, an extern far from home who cannot pass the entrance exams to the university, is in love with Chana, a local governess and the daughter of his former landlady. Chana, in turn, is in love with a soldier. Rachel, also an extern and a colleague of Sender's, is in love with Sender Ziv. Chana and Rachel go on vacation to a nearby resort town—Rachel with her tutorial students, Chana with the children for whom she is governess. Rachel invites Sender Ziv to join her there, tempting him to come by guaranteeing a meeting with Chana. He takes Rachel up on her offer, but his visit is short-lived because he dies, falling off a precipice after spotting the soldier with whom he imagines Chana to be in love.

The only articulated desire in this story is Sender's. He is, after all, a talush, and according to convention, the talush must be in love. Unlike the conventional talush narrative, however, this story is rendered in the third person, and the dominant point of view is Rachel's. As I mentioned earlier, the "Rachel" characters in Berdischevsky's and Brenner's classic talush texts are narratologically and thematically simply foils to the male talush. In Baron's story as well, Rachel's subjectivity is never fully developed. It is in fact seriously circumscribed, operating primarily in order to grant us insight into Sender Ziv's character as a talush.

Yet even as Rachel represses her own consciousness in order to serve as a vehicle for Ziv's, she distinguishes herself from the Rachels in the stories by Brenner and Berdischevsky. This separation can be illustrated by two passages toward the beginning of the story. We read:

Rachel Feinberg, the elderly private tutor Rachel Feinberg, who had taken the exams along with Sender Ziv and had also failed by one mathematics problem, entered his room at one such twilight hour and the sight that appeared before her eyes shook her so deeply that she remained transfixed at the door and couldn't move from the spot. Sender Ziv, short and gaunt, sat shrunken and alone at the large desk, his face buried in the textbooks before him, and his body shook with such odd shudders that it looked as if he were in the throes of some kind of seizure.[26]

This passage is our first introduction to Rachel. We are immediately given reason to believe that she, like Ziv, is a classic talush simply by virtue of the fact that she is an extern who has failed her exams. The moment she enters the story, however, she does so not so much as a protagonist in her own right, but as an omniscient observer of Ziv. Indeed, Ziv reflects later on the experience of having been barged in on by Rachel: "Suddenly he felt acutely that if he didn't hurry to get away from this harbor and from these people around him, they would all witness the same thing that had once overcome him in his room, the time Miss Feinberg had come to see him and he had forgotten to close his door properly." [27] Rachel has violated Ziv's privacy, has witnessed what she is not supposed to witness. Although Rachel gives us privileged access to Sender Ziv, she also gives Ziv privileged access to Chana, acting again as an omniscient narrator in the text of his life. Here we are given a description of the view from the window of a room Rachel deliberately rented for herself so Ziv could use it to glimpse Chana: "Through one of these windows the little garden, Dr. Starkman's flower garden, across from the big park, could be seen in exquisite detail, the garden with its narrow footpaths of freshly raked sand that wound their way among the flowerbeds and the governess, the Starkman children's governess, who was now strolling along those sandy paths." [28] The Starkmans' governess is Chana, Sender Ziv's beloved. Rachel, situated between Ziv and the reader, also situates herself between Ziv and Chana; she functions, if not narratologically, then thematically, as a stand-in for a narrator, negotiating not only the reader's but also Sender's perspective on the unfolding drama.

It is important to emphasize that Baron foregrounds Rachel's position in the story by not writing a first-person narrative from Sender Ziv's point of view. At the same time, she does not write a first-person female talush narrative from Rachel's point of view. She avoids the first person, because she, like Henry James, wants to avoid the "large ease of autobiography." [29] By making it a point not to employ the first person, Baron reconstitutes the autobiographical premise of the talush into a fictional one, suggesting that someone on the outside, someone marginal to the experience of tlishut, must be the real author of the talush text.

In a very real sense, Rachel is the writer that Ziv can never be: "He did not have the gift of expressing himself in words, no. He couldn't write, develop his thoughts on paper, not even as well, for example as that kind spinster, the external student Rachel Feinberg, who not long after began to write and send him short, beautiful letters from the summer resort every day." Rachel's desire for Ziv is articulated not in the content of her letters, explicitly, but in their context. Linda S. Kauffman has argued that in the tradition of epistolary literature, letters are a way for women to transform themselves into writers. She has further discussed the conjunction of epistolary discourse and discourses of desire, arguing that "desire is infinitely transcribable, yet ultimately elusive." [30] Thus, the letter is the perfect way to communicate the sublimated or unrequited nature of desire because it is one part of a dialogue that may or may not be completed. In other words, Rachel transforms herself from an extern into a writer via her letters to Ziv. As she begins to articulate her desire, she learns subterfuge, art, and convention. Whereas Ziv never moves beyond his desire for Chana, in her frustrated acknowledgment that Ziv will never reciprocate, Rachel becomes the author that Ziv will never be.

By the story's end, Rachel goes so far as to be the only guarantor of any kind of text on Ziv's life as she saves money to inscribe his gravestone after his death, even if it is only a "simple headstone with the cheapest inscription in small letters." [31] How are Rachel's letters and her inscription on Ziv's grave interconnected within the context of Rachel's unfulfilled desires? The rhetoric of "revival" that characterized Baron's literary milieu implied a cognizance of death; the Hebrew language was seen as a dying monster, a formidable tradition without the vernacular or cultural apparatus to survive national modernization of the Jews, and the modern Hebrew renaissance was a way of pulling Hebrew from its early grave, breathing life into its nostrils before it died completely. Throughout her corpus, Baron questions the marginal position of women's voices within the life-and-death culture of the modern Hebrew renaissance. Here, by having Rachel inscribe her desire for Ziv onto his gravestone, she confirms the death of the talush and all the sublimated desire that went into making him a talush by writing a commemoration for him. She does not revive him as much as she buries him and writes, alive, beyond him. Some things, Rachel indicates in unison with Baron, are best commemorated though not resurrected. Within the "revival" rhetoric of the modern Hebrew renaissance, Baron indicates that there are certain textual traditions—perhaps Haskalah autobiography with its apparently compulsory maleness—that should be laid to rest in order to make way for fiction writers of a new generation, women as well as men.

Rachel's ability to inscribe Ziv's grave, even in the simple manner described, is positioned in direct contrast to Ziv's inability to do the same thing for his own father. The story opens when Sender Ziv receives a postcard from his sister. Her postcard is our first introduction to him:

> In a foldout postcard from his little shtetl, Sender Ziv's younger sister, the married one, once asked him when his troubles and wanderings in the distant, foreign city would finally come to an end. The grave—she wrote to him—their father's grave had been without a stone or marker for over two years now. . . . Just that week their wealthy cousin had returned from the city and whom had he bumped into there but Sender her brother, and he had seen him walking around the city the picture of gloom, dressed in rags, because he had no tutoring jobs to support him and no hope of getting his diploma, no prospects at all—and when, she would like to know, would all of this finally end? Wasn't it high time already?[32]

In the paragraph following the introduction of the postcard, an omniscient narrator describes Ziv in exactly the same language. As in his sister's account, Ziv is presented as "the picture of gloom, dressed in rags," and his consciousness is portrayed in a replication of her language of it being "high time already" for Ziv to move on. Ziv, from the story's outset, has been written about by someone else. In this case, it is his biological sister. In time, he is also written about by his spiritual sister, Rachel, the female extern who calls him, as we shall see in the next passage, her "soul brother."

At moments, the distance between Rachel's letters and the narrative is abolished. Her subjective recording of certain experiences in the form of a correspondence with Ziv becomes the text of the narrative itself:

> And here too, she wrote to him, there are small flower gardens beside the larger houses and gazebos and paths, narrow footpaths strewn with sand

where one can go for a pleasant stroll at sunset. In the leafy arbors deep within the forest it was almost always dark and quiet, a cool and sweet darkness, but at the same time the large meadow near these arbors, by Dr. Starkman's house, was full of radiant sunlight and children of all ages and the doctor's children, let by their governess—was there any need to ask him yet again if he would pay a visit here soon? Certainly he would come, her soul brother—she finished her letter with a quote from Nadson's poetry.[33]

The shifting tenses, from present ("there are small flower gardens") to past ("in the leafy arbors deep within the forest it was almost always dark and quiet") indicate a movement from the voice of Rachel's letter to the preterite convention of omniscient narration.[34] But in the continuation of the paragraph, as we encounter the question "Was there any need to ask him yet again if he would pay a visit here soon?" we are alerted to Rachel's idiom and her consciousness. We are not sure if she has written this passage or if she is thinking it, but with the next line ("Certainly he would come, her soul brother—she finished her letter with a quote from Nadson's poetry") we are reintroduced both to the text of her letter and the distancing effect of omniscient narration. She writes the "soul brother" quote to Sender, and then the narrator takes over, describing it as such. The epistolary convention for female subjectivity is employed by Baron here to transform the female letter writer into the female author. The talush may be a frustrated writer, but Baron's female protagonist is not. Even so, Rachel does not use her writing to express her own desire. Rather, she displaces her desire onto Sender's yearning for Chana. The birth of a female talush or a tlushah is rendered problematic in this paradox. Even as she exists alongside Sender Ziv, fully embodied, fully desirous, Rachel can only write his desire, his needs. The letter she writes to Sender inviting him to join her, as we have already seen, is all about Chana.

Not only can Ziv not write, but he can live only inasmuch as other people's scripts for him will allow. Just as Rachel scripts Ziv's meetings with Chana, a friend of Ziv's scripts his death:

One of Sender Ziv's acquaintances, an external student who penned stories that he submitted to a Hebrew literary journal, mocked Sender Ziv and shrugged his shoulders when the latter unburdened his secret love once to him. "Believe me, my friend," the young story-teller told him, "that if we were to put down in writing a description of a bachelor over thirty, a man with no social position and no solid ground beneath his feet, dried up and dirt poor, losing more of his hair every day, a broken shell of a man, and he, this bachelor, his only ambition is just for the shadow of a fair young girl, and he daydreams about her and paces underneath her window at night like a schoolboy—if we were to write like that, they would say that we were falsifying reality, that this was fanciful and beneath criticism." [35]

In this passage, Ziv's writer friend discusses how ridiculous Ziv's desire for Chana is because of its untranscribability. No one would write it because no one would read it, he quips; it is simply too absurd. In communicating this feeling to Ziv, however, his "writer friend" actually inscribes Ziv's death, using the language of Ziv's own demise in his fictional projection of the doomed nature of such a tale. He calls Ziv a "broken shell of a man" in a foreshadowing of the way his death will be described at the end of the story: "For an instant it seemed that he was about to escape into a nearby trail which was across from him now, but then he changed his mind and flinched violently, and losing his balance, slowly pitched backward from the ridge path and tumbled to the boulders below, where he lay, his body a broken shell." [36] Although even Ziv's friend, who is identified as someone who "penned" stories, does not actually write down the tragic story of Ziv's life, Rachel does. In the final analysis, Rachel is figured as the only writer of Ziv's life as she saves money for the inscription on his gravestone. As someone who does not dwell on her own failures, does not claim to be unable to write, is not constructed as a model for an entire generation, and never expects to have her misdirected love reciprocated, Rachel does not live up to the conventions of the talush. But she lives and writes while Ziv dies.

One thing that sets Ziv apart from other talush figures in works by Brenner and Berdischevsky is the fact that he does not recognize his own talush status: "He had never thought about whether he was being true to life or falsifying reality, but the fact that his heart swelled inside him and choked him with pain and longing no less than the heart of some schoolboy—of that there could not be the slightest doubt." [37] Because Ziv is not writing his own story, there is a lack of self-consciousness on his part that undoes the conflation between the Hebrew modernist literary "type" and the autobiographical male writer in the first-person talush texts of the modern Hebrew renaissance. Perhaps this lack of insight on his part mercifully strips him of his status as a talush because, in the end, he does have a way out, unlike his endlessly self-reflexive peers. On the other hand, perhaps this lack of insight is what distinguishes him as the ultimate talush, the one who is killed because he can exist only in a text.

Baron suggests, in killing off Sender Ziv, that he is nothing more than a fictional whim, significant only inasmuch as he expresses the desire of Hebrew writers to affiliate with the modernists and for the Hebrew reading public to see their narrative of apostasy and alienation writ large. But to render the talush the only possible autobiographical subject, to make him the sign of Hebrew modernist aspirations, she reminds us, is impossibly reductive. Despite the talush's unitary presence in the prose fiction of the modern Hebrew renaissance, Baron proposes that he is nothing more than a literary convention. Baron sees no advantage to crafting a female equivalent for the Hebrew modernist type or to the national autobiographical subject. Rather, she asserts the staying power of a figure that defies convention. A literary figure like Rachel who cannot be identified as synonymous with the subjects of the other talush texts of Baron's generation, partly because she does not fit neatly into their literary conventions but also simply because she is a female subject, actually provides a welcome perspective on the impossibly solipsistic and self-defeating nature of collective literary figurations such as the talush.

Having rejected the possibility that Baron represents a female tlushah as parallel to the male talush, we find ourselves asking, at this juncture, whether Baron develops figures in her work that qualify as talush in a different sense. Who, in Baron's work, was geographically disoriented, authorially figured, alienated, isolated, and reflective? In Baron's more mature canonic work she does not create a female tlushah that parallels the male talush. Rather, she weaves the notion of tlishut, or "uprootedness," into her work in the guise of a variety of women who narrate and are featured in her stories: the rabbi's daughter, the child of the shtetl, and the displaced European women of the new Yishuv.

2

Strange Sympathy

The Talush Imperative

> Literary representations of the shtetl demonstrate the tendency for poets to turn, time and again, to the landscape of their upbringing for literary material. This tendency, viewed by many in our midst as the proof of an inability to shoot roots down into our new soil, can sometimes be justified.—Yitzhak Ogen, "Dvora Baron" (1943)

> If one day the painful image presented by David Frishmann should come to pass, and a massive deluge should eradicate Eastern European Jewry, and our nation should want to preserve in a museum an artistic reproduction of that lost world, it won't be enough simply to include the works of Mendele alone. . . . Dvora Baron's "trifles," the details that she depicts, are needed to complete the portrait.—S. Y. Pinles, "Mah she-Hayah" (What Has Been [1939])

DESPITE THE PRESENCE in her corpus of three stories focused on a talush named Sender Ziv, Baron has never been included in the "brotherhood" of authors who wrote about the talush as a literary, a cultural, or a modernist trope. In this chapter, I consider Baron's subversion of the talush not strictly in terms of his own self-defeating solipsism but also in terms of the critical establishment's inability to recognize "tlishut," or uprootedness, in figures or discourses beyond the monolithic male protagonists of the modern Hebrew renaissance. Indeed, the figure of a rabbi's daughter, both as a child witness and as an adult narrator, articulates the quintessential voice of tlishut in Baron's work. Similarly, the women inhabiting the new Yishuv in several of Baron's stories set in

Palestine serve as models for a new kind of tlishut in modern Hebrew literature—an uprootedness borne of experiential continuity despite abrupt geographic fissure.

Gershon Shaked has explicitly stated that "[Baron's] characters are not talush. They are simply downtrodden figures life has treated poorly. While she creates figures similar to those that were created by her contemporaries and the fate of her characters is no better than the fate of the standard talush, the narrator judges them favorably, allowing them a way out of their distress." Shaked points out that a "favorable judgement" on the part of a narrator is one of the most important criteria for disqualifying a text from inclusion in the talush literary corpus. According to Shaked, Baron's narrators "judge" her characters too "favorably" to allow them to evolve into actual *tlushim*. As articulated by one of Baron's earliest reviewers, Y. Uvasi, Baron's narrators know (seemingly too well) how to "extract light from all the darkest corners and hiding places" of the human psyche.[1]

But it is precisely that "sympathetic" presence, the grace granted her suffering protagonists, that constitutes the strongest argument for the presence of a talush in Baron's work. I propose that Baron creates a distinctly talush presence in many of her works, not as a tlushah or the female equivalent of the modernist or nationalist type, nor as a character type such as the extern. Rather, Baron's talush figures are her "sympathetic" narrators who, despite their purported compassion, keep their distance from the narratives they voice.

Writing in a literary climate in Europe wherein the shtetl was represented primarily as a quagmire of corruption and ignorance, and in Palestine after her immigration where the ideal literary texts focused on the rehabilitation of Jewish identity in Palestine, Baron's texts that continued in some form or another throughout her career to communicate a "sympathetic" view of the shtetl were ambiguously framed by narrators who found it necessary to negotiate a variety of contradictions. Aside from her rejection of the imperative to depict the decline of the shtetl and her resistance to writing about agricultural collectives or socialist ideals in Palestine, Baron's narrators posed, when embodied within the narrative text itself, as female authors, largely unprecedented beings in the literary culture of the modern Hebrew renaissance.

Baron's narrators in her canonical later works are, more often than not, homodiegetic—present in the narrative as characters. Not wholly participating because, like Sender Ziv's roommate in "Exams," they are generally unnamed, they peep in and out of the stories, interacting in a limited fashion with other, named, characters. And they are, indeed, frequently sympathetic to the plight of their fellow characters. But that sympathy or compassion is rendered from an uncomfortable distance. The narrator in these particular stories expresses a seeming desire to be more involved in the unfolding narrative but demonstrates restraint. In so doing, the narrator is betwixt and between—neither a character nor an omniscient narrator, neither wholly present nor wholly absent, both sympathetic and distant.

The talush, as we recall, is a social chameleon whose colors never change quite rapidly or thoroughly enough to allow him to blend into any of the contradictory yet simultaneous worlds he inhabits. He has pious sensibilities and apostate practices, is an old man in terms of life experiences, and is a little boy in emotional maturity. He is a keen observer of others who is nearly oblivious to his own shortcomings. The talush, most important, is never wholly in any world and is thus always on the outside looking in—like a narrator who is neither omniscient nor entirely implicated in the plot of the story. There are things that Baron's narrators cannot know and cannot tell us, whereas there are other things to which, given their lack of omniscience, they seem to have uncanny access. It is here that the sense of tlishut becomes fully developed in Baron's works.

Most notable among these cagey homodiegetic narrators is the figure of the rabbi's daughter. Because Baron herself was a rabbi's daughter, this narrator has come, in the critical literature, to be identified with Baron herself. Baron's rabbi's daughter is an extension of the rabbi in many instances because she is the mouthpiece for traditional texts and the bearer of knowledge to her friends and other community members in a variety of settings. As Ruth Adler has articulated, this rabbi's daughter is, as the daughter of the figure at the center of the shtetl's social and intellectual gravity, also the "daughter of the shtetl."[2] It is the synthesis of these two roles that serves as the primary locus for Baron's voicing of tlishut. The rabbi's daughter or daughter of the shtetl indicates, in a variety of narratological and thematic ways throughout Baron's corpus, that she is, at the time of the story's composition, caught in a spatial and temporal vortex that keeps her from being comfortable either in the world of the narrative or in the world beyond the narrative in which the narrative is written.

Baron's story "Mah she-Hayah" (What Has Been) (1939) begins in the following way:

> Of all the youngsters I went about with in my home-town, the one dearest to me was Mina, our neighbor's girl, who was nicknamed "Spotty" on account of her freckles. Mina was hardly what one might call a pretty girl; but, we all know the saying that it is in the earthenware jar that the best wine is preserved, and have we not seen the living word of God inscribed in a simple scroll? Yet, as I come to tell about her I find I cannot abstain from sketching in details of the life surrounding her, just as it would be inconceivable for a painter to draw any object, living or inanimate, without setting it in an appropriate background.[3]

In addition to posing as an eyewitness to and interpreter of the culture of the shtetl, by invoking first midrash ("it is in the earthenware jar that the best wine is preserved") and then the Torah ("the living word of God inscribed in a simple scroll"), the narrator prepares us for her dominant role in Mina's acquisition of literacy. Midway through the story, we read:

> From the way I once saw Mina turn over the pages of a book, I gathered that she didn't know how to read. I, then, offered to teach her, and in our spare time, usually in the afternoons, I began to show her how to make out the different letters. We started with the alphabet, and once she was able to form syllables, we passed on to the prayer book. It was not long before we were reading the Bible, which was used at the time as a textbook for Hebrew lessons. . . .
>
> Seeing how great was her yearning for knowledge and since her vocabulary was still too poor for her to be able to read in Hebrew, I brought her any book in Yiddish I could lay my hands on at home. These were no great words, to be sure, yet they faithfully mirrored life as it was and bore the rough stamp of truth. And she, like all of us when we first begin to read, seemed to plunge into a new dream world.[4]

This narrator is the vehicle for our encounter with Mina because she is framed as the author of the story. At the same time, she is the vehicle for Mina's encounter with literature, teaching her to read. This presentation of a narrator as a literary mediator, both for the reader of the text and for the protagonist within the text, is reminiscent of the double mediation we observed in the case of Rachel in "The End of Sender Ziv." As we recall, Rachel gives the reader insight into Sender Ziv's character in ways that only an omniscient narrator should be able to do. Similarly, she textually mediates Sender Ziv's life in ways that he cannot, by serving as a literary go-between for him and Chana, and finally by inscribing his gravestone. Here in "What Has Been" a narrator, inflected as a writer, looking back at the figures from her hometown, reflects on her own role in bearing literacy to one of its inhabitants. The rabbi's daughter as teacher of literacy within the story and as narrator of the story is a pivotal figure in the protagonist's as well as the reader's literary experience.

The figure of the narrator, teaching the protagonist to read, is inflected differently in the story "Mishpahah" (Family) (1933). Here the roles of erudite narrator, literary author, rabbi's daughter, and daughter of the shtetl most explicitly converge. Although I will deal more extensively with this story as I explore the place of Baron's fictional sermons in the construction of a literary vernacular during the modern Hebrew renaissance, here I will focus on the placement of a first-person narrator—a rabbi's daughter—at a particularly self-consciously literary juncture of the narrative. "Family" tells the story of Dina and Baruch, a young couple who cannot conceive a child and are forced, after ten loving and peaceful years of marriage, to divorce. During the divorce proceedings, the first-person narrator, unnamed as in "What Has Been," appears in the following way:

> There was no joy in our house—which served also as the community house—whenever a divorce was due to be arranged. "The deed of divorce," my father the Rabbi would say, "is called a sefer keritut, a 'deed of excision,' for by it one soul is cut off from another soul."
>
> He never touched any food that day, and he would stay up most of the previous night poring over his books, checking the names of the parties

and the grounds, or re-studying the Talmudic tractate dealing with the whole subject of divorce.

The sages of old held divergent views on the matter. When, later in life I studied their dicta, I could well imagine with which of them my father sided. A kind-hearted man, he no doubt held with those who, like Rabbi Eliezer and his school, condemned separation, and he was probably deeply affected by the eloquent parable by which the very altar in the temple was said to shed tears for a divorced woman. Yet, on the other hand, he must have remembered also that wondrous night vision, when the Lord had led Abraham outside, and he must have felt the forlorn anguish that made the patriarch cry out: "Lord God, what wilt though give me, seeing that I go childless!"[5]

The narrator places herself (grammatically gendering herself as female, as one must do in Hebrew), in the last pages of the story, into the middle of Dina and Baruch's divorce proceedings. She does not appear earlier in the story, and she plays no role here other than to demonstrate knowledge of the emotional state of her father rabbi on the eve of having to oversee a divorce. This narrator does not teach her father traditional texts in the way that she taught Mina how to read, but she presents her father's emotional state and subjective consciousness vis-à-vis an overview of the traditional rabbinic texts that contribute to his sense of the tragedy of divorce.

The narrator of both stories—appearing belatedly but eruditely in "Family" and consistently but namelessly throughout "What Has Been"—is inscrutable. Who is she? From whence is she returning? Does she have a name, a vocation, a reason for returning? At the end of "What Has Been," the narrator orients her readers to her whereabouts in the present:

For a long time I—now settled in my new homeland—heard nothing of the family. News began to reach us of the horrors that befell our brethren, and many believed that all had perished; yet I, in my heart of hearts had faith that He who keeps alive the seed of grain under the winter snow and gives strength to the tree-trunk to weather the severest storm, had preserved some survivor of this family.

Years later, there came to see me a young lad from my home town; and I immediately saw that he was a sturdy fellow of fine mettle. In reply to my question about his parentage, he told me his mother's name was Mina and his father had been a miller in the village of Libidov. He himself had just arrived in the country with a group of immigrants.[6]

Linking her personal past to her literary present, the narrator presents herself and the son of her friend Mina on the same (unnamed) shores as the only remnants of a destroyed culture. A link has been established not only between places, because the narrator is now located in a "new homeland," but also between generations, because she is interacting with the child of the friend she taught to read and whose story she has communicated to the world in writing. The narrator, a gentle, subtle presence throughout the story, has become the final, dominant voice in the story, reminding us that she is the ultimate arbiter of this text. Still, in her namelessness, in the anonymity of the aforementioned homeland, in the cursory and sudden allusion to cataclysm, this narrator leaves many loose ends. There is, to her voice, a sense of "uprootedness," a sense of the wholly literary like the talush in the Sender Ziv trilogy who, in the final analysis, is lost in the literary shuffle of his own exemplarity on the horizon of European modernism.

The rabbi's daughter as the narrator and author of many of Baron's texts presents herself, self-consciously, as a singularly literary figure. In the same way that Baron kills off Sender Ziv because he is nothing more than a text written by others, in the case of the rabbi's daughter, we see the opposite effect. No one but the rabbi's daughter seems to be capable of generating many of Baron's texts. Even in the case of a seemingly omnisciently narrated story like "Family," the rabbi's daughter steps in belatedly and presents herself as an important source of literary knowledge and perhaps the author of the story itself.

The narrator's identity as a variation on the classic talush grows out of her position as an insider—the rabbi's daughter, no less—in the destroyed culture of the shtetl. Like the classic talush, the rabbi's daughter here is implicated in the authorship of the text that seems, in some ways, to exist independently of her but in other ways to depend wholly on her as its literary channel to the outside world. In other words, just as talush texts are said to be spoken in the voice of the talush, even as he laments his inability to write, so too, in the case of the rabbi's daughter as narrator, the text depicts a world that she has left behind long ago. Its existence, it seems, is wholly dependent on her decision to depict it in literature.

Dan Miron, in his important essay "The Literary Image of the Shtetl," entirely omits Baron from his catalog of shtetl writers.[7] Nevertheless, in a survey of early reviews of Baron's collections *Ketanot* (Trifles) (1934), *Mah she-Hayah* (What Has Been) (1939), *le 'Et 'Atah* (For the Time Being) (1943), and *Parshiyat* (Tales) (1951), most discussions of Baron's work focus on her treatment of the shtetl.[8] Critics, for the most part, were unable to see beyond Baron's shtetl and viewed it not simply as the setting for, but as the subject of, her work. The consensus among these early critics is that Baron gives us access to women's experience in the shtetl, to the intimate rhythms of its daily life, to the beauty beneath its poverty, and to the holiness beneath its vulgarity. Although one early critic, Yitzhak Ogen, explicitly argues that Baron's shtetl is presented from a "female" point of view and therein lies the difference between hers and all the other shtetl narratives that are told from a "male" point of view, Y. Uvasi wrests narrative agency altogether from Baron's supposedly "female" narrators and "female" perspective and argues at one point that it seems as if the shtetl itself narrates Baron's stories.[9]

Ogen, in a 1943 review of Baron's *For the Time Being*, remarks, in a somewhat underhanded fashion: "Literary representations of the shtetl demonstrate the tendency for poets to turn, time and again, to the landscape of their upbringing for literary material. This tendency, viewed by many in our midst as the proof of an inability to shoot roots down into our new soil, can sometimes be justified when it is used as the basis for a profound subjective vision."[10] Beginning his review in this way, Ogen betrays his own anxiety over literary works featuring the shtetl authored by writers on the new Yishuv. He valorizes what I would call "local mimesis," or the presentation in literature of the locality in which the literature was written. In his 1950 essay "Concerning Our Literature," Dov Sadan introduces a precursor to "local" mimesis in Zionist nationalist thought when he discusses the well-known notion of literature as a model "for" as opposed to a representation "of" reality. This particular variety of mimesis—not a reflection, but rather a blueprint of reality—became essential to critical understandings of the role of Hebrew in the construction of an "imagined" national community for Jews on Palestinian ground. Sadan formulates his sense of mimesis in a Hebrew literary context in the late nineteenth century as an "as-if" mimesis—a prescription for what could grow out of a fully realized commitment to the transformation of textual culture into a living one.

As we know from the contemporary discourse of mimesis, most mimesis is, in fact, a form of as-if mimesis, or the scripting of a future reality on the basis of an imagined one. Even the earliest theorists of mimesis—Plato and Aristotle—viewed the act of representation as a "shadow play" in which representation is far from a direct, hierarchical, transparent act of depicting reality in art. Nancy Armstrong points to the dynamic introduction of a bourgeoisie ideal in eighteenth- and nineteenth-century England via photographs, that most purportedly mimetic of the arts. Rather than simply reflecting ideals and disseminating them, she argues, photographs were the vehicle by which those ideals were generated.[11] Even now, the photographs of hyperslender models, as we know, have dictated the terms of beauty to generations of women of more ample proportions who have proceeded, dangerously, to shape themselves accordingly.[12]

Sadan discusses the relationship between the creation of an as-if reality in Hebrew letters during the Haskalah and the use of the Hebrew language in life: "The Enlightenment writers can be seen as the unconscious servants of reality, more than they could ever have imagined. A reality blossomed, naturally, out of and into their language and literature."[13] According to Sadan, Hebrew life as represented in Hebrew literature served as a model, albeit unintentionally, for the subsequent construction of a Hebrew-speaking society in Palestine. Hebrew letters created an as-if reality that Sadan hoped, in time, would become "locally" mimetic, would represent in Hebrew a physical and linguistic milieu that actually existed in Hebrew. In other words, Hebrew literature would become a mirror and not just a projection of Hebrew life in the Jewish homeland.

Dvora Baron did not write an as-if literature, describing the national revival in the present or projecting a revived culture in the future. Neither did she write a locally mimetic literature, describing (for the most part) the fledgling Jewish milieu of Hebrew Tel Aviv where she lived for most of her literary career. Rather, in choosing the shtetl as the setting (and as we saw above, according to many, the subject and voice) for much of her work, she constructs a different kind of "imagined community" from the one that was being promoted in her literary milieu. She creates a sense of geographic continuity and communal imagination that includes the shtetl as opposed to the kind of local mimesis that promoted a fixation on the communities living on the Yishuv in the present, or an as-if mimesis that promoted a fixation on the communities imagined in the future of the Yishuv. Rather, particularly in her depiction of the shtetl, Baron employs what I would call a mimesis of transition.

Before I define what I mean by a mimesis of transition as it distinguishes itself from as-if mimesis and local mimesis, I would like to reflect for a moment on why I call the dynamic evolution of representational values during the period of the modern Hebrew renaissance mimetic as opposed, simply, to representational. Why, in other words, don't I formulate a taxonomy of representational classifications as opposed to mimetic classifications, employing, for example, the terms "reverse representation," "local representation," and so forth?

As Sidra DeKoven Ezrahi has argued, Judaism has been a particularly mimetic culture for millennia. She claims that Jewish art is an art of desire and longing, an art of distance from the sacred object, and as such is predicated either on the disappearance or on the unobtainable nature of the original. Modern Jewish culture, as we know it, is built upon the "cornerstone" of primordially imagined cultures such as the biblical and the temple periods. Alternatively, it is focused on a future culture of messianic redemption and geographic homecoming to the promised land. When Jewish culture fails to be mimetic, to represent some ideal history or aspiration intrinsic to its sense of self, it can no longer, according to DeKoven Ezrahi, be called "Jewish." When Jewish culture claims to have

achieved its teleological goal of "homecoming," it has ceased to be desirous and to represent its fantasy of what awaits it in some eternally deferred future or some mythical past, and it fails to produce "Jewish art."
"Jewish exile," says Ezrahi in the spirit of George Steiner, is a "kind of literary privilege."[14]

According to this theory, the language of Jewish literature is automatically "surrogate" and as such is automatically mimetic. As we know,
metaphor and metonymy are both tools of a mimetic imagination, the
need to liken something to something else or to link something to something else in order to illuminate both sides of the poetic exchange of images. A further development of this notion, however, posits that
literalization, or the breakdown of the metaphoric or metonymic relationship, augurs the death of poetry. The desire for poetry is akin to the
desire for mimesis, and both are signs of artistry. The Jewish artist, in this
formulation, is committed to a mimesis of distance and destruction. It is
the practice of creating textual surrogates for what can no longer be reconstructed in "reality" or for what cannot be obtained in the future or
both. Ezrahi concludes her discussion of the classical Jewish quest for the
creation of "sacred space" by mimetic means in the texts, both of the tradition and of the modern pre-Zionist or anti-Zionist Jewish imagination, by arguing that "the triumph of the Zionist enterprise in the
aftermath of the Holocaust implied certain strictures on this form of
imagination. The force of a collective homecoming and of a utopian vision put the entire mimetic project of exile into question. . . . The return
of the exiles seems to involve a repudiation of the aesthetic principle that
allowed us to create images in all the lands of our dispersal."[15] In this
vein, the development of a local mimesis or an as-if mimesis, which are,
respectively, posited on the representation of things "as they are" or as
they "will soon become," demonstrates a striving for the fulfillment of
age-old desires. As such, they are antithetical to the kind of mimesis that
pertained in Jewish thought for millennia. More important for our purposes, they place an artist like Baron at a crossroads. As a Zionist she was
expected to produce a fiction that would represent the flavor of local life
as a means of effecting, in a kind of as-if mimesis, the future development of a Hebrew vernacular and a real culture. But Baron saw herself

first and foremost as a "Jewish" writer caught in the maelstrom of the modern revolutions and destructions of early-twentieth-century Jewish life. Particularly as a "rabbi's daughter" within the secular Yishuv, and a "daughter of the shtetl" within the urban Zionist environment of Tel Aviv, she practiced a particular type of mimesis of transition that exemplified the struggle between the "rooted" and the "uprooted" (the talush) in the literature of the modern Hebrew renaissance.

Baron's mimetic commitments depend on a narrative persona who claims to be recalling a past reality but is doing so from a transitional position, a place between worlds. There can be no verification of the verisimilitude of the subject of the mimetic work conceived within a transitional mold, because that which is being reconstructed has been superceded by the process of reconstruction itself. The depiction of the shtetl, in other words, has become not a representation but a replacement for the shtetl. The fact of the literary transcription of the shtetl is, in a sense, the shtetl's death knell and could even be seen as the very act of extinguishing that culture. Transitional mimesis can also be viewed as the documentation of transition from one set of mimetic concerns to another. In Baron's work—spanning a fifty-year period and a broad geographical distance—we see a shift from a local mimesis, in that early in her career she depicted a milieu in which she lived (the shtetl), to a mimesis meant to depict a disappeared world. Here I propose that a mimesis of transition conflates death with the act of textual representation. Before we can memorialize a lost culture, in literature or otherwise, it must be lost. Transitional mimesis documents the process of that loss not by depicting, for example, pogroms or the Holocaust, the displacements of World War I, or the like. Rather, texts written in a transitionally mimetic vein document their own textualization of a real culture just as it is being snuffed out, and they take partial (if not full) responsibility for the extinction of that culture through their very textualization of it.

By writing about the shtetl "as it was," Baron is not memorializing it. She is, rather, documenting the transition of the shtetl from one kind of literary trope to another. Baron is in fact the third generation of shtetl writers—the first being the Haskalah satirists and memoirists such as Joseph Perl and Yisroel Aksenfeld, the second being the bathetic comics such as Sholem Aleichem, Mendele Mokher Sforim, and, a bit later, Y. L. Peretz. Finally, in Baron's generation, the shtetl was described by Y. H. Brenner, M. Y. Berdischevsky, D. Berkowitz, U. N. Gnessin, and others as the terrible locus of bourgeoisie impassivity, abject poverty, and social and intellectual philistinism. Baron, on the other hand, as we earlier observed in Shaked's remarks, depicts the shtetl "sympathetically," shining a harsh light on the imperfections and inequalities of traditional Jewish life but maintaining a general sense of the integrity of that world. Baron presents the shtetl in its transition from an object of social critique and scrutiny to a mythical construct. The shtetl, in her work, is a new literary incarnation, ever further removed from the depicted object "as it was," "is," or "will be."

The "transition" the shtetl is undergoing in Baron's work is a transition from one kind of literary trope to another, and as such, it is moving further from the "real" referent. According to rabbinic law, once something is presented in a particular fashion three times, it is, by force of the strength of precedent, permanently to be understood in that state. As one of the third generation of shtetl writers, Baron's work embodies the transition from a literary preference to a literary imperative, from the possibility of resonance within the real world to the solipsistic enclosure of shtetl depictions within a limited literary universe.

The discourse of the shtetl and the discourse of the talush overlap in a startlingly vivid fashion in Baron's work through the dynamic of transitional mimesis. To illustrate this dynamic, I will briefly outline Dan Miron's paradigm of "classic" and "anticlassic" shtetl narratives authored during the modern period of Hebrew and Yiddish literature, in his schema from the 1870s to the 1920s. Beginning with Sholem Aleichem and S .J. Abramowitz's "classic" shtetl narratives that feature the well-known shtetls of *Glupsk, Kabaznik, Tuneyadevke* (in Abramowitz's Hebrew and Yiddish works) and *Kasrilevke* (in Sholem Aleichem's corpus), Miron moves on to analyze an anticlassic fictional shtetl tradition best represented in the work of M. Y. Berdischevsky's talush narratives in Hebrew and David Bergelson's Yiddish works.[16]

When viewed in the context of the discourse of the talush, what emerges from Miron's schema is the sense that the literary opposite of the talush is the shtetl not just in thematic terms but in stylistic terms as well. What makes Sholem Aleichem's *Kasrilevke* stories classic shtetl narratives, whereas Berdischevsky's "Two Camps" is an anticlassic shtetl narrative? Sholem Aleikhem's stories are about the collective culture and the disintegration of the eastern European Jewish shtetl, whereas Berdischevsky's narrative is a description of the atomized, existential aftermath of the escape from the shtetl as it affected isolated individuals. The classic shtetl texts, in other words, document the birth of communities of *luftmenschen* (homeless, groundless Jews), where the anticlassic shtetl texts respond with the creation of the talush (the miserable shtetl escapee subsisting in clusters, but not communities, of young men, and women, who have similarly fled the shtetl).[17] Whereas the classic shtetl is emptied out all at once by expulsions and fires, the anticlassic shtetl is cleared out gradually and insidiously by enlightenment, secularization, and disillusionment. There is, in this latter instance, no sense of collective identification and the kind of comfort and humor borne of that kind of identification. As we recall in "Exams," Baron's satire of the conventional talush narrative, Sender Ziv is horrified that more Jewish young men have arrived to take the exams alongside him. He articulates no sense of identification with or sympathy for them.[18]

Miron demonstrates, as do Gennady Estraikh, Mikhail Krutikov, David Roskies, and Ben Cion Pinchuk, that the "shtetl" in contemporary literary and cultural discourse is a literary construct more than a historical fact. Responding to the contemporary tendency to read all of eastern European Jewish life as a distillation of the popular American film *Fiddler on the Roof* (based on Sholem Aleichem's *Tevye* stories) or the paintings of Marc Chagall (modeled on his hometown, not shtetl, Vitebsk), Miron, from a literary perspective, and scholars such as Pinchuk, from a historical perspective, attempt to reclaim the shtetl from the catch-all "state of mind" or "magic circle" it has become. Miron tries to demonstrate that the shtetl, as we know it from the "classic" works of Abramowitz and Sholem Aleichem, is a wholly literary construct out of which all non-Jews have been excised. Krutikov, in a related vein, demonstrates that Abramowitz's *Glupsk,* said to be modeled on the Belorussian city of Berdichev, was actually inspired by the city of Glupov in the Russian works of Mikhail Saltykov (N. Schedrin); Abramowitz's literary shtetl was based, in its turn, on a literary shtetl and not on an "actual" one.[19]

Popular culture has pitted history and fiction against one another in the discourse of the shtetl. Steven Zipperstein has pointed out that "literature rather than historical research has molded the shtetl's image as an ideal Jewish town." Pinchuk remarks that "most contemporary writing on the shtetl is done by students of literature and linguistics rather than history." As such, "what is considered fact and common knowledge is frequently literary invention, cliché, stereotype, and even prejudice." The notion of the shtetl as an "actual habitat," Pinchuk concludes, "fell victim to a paradoxical combination of ideological animosity that pictured the small Jewish town as negative and repulsive. It also fell victim to the nostalgia and feelings of guilt that idealized its lifestyle and people."[20]

Although Mendele and Sholem Aleichem did nothing to hide the countless physical and spiritual shortcomings of the shtetl, they did maintain a certain intimate connection to the shtetl through their means of representing it. Their narrators are in the shtetl with the shtetl dwellers, gathering their stories and relaying them either orally or literarily to the audience of their readership. Berdischevsky and Brenner, for their part, develop talush characters who have left the shtetl behind and imagine it as an impossible place to return to (Berdischevsky's "Two Camps"); if they return (Brenner's *In Winter*), they tend toward suicide.

Baron's shtetl, on the other hand, was read as neither idyllic nor hellish. In a review of Baron's work in 1941, M. Gil describes Baron's shtetl in the following way:

There are authors who have illuminated the shtetl in all its broad, far-reaching aspects that touch upon the deep conflicts within the human soul that were harbored within its confines. There are other authors who have looked at it with a skeptical eye and reveled all its sicknesses of body and spirit. Here, in the work of Baron we see a further development in the depiction of the shtetl. Her work shares all the features of the shtetl depictions we all know so well. But she doesn't try to make generalizations. She acquaints us, in her work, with new details about the shtetl. She shines a delicate light on the shtetl where we see from the vantage point not of a lighthouse, but from behind a sort of flashlight. We look at the small things, not at the big ones.[21]

Later in this review, Gil argues that Baron studies the depths of the shtetl, not its surfaces. Baron maintains a sense of detachment from the social problems that the other shtetl writers "took a stand against" in their depictions of the shtetl and enters, instead, into an intimate view of the "spirit" of the shtetl. This detachment is the sign, perhaps, of an outsider like the modern reader. Or one could interpret it as the view of an "insider" unable to see the forest for the trees.

Another way to consider this literary stance vis-à-vis the shtetl is to imagine it as the perspective of a simultaneous insider and outsider—a shtetl dweller who left it behind and could revisit it only by writing about it. Unlike Sholem Aleichem and Mendele who are temporally and spatially located in the shtetl in their narratives, or Brenner's and Berdischevsky's protagonists who have left the shtetl and resist returning to it because it still exists, Baron's narrator of the shtetl is someone who could not go back physically if she wanted to. The shtetl has been more or less destroyed. Whereas, as we recall, the shtetl in its literary form was never a representation of a "real" place, in Baron's lifetime the literary representations of the shtetl were transformed by their readership into the only real address for a world that was being destroyed. The text turned into the eastern European homeland itself while it had originally not even pretended mimetically to represent a "real" object.

During Baron's writing career, real *shtetlakh* were transformed from many geographical locales to a literary memory. Their imagined death, in the stories by Berdischevsky and Brenner, became a real death in the interwar period when Baron began publishing her collections of stories in 1927. Historians, as discussed above, began, because of the magnitude of the tragedy that destroyed real *shtetlakh*, to rely on literary representations of the shtetl in order to reconstruct it. As Pinchuk acutely observes, "The image of the shtetl and its place in history was determined by the people who abandoned it and did not care to ask what precisely happened in the small towns they had left behind." Critics finally are coming to terms with the fact that we have very few reliable factual resources about the culture of the shtetl. A new area of historical study must come to replace all the guilt, trauma, and romanticization that has overlaid images of the shtetl as it was presented in literature. Miron describes the shtetl presented in narratives from the classical period of modern Yiddish literature (1870–1920) as a "pure, unalloyed and undiluted Jewish world." He concludes that "as both object and subject [the shtetl] amounted to a tremendously potent myth that nourished and sustained an alienated, nostalgic, modern Jewish community (in essence, an emigrant community) that desperately needed both to remember the idealized old home (which had never existed in a historical sense) and at the same time to justify the modern Jew's betrayal of the old familial home he had left, hurtling himself into the cold, harsh, individualistic and egotistic world of modernity." [22]

The dilemma of locating the "real" beyond the "fictional," of finding the "facts" about the shtetl behind the "myths," is strikingly similar to the dilemma of finding the real Jew behind the abstracted "jew" in European culture, or the Jewish woman who has been subsumed by the feminized Jewish man. The imagined death of the shtetl and the real death of the shtetl are negotiated in Baron's stories from the vantage point of a narrator, the rabbi's daughter turned writer, situated across a historical and geographic chasm who uses her pen to revisit a world to which she could not choose to return even if she so wanted.

As we will see in the fourth chapter of this study, the dominant metaphor for exile and displacement in rabbinic culture is the image of a woman abandoned by her husband. The sacked city of Jerusalem in the book of Lamentations is likened to a menstrual woman sitting, shamed, on her stained skirts or to a merciful mother cannibalizing her own children. The quintessential lamenter of exiles is, in Prophets, the matriarch Rachel, weeping on the road to Bethlehem, where she died giving birth to her younger son and the child of her husband's old age, Benjamin. In the culture of classic shtetl narratives, women play a central role in emphasizing the tragedy and pointlessness of shtetl existence. In Sholem Aleichem's *Motel Payse: The Cantor's Son,* the protagonist's mother is rendered ridiculous in her incessant and ugly weeping as her shtetl is dismantled and the majority of its inhabitants emigrate to America. Motel Payse's mother is presented here as the metonymy for the shtetl's grief at its own end, its fear over emigration, its unrefined mannerisms. She is grief stricken and bleary eyed throughout their departure, running back and forth across town to say good-bye to just one last person, again and again. Dvora Baron, in her presentation of the rabbi's daughter returning in writing to the shtetl she left behind, yokes together a whole system of metaphors—from the classical rabbinic to the classical modern. She turns the lamenting woman from a weepy idiot into an erudite narrator and poses the possibility of reassessing the symbolic terms of Jewish discourse, for the first time, from a woman's point of view.

In 1939 S. Y. Pinles, in a reference to David Frishmann's oft-quoted statement that Mendele's literary shtetl would one day serve as the witness to a world that was soon to be wiped off the eastern European map, observed:

> If one day the painful image presented by David Frishmann should come to pass, and a massive deluge should eradicate Eastern European Jewry, and our nation should want to preserve in a museum an artistic reproduction of that lost world, it won't be enough simply to include the works of Mendele alone. Even clips from the works of Yehudah Steinberg, Sholem Aleichem, Berdischevsky, Agnon and Barash will not complete the picture. Dvora Baron's "trifles," the details that she depicts are needed to complete the portrait.[23]

During the 1930s and the 1940s the shtetl's cultural demise and eventual destruction was becoming increasingly evident and inevitable. Early reviews of Baron's work reflect an awareness of the newly historical and commemorative role of Hebrew and Yiddish literature. They also forgive, for the first time, Baron's seeming reluctance (with rare exception, which we will discuss briefly below) to write about anything but the shtetl even after her emigration to Palestine. Although contemporary notions of the destruction of European Jewry often go no further back than the Holocaust, in fact the interwar period was an especially difficult time for Jews. Because of the shifting borders within the Pale and the Russian Revolution, Jewish life in the cities and shtetl life as well had become particularly tenuous. Baron's first collected works published, beginning in 1927, during the interwar period, contained eerie images of death and destruction that referred to the Jewish plight after World War I but were, interestingly, translated into English as references to World War II. In the end of Joseph Schachter's 1969 English rendering of "What Has Been," for example, he translates *zeva'ah* as "Holocaust": "For a long time I—now settled in my new homeland—heard nothing of the family. News began to reach us of the *holocaust* that befell our brethren, and many believed that all had perished." [24] Although the term "Holocaust" to refer to the events of World War II in the Jewish community finds its Hebrew counterpart in the term "Shoah," Baron used the Hebrew term *zeva'ah* in her original. Also, Baron's story was published in 1939, several years before either the term "Holocaust" or "Shoah" came into common usage.

Like the ideology of "revival," which was seen as a kind of disinterment of ancient Hebrew for modern use, the dominance of the shtetl in Baron's work reflects, to her critics, a shifty, almost supernatural, impossibility. Presenting anew the texts of an ancient culture to a modern readership (as in "Family"), and giving literacy over to the illiterate (as in "What Has Been") or at least the nonliterary (as in the case of "Sender Ziv"), Baron's narrators express the discomfort of a wholly literary presence disguised as an autobiographical persona who rejects the imperative to become the ethnographer and mouthpiece of a lost world. The "uprootedness" of Baron's narrators is like the unrest of a ghost being called back from the dead with the urgency of a renewed call for a different sort of revival—not a cultural one anymore, but a literal one. Hebrew was no longer the only thing that needed revival when Baron's collected stories first appeared. An entire culture was at stake. When Baron kills Sender Ziv off at the end of her talush trilogy in 1919, she gives birth, as it were, to a different kind of talush—the narrator of her shtetl stories— who will be pressed to write both from within the world of the shtetl and from beyond it.

One aspect of the talush that I have not yet elaborated upon is his identity as a somewhat unusual figure for the experience of modern Zionist nationalism. Perhaps if we were to consider the talush as a "real" response to the "ideal" Jew who was being touted by the Zionists, we would better understand why a generation of writers would choose the talush as a metonymy for the experience of nationalism. The talush may, perhaps, have been a fledgling stab at the impossibility of the "muscle Jews" being promoted and disseminated by Zionist thinkers such as Max Nordau (1849–1923) or the "new Jew" advocated by a wide variety of Zionist ideologues such as Zev Jabotinsky (1880–1940) and David Ben Gurion (1886–1973).[25]

With the exception of a few scattered references to the different "isms" circulating in the Jewish community at the end of the nineteenth century throughout the works of writers such as Brenner and Berdischevsky, the talush is never appointed as a "spokesman" for any collective movement. Rather, the talush scorns collective ideologies. Nevertheless, it is clear that those ideologies, coupled with the remnant of the Haskalah philosophy of communal advancement through individual improvement gave these talush protagonists license to leave their provincial lives and their religious practices behind, exchanging a Jewish intellectual world for a European secular one. In Brenner's classic text of a European talush, *In Winter*, Yirmiyahu Feierman is witness to (if not an active participant in) numerous debates pitting Zionism against socialism. Feierman's good friend, Haimowitz, a revolutionary, raised in a financially and socially privileged secular Jewish home, challenges Feierman repeatedly for being so "Jewish." Why not work on behalf of the proletariat as opposed to the Jews? Why bother with Hebrew when no one understands it?[26] Feierman does not defend his own position. Even as he clearly embodies the Zionist values that led him to write his account of these conversations in Hebrew (the narrative is figured as Feierman's diary), he does not articulate his particular allegiances to any one political group—socialists, bundists, Zionists, or anyone else. In typical talush fashion, Feierman is simultaneously conscious and unconscious—conscious of the political discussions raging about him, unconscious of his own implication in them.

One of those discussions, not thematized in the literature but stylistically exemplified by it, was the role of the "Jew" in the discourse of modernism. Paradoxically, whereas Georg Lukacs (during his Marxist era) argued that the problem with modernism was that it was too idiosyncratic and self-indulgent to foster instructive "types" for a readership seeking characters with whom to identify and upon whom to base "model societies," in the Hebrew case modernism itself motivated the birth of a literary "type."[27] In fact, it was in the figure of the talush that Zionism and modernism converged.

In Brenner's seminal article "The Land of Israel Genre and Its Accouterments" (1911), he argues that the Yishuv lacks the "stability and typicality" necessary for the establishment of a literary genre particular to that time and place. The article was written in response to a scandal that arose with the publication of Brenner's earlier story "From Here and from Here" (1910), which was interpreted by many as a loosely veiled satire of the literary establishment in Palestine and its attempts to foster an ideologically motivated "local" literature. Todd Hasak-Lowy eloquently argues that Brenner's notion of "genre" does not refer to literary historical conventions.[28] Rather, in discussing the impossibility of a "Land of Israel" genre, Brenner articulates the unsavory conditions for the establishment of local literary "types."

In reflecting on the literature of Sholem Aleichem and Mendele Mokher Sforim, Brenner argues that what made their Yiddish and Hebrew stories so distinctive and successful was the fact that they were able to depict types that were instantaneously recognizable by their readership as "condensations" of a particular locale, time, and place. Brenner argues that these authors' writings were distinguished not by their creation of new types, but by their ability to put a fresh face on old "types" and make them resonate with their readers: "When our elder Mendele describes Rayze the shopkeeper, we are already familiar with her as a 'type.' We are astonished by the capacity of the artist to give us his own particular portrait of an already familiar face. In the same vein, when Mendele depicts Reb Abraham Ba'al ha-Zohar. It doesn't matter if Abramowitz ever actually saw a Jew like him or not. Rather, before us stands a slice of life from a locale and a generation familiar to all of us."[29]

In order to forge a unique Palestinian "genre," the geographic locale within which that literature is produced must provide a modicum of stability and even stagnancy for the creation of literary "types" or conventionalized personalities. The Yishuv, according to Brenner, could not hope to generate a distinct, resonant Palestinian Jewish literature until the culture was sufficiently stabilized. Early Hebrew renaissance authors (like Mendele) never attempted, according to Brenner, to promote the impression that they were writing about a place that was infused with Zionist values. Rather, much of Mendele's corpus was self-consciously written in Hebrew as a sort of aesthetic and cultural exercise. Focused on traditional Jews in Europe and set, most often, in the shtetl, Mendele's Hebrew corpus—bridging the Haskalah and the renaissance—was linguistically Hebrew but not obsessively oriented toward conciliation between the language in which it was written and the culture it represented. Brenner ridicules the literature written in Palestine during the first decade of the twentieth century that fancied itself a simultaneous representation of and product of the newly Hebraic spirit that was capturing the Yishuv. He argues that although writers writing in Hebrew in Palestine like D. Shimoni (1886–1956), Y. Barzilai (Eizenstat) (1855–1918), and even S. Y. Agnon (1880–1970) may have thought they created an indigenous literary form that expresses the spirit of an organic Hebrew life in the Jewish homeland, in fact there is no sense of the resonance or recognition that is requisite for the establishment of what he calls a genre.

As I will further explore in the next chapter of this study, the fixation on representing things "locally" (in my terminology) or "things as they are" (in the language of Hebrew renaissance writers themselves) in the literature of the modern Hebrew renaissance was partly an attempt to rise to the challenges posed by a fledgling literary language that was only beginning to flex its realist muscles after millennia of wholly scholarly use. The need to represent "things as they are" was also, in part, motivated by the nationalist fervor fueling much Hebrew literary production, particularly in Palestine, during the period of the second aliyah. This found its expression, as we have discussed, in a kind of local mimesis. Many authors viewed it as their responsibility not only to represent "things as they are" in the Palestinian Yishuv for perusal in Europe as a catalyst for interest and immigration but also to script a Palestinian reality, to propose things as "they should be" for those people anticipating immigration.

For purposes of this discussion, let us focus on Brenner's despair over what he perceives to be the lack of a suitable climate—social, political, and literary—to craft the types that would establish a "Land of Israel Genre." Dvora Baron, as we recall, emigrated to Palestine in December 1910, just months before Brenner's essay "The Land of Israel Genre" was published. Indeed, Baron, as has been documented by Nurit Govrin, was sorely criticized by a wide variety of readers and critics for not providing a "looking glass" into the lives of youth making a go at agricultural life in Palestine. Baron wrote almost exclusively about the European shtetl or the urban setting of the old Yishuv (the Jews living in Palestine for several generations who had not immigrated for secular nationalist purposes, but for wholly religious reasons and were not agriculturalists but were, rather, pious city dwellers). Does Baron prove Brenner's point about there not being a climate for the creation of a "Land of Israel" genre by writing almost exclusively about the shtetl even after having emigrated to Palestine? Does Baron's particular construction (and subversion) of the figure of the talush help us to identify a call, in Brenner's rhetoric, for a character who can bridge the geographically, spiritually, and intellectually polarized worlds of the writers of the modern Hebrew renaissance? Brenner, in this light, may not be searching for a character type that grows indigenously out of the Land of Israel. Rather, he is searching for a character type that can embody the myriad disjunctures that characterized Jewish life in transition between Europe and Palestine at the turn of the twentieth century. Baron, in several of her stories set in Palestine, presents us with that type in the guise of Jewish women emigrants to Palestine, displaced in all cases, disfranchised in most, and surprisingly resilient in others.

Baron's "ka-Aleh Nidaf" (As a Driven Leaf) (1949) tells the story of a young woman who is sent to Palestine from eastern Europe because her mother believes that she is more likely to find a husband there than in her hometown. In the literature of the period, anyone who emigrates to

Palestine without a conjugal partner never finds one. Agnon's stories such as "A Hill of Sand" (1931) or "Betrothed" (1952) and his magnum opus, "Only Yesterday" (1945), all feature single men and women who have emigrated to Palestine and find themselves wandering aimlessly through the streets of Jaffa and Jerusalem. They are only sporadically employed and are constantly in love, but never find themselves in a position to marry because they do not have the financial stability to do so. In "As a Driven Leaf" Baron presents this narrative from the perspective not of the men, as was done in the works of Agnon and others, but from the perspective of the young woman, never named in the story, who relocates from Europe to Palestine only to find herself in a reconstructed shtetl. The story begins:

> The greengrocer from the southern neighborhood brought the girl to the house of the widow Pin. Of all the places where she herself had worked as a younger woman, this one seemed the most appropriate.
>
> "Here you won't be mistreated," she explained to the frightened girl, a new arrival from her own village in Europe. "The customs here are just like those of the Sdoveski household back home where we come from, and the food is simple and homey: cutlets and vinegar and pickles." [30]

The protagonist of this story longs for her mother, and for her hometown in Europe, but in the end commits suicide. Her decision to do so is made after her employer's son, who has led her to believe that he is romantically interested in her, becomes engaged to someone else.

Baron's nameless protagonist did not emigrate in order to work the soil in the Land of Israel or revive the Hebrew language. She did so in order to make a good match. She has been, quite literally, "uprooted" by her mother from a world with which she was quite content and, unbeknownst to her mother, transplanted in an identical world. The food is the same; the class structure is the same. The only thing that is not the same is the longing she feels for her mother because they have been so brutally and unjustifiably separated. In a conversation with the greengrocer, the girl expresses her homesickness, and her confidant replies:

Only death can separate people for eternity, but not geographic or temporal distance. The ways that led you here have not been erased, and others
can follow the same path behind you. Not a few parents have come after
their children even to non-Jewish countries. Even more so to this country
where the elderly come to die even if they don't have anyone here to meet
them. Get used to it here and save money from your salary so your mother
can prepare herself. The day will come when you will replace the sorrow of
parting with the joy of reunion.[31]

This presentation of life in Palestine as part of a geographic and temporal continuum finds its way into Baron's novella *ha-Colim* (The Exiles)
(1970) in which a community, transplanted from Europe to Palestine
during the second aliyah at the turn of the twentieth century, is once
again uprooted from Palestine and relocated to Egypt during World War
I. Whereas the men in the community are entirely focused on returning
to Palestine, their new "homeland," the women in the story are intent on
maintaining the home life that they have carried with them all the way
from Europe. Orly Lubin argues that *The Exiles* is a veritable cookbook of
Lithuanian favorites, as Nechama Rothstein, the local *balebuste* (home-
maker), feeds her way into the hearts of all the homeless, starving, traumatized, and ill people who pass through her various kitchens as she is
exiled, along with them.[32]

Toward the end of the story, Naomi Rabin, a little girl who has grown
up in Egypt, returns to Palestine with her mother, Chana, and visits with
Mina, a friend, in a northern agricultural settlement. (There seems to be
a law of conservation of names in Baron's corpus—Chana and Mina
recur frequently.) Instead of celebrating their return, however, they discuss their "true homeland," the European world they left behind:

Mina served some more coffee brewed with chicory in the Lithuanian
style, and with that Chana Rabin began preparations for their departure.

"Already?" Naomi asked, disappointed. "And I thought you would
continue to talk!"

"About the world 'over there?' Mina's eyes sparkled. "Sweetie, you
should go see it with your own eyes. You can still find something there, and

the way is not too long. Now that it is 'paved,' it is really quite close," she said thoughtfully. "Back when they used to talk in the community house about Palestine, it seemed to them that it was somewhere at the end of the earth, and the return to Zion was imagined as an endless path filled with loaded carts at the head of which was the neighborhood synagogue."[33]

The seamless path between Zion and Lithuania is traversable in either direction, according to Mina. Throughout Baron's work there is a sense of internal geographic coherence across the great divide of what was traditionally thought of as the Jewish diaspora and the Jewish homeland. In "As a Driven Leaf," emigration to Israel for the young protagonist is a profound form of exile from her mother and her hometown, whereas in *The Exiles* the movement to Egypt, for the women in the community, is only one step farther removed from the European landscape they long ago left behind and continue to re-create in their kitchens and their conversations. Their exile to Egypt, in other words, is not from their newfound Jewish homeland, but one step farther away from their original hometowns in eastern Europe.

Baron's "Palestinian" narratives, not unlike her narratives of the "shtetl," invert the conventional notions of exile and redemption. The immigrants are women seeking out families or nurturing them or both, and they feel that they would be better served had they stayed home. The rabbi's daughter in Baron's shtetl narratives, similarly, seems to grasp for the familiar as she recollects the world she left behind for distant unnamed shores. Although Baron early on kills off the classic talush in her work, rejecting the assumption that the talush was the national autobiographical subject and also reminding Hebrew modernist authors that they were, in embracing their own exemplarity, contributing to their own essentialization within the European imagination, we find the features of that talush recuperated in the narrators of limited omniscience, such as "the rabbi's daughter," who seem to be trying to reconstruct a lost world from a great geographic and temporal distance. This narrator shifts in and out of sight within the confines of the narrative, unwilling to leave the shtetl entirely behind yet unable to return.

3

⎯⎯❧❧⎯⎯

Things as They Are

The Mimetic Imperative

What is the itinerary of desire that has so insistently positioned the camera upon the throne of truth in representation?—Scott Mcquire, "Visions of Modernity" (1998)

This is a simple realism, with clipped wings, a creeping, photographic realism.—Y. H. Brenner, "From Here and from Here" (1911)

IN THE 1920S the *Yiddish Forward* in New York inaugurated a regular feature of photo-essays from the Old Country. These photographs were, by some accounts, meant to ease the pain and guilt of separation from families and communities by reinforcing the backwardness of the world left behind; photographic images of poverty and piety served as reminders that no matter how poor or misunderstood were the new immigrants in the United States, they still had it much better than did their countrymen who had remained in Europe. Photographs traveled in the other direction as well. New immigrants sent photographs back home in order to confirm the magical transformations wrought by the influence of the New World on the sons and daughters, husbands and fathers, who had gone to find better lives. A fantasy of instant financial success, of American streets paved with gold, was fostered by the photographs sent back to the Old Country in the well-clothed bodies and well-fed visages peering out of the photographic frame. The fictions created by the photographs sent back home as "evidence" of success belied the facts.

Whereas in the photographic exchanges between eastern Europe

and the United States photographs of the Old Country served to ameliorate the guilt of those individuals who emigrated and to arouse the envy
of the ones who did not, according to Vivienne Silver-Brody, photographs of the Palestinian landscape were used in eastern Europe as early
as 1884 to encourage Jews to support land purchase in the Holy Land
and to galvanize migration.[1] In some cases, photographs of Jewish work-
ers tilling the soil, of new settlements and fruit groves, of modern buildings being constructed on barren and ancient ground, served as
acknowledgment of donations to a variety of organizations such as the
Lovers of Zion organization in the late nineteenth century and the Jewish National Fund during the first few decades of the twentieth. These
photographs were part of the oft-documented process of "nation building" in that the age-old fantasies of life in Zion were fed and furthered by
modern images of that land.[2]

One of Baron's most striking allusions to photography appears in
"Bereshit" (In the Beginning) (1927) when a photographer passes
through Khmilovka, one of Baron's fictional shtetlakh, on the eve of a
Sabbath. The photographer's alien (and alienating) gaze is a corollary to
the gaze of the story's protagonist—a young rabbi's wife—as she surveys
her new home with chagrin:

> The young rabbi . . . asked her whether she had seen the charity boxes in
> these poor houses yet. And, indeed, in the very same spots where the racks
> for the cheese were attached to the outside of the houses could be found,
> on the other side of the wall inside nearly every house, a whole shelf full of
> tin cans, with acronyms of all the yeshivas in the world inscribed on their
> rounded sides. Precisely how coins were deposited into these cans was
> captured, to the consternation of the locals, by a roving photographer
> who came through here once on a Friday afternoon.
>
> He, the stranger, standing at the threshold of his inn as the sun was
> setting, was fascinated to see the landlady take some copper coins out of a
> special pouch and arrange them on the tabletop, from which she had
> folded the tablecloth back for that purpose. The house had been straight-
> ened up and scrubbed. At the head of the table, under a satin Sabbath
> cloth, lay two loaves of challah while across from them, at the other end of
> the table, the candles stood ready in their candlesticks for light, and she,

the woman, sweeping the coins into her hand and raising her youngest child in her arms toward the charity boxes, was handing him the coins to toss into the slots when, suddenly, turning her head, she caught sight of the case in the visitors hands and saw what he was doing to her and to her son. She collapsed onto the bench before her and burst into tears.[3]

Did Dvora Baron see herself as akin in any way to the roving photographer in Khmilovka? To what degree did the historical circumstances affecting the Jewish shtetl determine the direction of Baron's fiction at its inception, and to what degree were those circumstances read, belatedly, into Baron's work? In my discussion of Baron's "transitional" mimetic poetic, I focused on Baron's sense that her shtetl stories, authored in Tel Aviv, were partly responsible, in their mythical representation of the shtetl as opposed to their ethnographic representation of it, for the shtetl's destruction. Also, in my earlier discussion of Baron's conflicting ethnographic and fictional impulses, I pointed to Baron's ambivalent attitude toward her relationship with women in the historical shtetl, being, as she was, one of the only writers to present them as literary subjects in their own right, even as she may have resisted being known as a woman writer of women. Baron creates links between disparate times (pre- and post-Holocaust), disparate places (eastern Europe and Palestine), and disparate impulses (ethnographic and fictional) in her stories that introduce a photography motif, even as she emphasizes the impossibility of using transparently mimetic or realist premises to create historical meaning within a literary context. In these stories, Baron positions her narratives, and, as we will see, her narrators, on the border between historical communities and imagined ones as she challenges the "mimetic imperatives" of the modern Hebrew renaissance.

As I demonstrated in the previous chapter, writers and ideologues of the modern Hebrew renaissance were preoccupied with reality and its literary "representation" in Hebrew. The desire to create a geographically localized and linguistically vernacular Hebrew culture on the basis of literary experimentation contributed to the development of rich and complex mimetic hierarchies in the literary discourse and the literature of the period. Some of the trends in mimetic thought within a Zionist nationalist modern Hebrew literary milieu that proved relevant to our discussion of Baron's response to the "talush imperative" included "local" mimesis, "as-if" mimesis, and a mimesis of transition. Here we will expand this discussion in order to probe Baron's attitude toward the more generalized "mimetic imperative" of the modern Hebrew renaissance. I will introduce several new mimetic categories in order to lay the groundwork for Dvora Baron's poetic alternative to mimesis: a poetics of mediation.

The gathering momentum of realist stylistics during the period of the modern Hebrew renaissance can be understood as mimetic imperatives as opposed to mimetic "tendencies" or mimetic "trends" because, as in much of the stylistic discourse of the Hebrew literary milieu at the turn of the twentieth century, overtures toward mimesis became "imperative" for canonization or at least serious consideration. The notion of mimesis, or in Hebrew the representation of *dvarim ke-hevyatam,* or "things as they are," shifted significantly throughout the modern Hebrew renaissance. At first, mimesis was designated an imitation of vernacular reality, or a "vernacular mimesis," and the successful construction of a Hebrew vernacular literary idiom was valorized. As we will further explore in the next chapter, S. J. Abramowitz was said to have achieved this vernacular success with his *"nusah"* literary idiom, a style that wove all levels of Hebrew literary discourse into an undifferentiated linguistic fabric that reintroduced the nuance and flexibility of a vernacular tongue into what had previously been a stilted, scholarly one.

A second type of mimetic success—a form of memorialization—also has been attributed to Mendele's work. David Frischmann said of Mendele in a passage that was echoed, as we saw in the previous chapter, by an early critic of Baron's:

> Let's imagine, for example, that some terrible flood came and erased every bit of that world from the earth, along with the memory of that world, until there was not one single sign of that life left and by chance all we were left with was "The Book of Beggars," "The Vale of Tears," "The Travels of R. Benjamin the Third," and "Of Bygone Days," along with his small

sketches and stories, then there is no doubt that on the basis of these sketches the critic could recreate the street life of the Jews in the Russian shtetl totally accurately.[4]

The successful conservation, and, later, memorialization, of "things as they were" in the shtetl is here credited to Mendele.

Avraham Leib Ben Avigdor, an important editor and publisher in the last decades of the nineteenth century, formulated another mimetic ideal modeled on the contemporaneous ideologies of the Russian positivists V. Beliniinski, N. Chernichevsky, and D. Pisarev when he said: "The pleasant and the pragmatic have to come together in a literature which must represent, as in a mirror, the life of the nation. We are not looking for articles filled with fancy language or entertaining plays full of riddles and sleights of hand. Rather, we are looking for living, clear pictures—true renderings taken from life we have not yet seen in our literature; the number of stories, pictures and original sketches from the life of our nation is paltry in our literature."[5] Ben Avigdor spearheaded a literary movement called the "New Way" *(ha-Mahalakh ha-Hadash)* that shifted the mimetic focus away from the valorization of a vernacular idiom and from a critically perceived commitment to historical commemorations of a disappearing world. He and the writers he championed sought a Hebrew literary style that would capture Jewish life in its urban, contemporary setting—raw and supposedly unaffected by excess concern over stylistics (as in vernacular mimesis) or history (as in memorial mimesis). Writers of the New Way were committed to the depiction of social struggle, of poverty, migration, and linguistic disjuncture in the here and now—"things as they are."

Baron's generation (including Y. H. Brenner, H. D. Nomberg, U. N. Gnessin, G. Shofman, and Yaakov Steinberg) followed the New Way by about a decade, distinguishing themselves as psychological realists and modernists from what they perceived to be the naturalism of their predecessors. Nevertheless, Ben Avigdor, through his book series (Penny Books [*Sifre Agurah*, 1891] and the Hebrew Library [*ha-Bilioteka ha-Ivrit*, 1897]), his publishing house (Toshiyah, 1896), and his journal (*Ahiasaf*, 1893–1896), was a crucial part of their literary landscape and their professional development. Dvora Baron via a mutual friend, Ben Zion Katz, negotiated for years with Ben Avigdor to have her first collection of stories published by Toshiyah, Ben Avigdor's press. In fact, the most frequently quoted account of Baron's unexpected popularity after the publication of her first story features Ben Avigdor. As told by Baron's friend Rivka Alper, after the publication of Baron's first story in *ha-Melitz* in 1903, "The well-known author Ben Avigdor wanted to meet the author. He took a detour to her village and went to their house. At that very moment Dvora Baron was standing barefoot by the water pump and busily washing the dishes. 'Child,' the man called to her, 'is this the Baron house?' She pointed to the house. After some time her brother called to her with excitement, 'Dvorka, He has come for *you!*' "[6] Despite his seemingly extreme interest in Dvora Baron, and Katz's reassurances, Baron's work was never published by the Toshiyah press.[7] Nevertheless, Baron's eagerness to be published in Ben Avigdor's series and Ben Avigdor's apparent eagerness to make Baron's acquaintance reflect his interest in and importance to young, up-and-coming writers at the turn of the twentieth century.

Brenner recalls the impact on his literary development of Ben Avigdor's movement and the Penny Books series that he used as a showcase for the New Way:

> When we first heard the word "realism," we didn't understand it, yeshivah boys that we were. But we knew that something really novel was happening, nevertheless. The stories published in Penny Books, for example, started right in with the word "he" and would put the hero on his death bed or at some other critical movement in his life and his entire history would flash before his eyes. These books were snatched up like first fruits before their time. These descriptions of reality "as it is," without really revealing internal worlds, were a giant step forward for the pathetic state of Hebrew letters that existed at the time.[8]

Although Brenner was not published in the Penny Books series, his first book was published in Ben Avigdor's Hebrew Library series in 1901.[9]

Ben Avigdor's brand of mimesis is a harbinger of what I called "local mimesis" in the previous chapter. Although his notion of "things as they are" was grounded in Europe, the rhetoric of local mimesis took on a life of its own among Hebrew writers in Palestine. The valorization of literary depictions of the Palestinian locale in which the narratives were physically composed can best be understood in light of Baron's critics' concerns over her continuing depictions of shtetl life even after her emigration to Palestine. This focus demonstrated, above all else, her "inability to shoot roots down into her new soil."[10] This local mimetic imperative, in turn, was yoked to as-if mimesis, the creation of a blueprint for Hebrew culture in Hebrew literature. As-if mimesis, as we recall, is the expression of a linguistic teleology—a belief in literature's capacity to effect the transformation of linguistic "imagined" communities into "real" ones.

Without belaboring this taxonomy of mimetic orientations, it is important to emphasize that Baron's poetic of "intimations," in which she gently and subtly engaged the "imperatives" of her generation, extended to mimesis. Baron's intense manipulation of mediating voices throughout her work—and particularly the voice of a rabbi's daughter—was, to my mind, her strongest antimimetic statement, even while it was widely interpreted as the measuring stick of her works' realism. The voice of the rabbi's daughter—sometimes named, sometimes not, sometimes featured as a character in the narratives, sometimes introduced obliquely into narratives and immediately abandoned (or silenced)—was construed as the signifier of Baron's autobiographical intentions, her ethnographic aspirations, and above all else her commitment to a form of commemoration. However, that voice is the tool with which Baron streamlines explicit articulations of ethnography, autobiography, and memory with fiction and fantasy, demonstrating that there is no such thing as the mimetic representation in literature of "things as they are." Instead, Baron posits a "mediational imperative" through her placement of a photographic idiom in the rabbi's daughter's mouth.

"Fradel" (1947), which we discussed in the Preface, is one of the best examples in Baron's corpus of layers of mediation. The conjugal misery of Fradel, the story's protagonist, is unstated by Fradel herself but is witnessed and narrated by a series of minor protagonists: the rabbi's wife (the rebbetzin), Crazy Gitl (the town lunatic), the neighbor women, Aunt Chana, and little Chana (the town rabbi's daughter). Little Chana is introduced into the story as a witness to Crazy Gitl's account of Fradel's unhappiness when Fradel's husband returns home one night following a late night of chess at his friend's house:

> "Crazy Gitl," Fradel's neighbor on the kitchen side, once saw him steal into the house through the back entrance, and then from inside came the sound of words and a moaning cry, and the next day she told the women about it at the community bench, where the relations between the couple was by now a frequent subject, and little Chana, who was playing there, listened to the story.
>
> In that place, in those days, they did not believe in shielding the eyes of a child by throwing an elegant prayer shawl over life's nakedness, and so, along with the song of sun-dazzled birds and the scent of dew drunk plants, she also absorbed impressions of daily life, bits of local color, of heartache and heart joy, which in the course of time—when they had been refined and illuminated by the light of her intellect, and experience had bound them into life stories—became for her, in the solitary nights of her wandering, a source of pleasure and comfort.[11]

We see three layers of mediation in this passage: first, there is Crazy Gitl, then Chana as a little girl listening to Crazy Gitl's account of Fradel's unhappiness, and finally, Chana, grown up, relates the contents of Gitl's story in the literary text we are reading. The contents of Crazy Gitl's remarks are, it is important to note, conspicuously missing. We do not know if Gitl has witnessed some kind of sexual scuffle or (given her purported craziness) is fabricating an account unsuitable for a child to hear. Nevertheless, this sketch is the story that Chana, as an adult, lays claim to and "illuminates by the light of her intellect and experience." What are we to make of the fact that in the case of "Fradel," the source of Chana's information is a supposed madwoman? Does this serve to authenticate the account Chana later transforms into the story we have before us, or does it serve to fictionalize it?

Baron articulates concern here that the reader recognize the literary material at hand is a transparent transcription of its source materials.

This concern is echoed in a passage from "The First Day," which we looked at in the Introduction, as the narrator purportedly recounts the first day of her life and says, enigmatically: "It's embarrassing to relate, but the events should be written simply, exactly as they happened."[12] Although this story ostensibly presents its contents as the autobiographical account of its narrator's first day, it is quite obvious that no real person could remember his or her first day. The pretense of "transparency" proposed by the narrator at the story's outset is undermined by the impossibility of a first-person, memory-based account of the beginning of one's life. Unlike "Fradel," which lays out the line of historical and literary transmission, "The First Day" does not posit any alternative witnesses to the child's birth that could provide the material necessary for a (later) literary recounting by the child herself. Baron, it seems, deliberately fosters a certain degree of incredulity in the very same narrative (indeed, the only narrative in her work) in which "transparency" is valorized. This same incredulity is built into the line of transmission in "Fradel." Can it be that Chana's only source of information and the basis of her narrative recounting is her memory of a madwoman's storytelling?

In another example of undermined transparency in Baron's work, she plays with the limits of verisimilitude in a narrative that purports to be "witnessed." "In the Beginning" is the story of a rebbetzin's unarticulated emotional journey toward adjustment to life in a small town. A chain of "witnesses" fills in the gaps left by the narrator's unwillingness to narrate the rebbetzin's emotional experience. One of those witnesses, Sara Riva, is the rebbetzin's housemaid who "described in detail how she, the rebbetzin, threw herself down in all her finery on the community bench and sobbed, while he, her rabbi husband, dressed in silk, paced the room—in consternation."[13] This same "witness" creates an important impasse in the communication of knowledge. The night that the child born at the end of the narrative is conceived, Sara Riva is once again invoked, but this time in terms of her silence and not her speech, her ignorance and not her knowledge:

> "Enlarge the place of your tent, for you shall break forth on the right hand and on the left," the rabbi rose from his seat and paced the length of the room, trilling his words in a mournful and tender tone—so mournful and

tender that the rebbetzin on the other side of the partition couldn't stop herself from standing up and holding her arms out toward the room. Is there any need to describe the things that passed between those two in the still of the night, in the raging heart of autumn? In any case there's no way of knowing all the details, since the old housekeeper had set up her bed that night in the kitchen, at the far end of the other room.[14]

Baron reminds us here that what we cannot know is as important as what we can know via the mediation of the marginal character she chooses for this important role. The commitment to realism implicit in the quest for an "authenticator" of narratives is, in some cases, the very thing that undermines the realist premise. Mediation, as in the case of Sara Riva or Crazy Gitl, creates an awareness of the reader's dependence on unreliable sources of narrative knowledge. The dissonance between what we want to know and what we can know because of the limitations of different critical mediators is typical of the dilemma faced not only by readers and writers of realist fiction but also specifically by Dvora Baron. And this point is where the rhetoric of photography and Baron's treatment of the discourse of realism reenter our discussion.

Chana, the narrator of Baron's "What Has Been," calls herself a "negative plate that remains alone after the photographed subject has been lost." She sees it as her "responsibility, for the sake of remembrance, to mark [her] impressions down on a sheet of paper."[15] In presenting Chana as a negative and not as a photograph, Baron goes back not to the original photographic moment—to the photographed object, the camera, the lens, the photographer, or even the photograph itself. Rather, Baron chooses to center the most cited and puzzled over metapoetic statement in her work on that thing which—in a representational economy of reality and its reproductions—is neither the object nor the subject of the reproduction. It is something in between, a kind of medium or mediator.

The negative was the key to the democratization of the art of photography as it evolved from an expensive and messy camera-driven art to a neater, more accessible, and in some cases even a cameraless art. The first notable photographic collection by a female "photographer" was that of Anna Atkins. In the 1840s and 1850s, she made photograms of seaweeds and pond scum and bound them in three volumes of a survey titled *British Algae.* There was no camera involved in this process.[16] Indeed, as discussed by Victoria Olsen in her biography of Julia Margaret Cameron (1815–1878), the first woman to make a name for herself during the early years of photography, "the negative enabled experimentation with the photographic process without requiring that the experimenter take any photographs his or herself."[17] Cameron did not get her hands on an actual camera until she had been experimenting with the process of developing negatives into different kinds of photographic images for a long period of time. The tools of the photographic trade were not fully accessible to her, so she made do with what she could obtain from a good friend—photographic negatives and processing chemicals. As we learn from the history of photography, the negative was the medium that rendered nonphotographers into photographic artists and facilitated the dispersion of photographic images at breakneck speed throughout the modern world.[18] What is the place of this image of the "negative" in Baron's presentation of her authorial narrator, Chana, and in her general discourse of photography throughout her literary corpus?

The contrast between the "negative" as the image in potential or the writer in potential and the "positive" as the final photographic or literary product is elaborated in Baron's presentation of Chana. Chana's tale, told in response to her perceived obligation to "commit some of my memories to paper as a memorial" to "those people who perished later in the great cataclysm," is a potential tale about a past world.[19] It is a tale for which only the dark contours exist and must, through gentle manipulation, through chemical treatment, and through patient evolution, be developed as is a negative into a photograph. That said, however, the process is essentially open to anyone. Chana's role as an artist is, in a sense, undermined by her characterization as a negative. She is the raw material for the evolving tale, but she is not necessarily the "photographer" with the inspired eye, or the "photograph" itself with the permanent image. Furthermore, calling her a photographic negative, as opposed to a photograph or a camera is, perhaps, Baron's way of locating Chana as both an "objective" voice on the culture of the shtetl and something else, less crystalline. At first glance, Chana's declaration of herself as a photographic negative in "What Has Been" seems to be a formulaic affirmation of the realism implicit in the story to follow. But Baron's use of photographic discourse at key junctures in her corpus has exactly the opposite effect. It acknowledges the value placed on the representation of "things as they are," or the "mimetic imperative" in the Hebrew literature of the modern Hebrew renaissance, then roundly rejects its stranglehold.

The ethnographic equation within which Dvora Baron and her work are usually placed can be reconsidered in light of the photographic negative with which she introduces her most complex and compelling metapoetic statement. Chana, as a negative, embodies the ethnographic pretense underpinning most post-World War II readings of fiction that feature the shtetl. That pretense is characterized by the conversion of the myriad specifics of eastern European Jewish life into a kind of consensual essence, a proliferation of details all converging on the same few points. The language of *Life Is with People: The Culture of the Shtetl* (1952), the post-World War II "ethnographic" study of Jewish life in eastern Europe that installed the term "shtetl" in the nostalgic vocabulary of American Jews, serves as a marvelous example of the typologizing and generic uses to which even a photographic idiom, or especially a photographic idiom, can be put.[20] In the preface to the book, the authors, Mark Zborowski and Elizabeth Herzog, say:

> It must be emphasized that this is a portrait of a culture and not a photograph or a diagram. Its subject matter is not ethnographic minutiae but rather prevailing patterns. It is, moreover, a composite portrait. Despite countless local variations, the Jews of Eastern Europe had one culture, possessing the characteristics that mark a culture: a language, a religion, a set of values, a specific constellation of social mechanisms and institutions, and the feeling of its members that they belong to one group. The effort has been made to capture the core of continuity running through the Jewish culture of Eastern Europe rather than the details in which localities and regions differed. Where forms are described, the most repre-

sentative one has been selected; or only the basic features have been re-
ported, minimizing the details that vary from place to place.[21]

In their explicit denial of the "photographic qualities" of their work,
Zborowski and Herzog are adopting the realist premises of photographic
discourse—that a photograph necessarily implies specific realities and
mimetic transparency. One of the dangers inherent in attempts to constitute a "composite" ethnographic "portrait" is, needless to say, the negation of the subject's specificity and therefore its identity. By denying the
photographic nature of their work, they deny the specificity of their
work, thus assuming, first, that photographs are inherently specific but
also that one cannot be specific in describing shtetl life to the American
public. When Zborowski and Herzog depict "the shtetl" for American
Jews, they present it in as schematic and streamlined a way as possible,
feeding into a nostalgia industry for whom a specific shtetl was too close
to home but a generalized shtetl was nonthreatening.

Reminiscent of Baron's own attempt to rescue the specific Jew from
modernist and European representations of "the Jew" (or later "the jew")
in *The Shtetl Book*, a 1975 portrait of Tishivetz, Diane Roskies and David
Roskies aim to "rescue the shtetl as a unique social organism rooted in a
specific time and place." In attempting, however, to reconstruct the map
of the shtetl through testimonies of its former inhabitants, Roskies and
Roskies run into a dilemma. As David Roskies puts it in a later essay,
"Since the actual inhabitants of the shtetl were capable of producing only
a redemptive or martyrological map of their imagined community, it
goes without saying that for subsequent generations of Jews who know
the shtetl second or third hand, even sketchy and primitive maps were
superfluous."[22]

Roskies, interestingly, employs the term "superfluous" instead of
"impossible" to describe the maps that could be reconstructed from the
memories of shtetl inhabitants and their offspring. What is implied by
the use of this particular term is the fact that specific artifacts or concrete
testaments to the dimensions and the construction of the shtetl could
not be reconstructed and were deemed unnecessary in light of the
shtetl's "afterlife," the life it took on in the imaginations of its descen-

dants. Here, in Roskies's response to *Life Is with People* and in the book itself, we see an articulation of belief that visual "reproductions" are the primary means, under normal circumstances, of communicating the physical minutiae of the past. But when that past is wholly erased, destroyed, and memorialized, visual proof of that world—in the form of maps or photographs—is deemed too specific or superfluous.

The myth of photography's monopoly on visual specificity is one major locus, both in Baron's work and in the discourse of photography, of photography's tenuous claim on realism. Many of the photographs taken of Jewish villages in eastern Europe during the interwar period by photographers such as Alter Kacyzne, Menachem Kipnis, Avrom Yosel Rotenberg, Henryk Bojm, Moryc Grosman, L. Przedecki, and Wilhelm Aleksandrowitz, published in Yiddish illustrated magazines or sent abroad to the United States and elsewhere, were captioned "Jewish Old Age," "A Woman at Work," or "The Community Synagogue."[23] Specific women, men, and synagogues became "types" over distance, over time, and certainly on the other side of cataclysm, when photographs taken before the war were published afterward.[24]

The "composite photography" of Francis Galton (1822–1911) in the late nineteenth century provides an example of the kind of "typologies" that grow out of the purported mimetic specificity and transparency of the photograph. In 1878 Galton described his intention to "obtain with mechanical precision a generalized picture: one that represents no man in particular, but portrays an imaginary figure possessing the average features of any given group of men."[25] Through a science of "double exposure," he produced a single face from several superimposed portraits. This effect, for our purposes, was similar to the effect of the ethnographic photography of the Jews conducted throughout eastern Europe at the turn of the twentieth century. When a specific woman becomes "Jewish Woman" and a specific synagogue "The Synagogue" of an unnamed town, photographs become denuded of their specificity.

If we compare the captions of two Alter Kacyzne photographs sent from Poland in the 1920s to the *Yiddish Forward*, we can see the unmistakable difference between a photograph conceived as a representation of particulars and a photograph forced into a typological, or generic, mold. In a famous 1926 photograph taken in Biala Podlaska, Lublin

4. *The Byaler Melamed, Binyomin Hirsh the Beard,* Laskarev, Lublin Province. *Courtesy of the Archives of YIVO Institute for Jewish Research, New York.*

Province, we see a *melamed* (teacher) sitting at a table in his schoolroom with several of his students (fig. 4). Gazing into the left of the frame, oblivious to a book he holds in his hands, he appears to be equally oblivious to his students. They look at their teacher, not at the camera, and their expression is inscrutable—restrained, resentful, respectful. Kacyzne's original caption (not published with the photograph in the *Yiddish Forward*) reads: "The Byaler Melamed, Binyomin Hirsch the Beard. More than once his students have nailed his beard—the longest in Byale—to the table when he has dozed off. Perhaps that's why he has such sad wonderful eyes." [26] All of the subject's identifying features are presented in this caption—his full name (Binyomin Hirsch), his professional role in the shtetl (the Byaler Melamed), and his nickname (the Beard). We are not given a generalized, "typical" image of the shtetl, but given a discrete piece of a particular man's life.

In contrast to this narratively ramified photograph, in an undated

5. Alter Kacyzne, *A Girl's Heder*, Laskarev, Lublin Province. *Courtesy of the Archives of YIVO Institute for Jewish Research, New York.*

photograph taken in Laskarev (Lublin Province), we see a "girl's heder" (fig. 5). It has no other identifying features—no narrative text, no year. The girls and their teacher, with the exception of one child on the far left of the frame, seem entirely absorbed by their work. No single figure in the photograph seems to be of central importance, and no relationship between any particular individuals seems preeminent. Rather, the overall effect is that of an ethnographic portrait, in which the photographer is drawing our attention to an institution rather than an individual. The tattered texts, identical page-boy haircuts, the dark hair, the rapt attention of the girls, and the teacher's close proximity to them instead of sitting at a separate table or standing above them are all left open to the interpretation and conjecture of the viewer because the caption does nothing other than offer a categorical identification: "A Girl's Heder." [27]

The relationship between these two photographs could be construed as a correlate to Baron's position as the only canonized woman writer of the modern Hebrew renaissance. She has, it seems, more often than not been presented generically as a female writer among male writers, as a soferet among sofrim. In her presentation of a metaphorics of photography, Baron is struggling with her own position in a pseudoethnographic literary culture of generic presentations and generic receptions. She may very well be more sensitive to the dangers of such a presentation or reception because of her own role as an "exemplar" or a "model" woman writer.

In *Family Frames,* Marianne Hirsch describes her experience, as a child, of going into her neighbor's apartment and looking at family photographs propped up on a side table in the living room: "These were pictures of Mr. and Mrs. Jakubowicz's first families—in my memory they have acquired a generic status of old looking studio family portraits." [28] Mr. and Mrs. Jakubowicz are Holocaust survivors, and their "first families" are gone. It is in this light that the photographs observed by the young Marianne Hirsch become not only depersonalized but also conventionalized. When the depicted personae in the photographs are not recognizable, they become wholly "generic," in Hirsch's terminology.

These photographs, aside from the Jakubowiczs' own memories, are all that remain of the dead. They explain, in the continuation of Hirsch's discussion of her neighbors' daughter (named Chana, like Baron's narrator in "What Has Been"), "how hard it must be for Chana to live in the shadow of these legendary siblings whom she had already outlived in age, whom, because she had never known them, she could not mourn, whom her parents could never stop mourning. I thought that their ghostly presence might explain Chana's pallor, her hushed speech, her decidedly un-childlike behavior." [29] Each of Chana's parents was previously married, and each of their families was killed during the Holocaust—husbands, wives, children, parents, sisters, and brothers. Chana's life is predicated upon and, unfortunately, facilitated by the death of the people in the photographs on her side table because her parents would never have married and had her if their first families were still alive. To Hirsch, these photographs reflect Chana's fate more than they reflect the fate of their own subjects. Their presence as a testament to death has come to replace their specific subject matter, as designated at the moment the photographs were taken.

Annette Kuhn, in her description of what she calls "memory work," echoes Hirsch: "Memory work undercuts assumptions about the transparency or the authenticity of what is remembered, treating it not as 'truth' but as evidence of a particular sort: material for interpretation, to be interrogated, mined for its meanings and its possibilities."[30] Kuhn's formulation of "memory work" as an act of interpretation, mobilization, and reconstruction is cast as a negation of the language of realism ("transparency," "authenticity," and "truth"). Memory work is, as in the case of Hirsch's understanding of Chana's family portraits, an act of appropriation and personalization that may not necessarily have anything to do with the actual historicity of the moment being "remembered" or the life narrative being recounted. The beholder of the photographs, Hirsch, projects onto the pictures the life experience of Chana, her playmate. Since she does not know the photographed people, and can never know them because they are now all dead, her own perspective becomes the dominant force not only in her interpretation of the photographs but also in the content of the photographs themselves.

Baron's Chana, too, as a "negative," is similarly inflected strictly on the basis of the extinction of "things as they were." Chana is not writing about herself per se, but everything she writes about reflects back on herself primarily because her subject matter reflects not its own life, but its own inescapable death. This point is where we revisit the notion of transitional mimesis, a process whereby the represented object is obliterated in the course of, and by sheer virtue of, its representation. Chana calls herself a photographic negative only after she asserts that "all these people, they say, perished later in a cataclysm: and I who knew them regard myself as a kind of negative that has survived long after the photographed object no longer exists."[31] Hers is not a nostalgic or mournful recollection. Rather, Chana as Baron's narratorial subject is the mediator of our awareness of the shtetl's extinction. Chana communicates the profound cataclysm responsible for her designation of herself as a photographic negative by failing directly to represent in the most conventional photographic form the world destroyed. No actual photograph, Baron seems to be articulating, can capture the cataclysm underlying her narrative, and so she designates her narrator, Chana, a negative. It is as if not only the photographed subject but the photograph itself has been destroyed.

At the end of "What Has Been" Chana says: "For a long time I—now settled in my new homeland—heard nothing of the family. News began to reach us of the horrors that befell our brethren, and many believed that all had perished in the disaster; yet I, in my heart of hearts, had faith that He who keeps alive the seed of grain under the winter snow and gives strength to the tree trunk to weather the severest storm, had preserved some survivor of this family."[32] Although Baron articulates Chana's role as a negative of a particular Jewish period and locale on the other side of a cataclysm, many critics view the Hebrew and Yiddish literature that depicts life in the shtetl as the archive of a lost culture, even though it was not conceived in that way. In other words, they appoint the literature itself as a photograph, unlike Baron who inserts the photographic image into the story. Perhaps, in so doing, rather than opening the story up to being viewed as a realist portrait, she forces the readers to consider it "real" on her (and Chana's) own terms. She enables the reading of "the disaster" between the lines of her narrative, in the silences of the narrative. But she avoids having that disaster become its raison d'être.

Though Baron mentions the cataclysm herself, in most contemporary readings of literature with the European shtetl as its subject, the cataclysm is projected upon it from the outside. Susan Sontag sums this point up beautifully in her reflection on the photographs of Roman Vishniac: "One's reaction to the photographs he took in 1938 of daily life in the ghettos of Poland is overwhelmingly affected by the knowledge of how soon all these people were to perish."[33] A gap develops, in such formulations, between what is to be found in the text and what comes to color all perceptions of the text.

Walter Benjamin, in 1931, theorized "the optical unconscious" as a visual corollary to the "unconscious impulses" of psychoanalysis. Photography, for him, is the expression not of the visible, the real, and the obvious, but of the invisible and the subtle. He claims that "a different nature opens itself to the camera than opens to the naked eye. . . . Even if one has general knowledge of the way people walk, one knows nothing of a person's posture during the fractional second of a stride. . . . Here the camera intervenes with the resources of its lowerings and liftings, its interruptions and isolations, its extensions and accelerations, its enlargements and reductions."[34] Benjamin, focused on the invisible and the ephemeral that the camera renders visible and permanent, expresses the belief that the picture accentuates its own fidelity to a real object or experience that is generally imperceptible. The photograph, which has come to be viewed as a synecdoche for the worlds it represents, is, in fact, an overdetermination of the fleeting image and the unseen gesture. It is only through the mediation, or, as he put it, the "intervention" of the camera, that we see those events or objects that we normally would not. This observation reverberates significantly in the context of Baron's emphasis, throughout her works, on the importance of narrative mediation. In her resistance to being identified strictly as a literary ethnographer of the shtetl, she is not denying the reality of the culture of the shtetl, or its precipitous demise in eastern Europe, particularly between the world wars. Rather, she draws our attention to the necessarily mediated nature of literary perception. Any depiction of the shtetl is to be understood as a depiction, not a transparent representation.

Baron may have been so intensely concerned with the distinction between the "reflected" and the "mediated" for several reasons. First, in her artistry she had earned the right to be considered a writer of fiction, not a social scientist, ethnographer, or autobiographer. Without denying the seed of the "real" in her work, because that source, after all, was a stylistic imperative of the modern Hebrew renaissance, Baron accentuates the artistic mediation that renders her work fictional. Also, as previously mentioned, Baron was regarded as eccentric and out of step in her decision to continue writing about life in the shtetl once she had emigrated to Palestine. Some critics argued that she did so because she could write about only what she "knew" as a woman with a narrow perspective. Again, through a thematic of mediation, even though she is writing about the shtetl in Palestine, Baron's artistic and aesthetic choices are accentuated.

Chana is the embodiment of Baron's affirmations of mediation throughout her work. She is, generally, a narrator-author who has left her home, only to revisit it, in text, years later. Her rendering of that "home" and the people therein is wholly contingent on her own faulty memory and her unreliable sources of knowledge. She was, after all, a young girl in her encounter with those personages and places she now, belatedly, depicts. As a young girl, her perception, her sources, and her process of encoding are, according to literary convention, deemed "unreliable." Also, by constantly emphasizing the female narrator's Jewish textual erudition within a gendered culture of female Jewish intellectual impoverishment, the mediated nature of these stories' evolution also is emphasized.

Chana, and not the reader, decides whether these stories are a representation of a lost world. Chana, and not the reader, determines which fleeting images are to be memorialized and are, ironically, to become narrative memorials. In so doing, Baron implicitly circumvents the tendency to read her stories as realist tableaux of historical memory, or, as I formulated earlier in the context of Mendele's later reception, as "memorial mimesis." She reserves the right to determine the realist reverberations of her narratives herself, or at least, in conjunction with Chana as the mediator between the story and its readers. By making Chana a negative, not only does Baron force her into the role of mediator between the story and its readers, but to a large extent she also forces the reader to consider the role of Chana's artistry, as a woman and a rabbi's daughter, in the construction of the Hebrew narratives that contain her.

Martin Sandler asserts, "Whereas art academies had always discriminated against women, photography required little formal training, and in fact many of the most successful women photographers would be self taught." Constance Sullivan argues eloquently, "When [photography] was first introduced to the world, there were hardly the standards for photographic practice or results to equal those of other disciplines. No one yet knew what the standards needed to be. Rewards went simply to those who succeeded and who were able to make their success known. The discourse was in terms of photography's potential and enthusiasts published lists of what photography might do. How it would occur remained to be seen. At this stage both sexes were on equal footing." [35] The notion that a "potential" art is more of an open art than a "realized" one resonates remarkably with the "as-if" mimesis implicit in the notion of

Hebrew literature as the expression of a "potential" Hebrew-speaking society. In light of this resonance, one would think that Hebrew literature would be open to the participation of anyone who wanted to try her hand at it.

Of course, only those individuals who know Hebrew can attempt to write in Hebrew, and the few who knew Hebrew well enough to do so during the modern Hebrew renaissance were generally educationally or socioeconomically privileged men. Furthermore, instead of broadening the horizon of participation, the idea that modern Hebrew letters were a prescription for Hebrew life actually made the culture of Hebrew letters more circumspect and less democratic than could be expected. The culture wars between those Zionist ideologues like Asher Ginsburg (or Ahad ha-Am, 1856–1927) who believed that Hebrew letters were a cultural heritage to be used only for the highest and most rarefied of intellectual purposes and those individuals like M. Y. Berdischevsky, Chaim Nachman Bialik, and A. L. Ben Avigdor who believed that Jewish normalization required the vernacularization and democratization of Hebrew belles letters succinctly represent the kind of tension surrounding the modern Hebrew literary endeavor.[36] Even those writers, however, who expressed a need to render Hebrew accessible and to recognize folk forms within the dense theological and legalistic codes of traditional Hebrew literature were somewhat cagey about what constituted an "appropriate" Hebrew literary form and what did not. The fact that Baron was the only canonized Hebrew woman prose writer of the modern Hebrew renaissance despite the fact that there were at least a handful of women writing (as described in the Introduction) attests to the troubled nature of the Hebrew literary democracy.

In a similar vein, although the ready availability of photographic technology for much of the twentieth century and certainly in the present should enable a kind of liberation from artistic conventions governing the visual arts and a democratization of photographic practitioners, in fact the opposite has taken place. Pierre Bourdieu illustrates the fascinating tension in photographic culture between the conventional and the creative:

> While everything would lead one to expect that this activity, which has no
> traditions and makes no demands, would be delivered over to the anarchy

of individual improvisation, it appears that there is nothing more regulated and conventional than photographic practice and amateur photographs: in the occasions which give rise to photography, such as the objects, places and people photographed, or the very composition of the pictures, everything seems to obey implicit canons which are very generally imposed and which informed amateurs or aesthetes notice as such, but only to denounce them as examples of poor taste or technical clumsiness.[37]

In other words, although photography could very well serve as the basis for the most democratic art, it, in fact, has been primarily channeled into a very narrow and specific range of functions—the family photograph, for example, and the documentary photograph. Similarly, only certain kinds of Hebrew narrative style were deemed acceptable and canonic. By focusing on the photographic negative, Baron may, indeed, be alluding to the ways in which her work serves as a kind of shadow or reversal of the "positive" or the idealized photographs that are the stylistic embodiment of the poetics of realism. As Pierre Frantcastle says:

Photographs are taken, even today, as a function of the classical artistic vision, at least insofar as this is permitted by the conditions of lens manufacture and the use of only one lens. The camera provides the vision of the Cyclops, not of man. We also know that we systematically eliminate all those recordings which do not coincide with a vision that is not real but rather more or less artistic. For example, we do not take a picture of a building from close up, because the recording will not correspond to the traditional laws of orthometry.[38]

In light of these assertions and denials of photography's democratizing potential, the uniqueness of Chana's identity as a Jewishly erudite female author of Hebrew narratives is simultaneously affirmed and undermined by her designation as a photographic negative. On the one hand, she is a living testament to the democratic potential within Jewish intellectual culture because she has managed to become a Hebrew writer despite her gender. On the other hand, her constant self-conscious affirmations of her erudition (to be explored in the next chapter) emphasize her unique identity as a woman who must assert her mastery of the necessary tools to become a Hebrew writer. In a similar vein, her self-declaration as an artistic negative both affirms her artistry and denies it inasmuch as, via negatives, artistic photographs can be made by anyone—even those who do not have access to a camera.

In his famous description of trying to find, after his mother's death, a photograph of her that captures her essence, Roland Barthes goes back to the first photograph ever taken of her when she was six years old. In that photograph, he claims to have found a "just image." "For once," he says, the photograph before him "contained more than what the technical being of photography can reasonably offer."[39] The winter-garden photograph (as he calls it) is a buffer between Barthes's mother and oblivion; it takes her back to her origins and gives him a glimpse of her existence as a being independent of him, a harbinger of her death wherein she once again exists on some other plane without him. For Barthes, the winter-garden photograph represents a realism divorced from the contingencies of sight and sound, and the dogmas of the "confirmable." Rather than bringing Barthes's mother back to him, the photograph mediates his mother for him; it creates the possibility of their coexistence in a universe that does not require that they both be present. As we conclude our discussion of Baron's treatment of the mimetic imperatives of the modern Hebrew renaissance, let us consider her 1951 story "Derekh Kotsim" (The Thorny Path) against the backdrop of Barthes's winter-garden photograph.

"The Thorny Path" is the story of a young woman, Mousha, married to a small-town photographer named Nahum. After the birth of her first child, Mousha is unaccountably paralyzed from the waist down. The child dies in early infancy, and thereafter Mousha spends her days lying in a bed that has been strategically placed by a window overlooking the central square of the town. Mousha's second child is born a few years after the death of her first child and the onset of her paralysis. Never having left the house, Mousha has presumably been unable to go to the ritual bath and observe the laws of family purity. After the birth of a child, as in the monthly onset of menstruation, there is a waiting period that must follow the cessation of uterine bleeding before a woman can immerse herself in a ritual bath and resume sexual relations with her husband. Since Mousha became paralyzed within days of her first child's birth, long before her postpartum bleeding would have stopped, she never seems to have had the opportunity to go to the ritual bath. It is assumed, with the birth of her second child, that she and Nahum have violated the laws of family purity that are central to traditional Jewish family life.[40] Consequently, the townspeople of Khmilovka boycott the circumcision ceremony of her second child, Muni (short for "Benjamin"), immediately after which he is sent to live with a wet nurse and her family because of Mousha's presumed inability to care for him. Mousha's stepmother has arranged for Muni's room and board with relatives of hers, on the condition that Mousha and Nahum have nothing to do with the child.

Mousha's gaze through the window of her house changes over time: "People who had to cross the square daily were getting tired of seeing her permanently framed in the window, regarding them with her smoldering eyes, as if they were to blame for having sound legs. They found this particularly irksome during their outdoor family celebrations when the sight of her wan, tragic face would suddenly mar the festive mood like a dark blotch against the bright background of their untroubled lives."[41] Whereas Mousha's gaze, at first, expresses anxiety, insecurity, and love as she attempts to follow Nahum through his daily routine with her eyes, it evolves into a gaze of surveillance, to match the surveillance of the townsfolk who believe that by ostracizing Mousha and Nahum they are upholding rabbinic law.

Nahum and Mousha spend years of their lives trying to reclaim their son, and only through the intervention of an old classmate of Nahum's are they able to arrange for him, when he is old enough, to become a photographer's apprentice and to leave his guardians' house. When Nahum dies of a heart attack, Muni returns home, as a young adult, to be reunited with his mother. He buys his mother a wheelchair and restarts the family photography business. It is at this stage in the narrative that Muni photographs his mother: "In this portrait he brought out and epitomized all her submerged traits, all her patient suffering and aching love, her repressed sighs and unshed tears, all the agony of her denied mother-hood. All these he captured and portrayed in every line and wrinkle of her prematurely seamed face. When he handed her the picture, she re-garded it in silence, then let flow the tears she had held back for so long. Her son laid a comforting hand on her shoulder, the hand of a long-lost son who had been restored." Barthes's quest, in photographs, for his mother's core characteristics, for that spark of the familiar and the com-forting after her death, echoes Muni's success at depicting his mother, Mousha, not for what she has always been able to present to the world but for what the world has not seen. Like Walter Benjamin's "uncon-scious optics," in the photograph shot of Mousha by Muni, "a different nature opens itself to the camera than opens to the naked eye." [42]

Baron posits an alternative to the mimetic imperatives of the mod-ern Hebrew renaissance in this image of Mousha. She breaks down the traditional notion of mimesis as a hierarchical relationship between something derivative and its original, something primary and its sec-ondary representation, something of the past or a projection into the fu-ture, and acknowledges the fundamental groping that takes place between the literary subject and the literary object, between the text and the world. There is, naturally, Baron posits, a sort of resignation behind every text—a resignation that accompanies recognition of irreconcilable difference and conciliation between the ideal mimetic capacity of the lit-erary text and the real mimetic capacity of the literary text. That recogni-tion and conciliation lead to a poetics of mediation.

In the well-known deconstructionist formulation of representation, the world does not become reflected in the literary text; the signifier text does not aspire to represent the signified object beyond the text. Rather, the literary text constitutes, in Barthes's terms, a "middle voice." When a literary text is understood as a middle voice, "the subject is constituted as immediately contemporary with the writing, being effected and affected by it." The middle voice, according to Barthes, facilitates a kind of "in-transitive writing," wherein "writing becomes itself the means of vision or comprehension, not a mirror of something independent, but an act and commitment; [it is] a doing and making rather than a reflection or description." [43] This intransitive writing is at the core of what I have called Baron's transitional mimesis, the designation of the literary text as

6. Dvora Baron seated. *Courtesy of Gnazim Archive, Ramat Gan, Israel.*

the crucible for that which is represented. Transitional mimesis like Barthes's intransitive writing is the recognition of the literary text's, like the photograph's, role in rendering the invisible visible and extinguishing the extant. The transitionally mimetic text takes on the life force of that which is represented in it, coming to replace it.

In "The Thorny Path," Baron presents her own version of a "middle voice," offering an alternative to the varieties of mimetic discourse during the modern Hebrew renaissance, gesturing to that which is intimated—present through its very absence and absent even when present. Baron, through her presentation of Mousha's disabled body at the focal center of the town of Khmilovka, inserts, as it were, an unmistakable yet illegible presence into the community. Is she there or is she not? She is visible, but she is not tangible; she has eyes, but can she see? And if she does, what does she see?

Chana, the rabbi's daughter become woman writer scattered

throughout Baron's work, serves as something of an illegible presence at the heart of Baron's corpus as well. As we have explored, Chana is presented in "What Has Been" as a photographic negative, not an actual photograph, and as such she represents Baron's stunning revision of the Hebrew renaissance's mimetic imperative. Via Chana, in Baron's literary universe, we witness the presentation of things not "as they are," "as they were," or "as they will be," but, in effect, as they come into being. Chana as a writer is born in the course of Baron's corpus. Baron does not create a "portrait of the artist as a young woman" in her development of Chana. Rather, she creates a "negative of the artist as a young woman," promoting the possibility of other young women artists, other scenarios of the birth of a female author.

Donna Haraway reminds us that "only partial perspective promises objective vision. All Western cultural narratives about objectivity are allegories of the ideologies governing the relations of what we call mind and body, distance and responsibility. Feminist objectivity is about limited location and situated knowledge, not about transcendence."[44] Baron, too, demonstrates, in her presentation of a thematics of photography, that even that which conceives of itself as the most transparently spectral, most "true" to life, or most unmediated witness is to be understood within the confines of a particular, finite, perspective. The true, Baron argues, is, in Haraway's term, only "partial." Particularly in the case of a woman writer writing in the company of men, obfuscating her obvious differences but also intimating them, we see in Baron's variation on the mimetic imperative a calling of the singular vision, of the pretense of unmediated literary engagement with literary reality, to task.

4

⋘⟡⋙

She Sermonizes in Wool and Flax

The Vernacular Imperative

> Writing is a lunacy, a kind of weakness and folly of the ego, like the compulsion of some people to step to the pulpit and treat the congregation to a sample of their gurgling.—S. J. Abramowitz, "Of Bygone Days" (1899)

> Reb Mendele, I can't understand you . . . I speak to you in a reasonable fashion, the way people speak to one another, and judge on the basis of what my eyes see, and you try to reveal the hidden through dialectics and deductions. You seem to be studying a page of the Talmud with me.—S. J. Abramowitz, "In the Secret Place of Thunder" (1887)

THE MOST DEFINING AND PERVASIVE "imperative" of the modern Hebrew renaissance was the "vernacular imperative." I have already described the vernacular imperative as an early, primary subset of the mimetic imperative. The successful fulfillment of the vernacular imperative through S. J. Abramowitz's creation of the nusah, his signature Hebrew stylistic innovation in which biblical, rabbinic, and postrabbinic Hebrew commingled to forge an idiomatic flexibility unprecedented in the Hebrew prose that preceded it, ushered in the fiction of the modern Hebrew renaissance in the last decade of the nineteenth century. Hebrew renaissance writers, beginning with Abramowitz, distinguished themselves from the Hebrew writers of the Haskalah by prioritizing the construction of a natural, spoken Hebrew register in their literary works. This style was in distinct contrast to the hypertextualized pastiches characteristic of Haskalah poetry and fiction. Because a living Hebrew did not yet exist in speech, the quest for a living Hebrew idiom in literature was, for the writers of the modern Hebrew renaissance, all-consuming.

When Dvora Baron sought, in the absence of a Hebrew-speaking culture, to create a Hebrew vernacular literature, or a literature that "spoke" Hebrew, how did her associations and choices differ from those of her male colleagues? To what extent did she declare those differences, and to what extent did she sublimate them? How do those differences nuance our understanding of the continuities and discontinuities with traditional textual and religious culture presented by an evolving Hebrew vernacular literature?

A student of Dvora Baron's father recalls Baron sitting alone in the kitchen, listening as her father gave lessons to his male students: "As if from a distance, she would call out questions, and her father and brother would answer her."[1] As a girl and a woman, Baron was never formally educated in the more sophisticated texts of her tradition. For her, literary production was a function of translating into text the oral process of Torah study as she experienced it, sitting apart from the men in her father's synagogue and calling out questions to her father as he taught male students. Because Baron's first exposure to literary texts was essentially oral, she was able to create literary texts that, despite their very textuality, could maintain and thematize orality or vernacular speech.

Baron, like several of her colleagues, forged a "speakerly" style in her fiction. A speakerly style acknowledges an oral motivation while gesturing to its necessarily textual trappings; a speakerly text "speaks" itself, implicitly acknowledging its wholly textual parameters.[2] The notion of a speakerly text was formulated by Henry Louis Gates Jr. in order to describe attempts to capture the colloquial rhythms of oral speech within African American literary works. According to Gates, speakerly texts can be distinguished from literary texts that simply attempt to communicate oral discourse in that speakerly texts privilege their textuality even as they poke fun at it; the juncture between the oral and the textual is simultaneously created and challenged. Speakerly texts speak their own process of textual transcription, privileging their textuality while commenting on it as if in voice.

S. J. Abramowitz, in several of his Hebrew short stories, bases his "vernacular" idiom on the synagogue liturgy that is canonized in text but performed in voice. Chaim Nachman Bialik, as part of his project of re-cuperating and collecting *Agadah* (legends gleaned from rabbinic litera-ture), argues in his essays for the essentially oral nature of *Agadah*. Baron's depiction of sermons, particularly in her story "Agunah" (Aban-doned Wife) (1920), also experiments with the identification and em-ployment of a speakerly literary form. Moreover, she develops unique and unprecedented oral-rhetorical strategies for modern Hebrew fic-tion, shedding light on the birth of a Hebrew vernacular literature.

Clearly, since modern literary Hebrew was evolving during Baron's lifetime and career, no literary texts from the modern Hebrew renais-sance can be discussed without attention to their linguistic fabric. In the work of each writer, we can observe the evolution not only of their own style but also of the modern Hebrew literary idiom that they created for themselves, for each other, and for subsequent generations of writers. The beginning of "Family," the first story collected in Baron's definitive anthology *Parshiyot*, deals with the link between generations of a family. I present it in as literal a translation as possible in order to capture its stylistic effect: "About the chain of generation, how it develops [*he-akh hi holekhet*] and comes into being, behold [*ki hineh*], the biblical record recounts in brief that behold, Ploni lived so many years and begot Al-moni, and after that Almoni lived so many years and begot sons and daughters."[3]

Baron often invokes different types of primary Jewish texts—the Bible, medieval rabbinic commentaries, Talmudic midrash—although she is most frequently acknowledged for her biblical allusions. Under close scrutiny, however, her biblical "allusions" are just that—allusions—but not quotations. The above passage folds into itself a biblical rhetoric through a paratactic style and through thematic suggestion, even though it does not directly quote the Bible. With the phrase *ki hineh*, (behold), Baron leads her reader to believe that she is about to quote the Bible. But she does not, because even though using the late biblical language for anonymous reference (ploni and almoni), she takes the anonymity of her statement beyond what we would expect from the Bible—"so many years"; by making the number of years as generic as her subject matter (ploni and almoni), she has resisted biblical norms and undermined the expectation of quotation.

In "Abandoned Wife," the story we are about to discuss, Baron frames biblical and rabbinic allusions within the voice of a preacher giving a sermon in a shtetl synagogue. Few of her peers write sermons as a means of mobilizing primary Jewish texts within a modern idiom.[4] Baron does just that—she takes these intertexts and makes them her own—by reframing them and rewriting them. Even so, she uses an overall style characterized by lengthy, paratactic, inverted sentences in which prepositions and modifiers frequently precede subjects and the reader must always account for the subject of the sentence through rereadings. Alongside a sophisticated lexicon that sounds somewhat archaic to a contemporary ear, this technique creates a generically "classical" effect that subverts any attempts to characterize her style on the basis of a specific intertext or a specific epoch.

The question that is frequently asked of writers from the modern Hebrew renaissance is whether they adopted, adapted, or rejected Mendele's nusah—his fluid synthesis of all different levels of Hebrew discourse for the creation of a vernacular effect. Nusah Hebrew was evaluated by subsequent generations as heavy-handed—almost too self-conscious of its own borrowings and its own innovations. It was, as its name means in Hebrew, "formulaic," insofar as it provided a formula for Hebrew literature that would maximize all levels of Hebrew simultaneously. It would be difficult to argue that any writer subsequent to Mendele does not have some debt to pay to Mendele's nusah as that which freed Hebrew from the shackles of the melitsah, or biblical pastiche style, broadly used during the Haskalah. As such, it is important to document what parts of the nusah are maintained in the style of subsequent generations and what parts are revised. Baron's style—simply by virtue of its invocation of all the different types of Hebrew texts—alludes to the nusah prioritization of all different linguistic styles simultaneously. But overall, Baron does not employ the style of all those texts as much as she refers to them thematically by invoking them or by rewriting them. In this chapter we will observe the ways in which Baron engages biblical and rabbinic texts in her literary performance of a sermon as her contribution to the post-nusah generation's struggle to create a vernacular Hebrew voice and the ways in which Baron's identity as the only woman writer of her generation contributed to her successful creation of that vernacular style.

Baron's career as a Hebrew writer reflects a process of textual acquisition based not exclusively on a scholarly engagement with traditional texts but, in part, on a gleaning of literary texts from oral encounters. Learning traditional Jewish texts orally and aurally, Baron was better equipped than her literary peers to recognize the importance of representing the juncture of voice and text in modern Hebrew literature. In her texts, she poses a number of crucial social questions about Jewish literacy as well as about vernacular literatures. Who is speaking and who is listening in traditional as well as in modern Jewish literary culture? Who chooses to read, and who chooses to hear? Who must hear because they cannot read, and what do they lose or gain in the process? Baron achieves a fine balance in her representation of the relationship between textually erudite orators and illiterate auditors, between the oral voice and the literary text.

Baron's narrators consistently display mastery of Hebrew scholarly culture in order to depict women's domestic lives in a language largely dominated by male scholarship and male literary biographies. It seemed incongruous, during the period of the modern Hebrew renaissance, to enter, in the language of the Bible and the Talmud, the troubled world of a barren woman, a woman going through a divorce, a neglected daughter, or an abused housemaid. In truth, the Bible provided ample precedent for literary depiction of such female predicaments. Hagar was exiled to the desert with Ishmael by a jealous Sarah; Dina's love for Shechem was foiled by her jealous brothers; Leah was not loved by her husband, Jacob; Rachel, Rebecca, and Samuel's mother, Hannah, all poignantly bemoaned their childlessness. But in the literary culture of the modern Hebrew renaissance (at its inception in Europe), texts seemed to move in one of two directions—either in the direction of the "folk" as conceived by the educated elite, such as S. J. Abramowitz and Chaim Nachman Bialik, or in the direction of the "self," on a trajectory of liberation from the house of study to the world of the academy or commerce, as in the work of Y. H. Brenner, M. Y. Berdischevsky, and U. N. Gnessin. Modern Hebrew manipulations of biblical and rabbinic language came to be associated with those two trajectories, and any thematic or style that seemed to veer off course, representing the "folk" not in a comic, deprecating, or sentimentalizing light and not from a uniquely disfranchised intellectual male perspective, seemed an anomaly.

The language necessary for the creation of any literary text seemed to be beholden to certain thematics and certain stylistics appropriate to the monolithic nature of the generation (they were almost all male yeshiva dropouts) that largely produced it. Baron's narrators occupy an alternative subject position, declaring alternative erudition and developing thematics unique to her generation. Her narrators situate themselves in the interstices of sameness and difference, forcing readers to ask whether it is necessary to read gender into Dvora Baron's narrative fiber or to question to what extent the circumstances of Baron's acquisition of traditional Jewish knowledge are encoded in the style of her fiction.

Traditional women were fairly familiar with biblical narratives, if not in the Hebrew original, then at least in the translations and synopses widely available in Yiddish. But women were expressly forbidden to study the Talmud and its associated texts by oft-quoted, and widely accepted, minority rabbinic opinions.[5] Despite this prohibition, or perhaps because of it, Baron's narrators consistently try to demonstrate textual skills within a rabbinic, homiletic mold. Biblical allusions are placed within an interpretive frame where the narrator can pose as something of a rabbinic exegete. In some instances, the narrator speaks in approximations, though not direct quotations, of rabbinic texts, and in other instances, particularly in the case of sermons, the narrator acts as an exegete-preacher or teacher, teaching biblical texts and speaking rabbinic ones.

Joseph Heinemann has argued that hermeneutic midrashim are transcriptions, to some degree, of synagogue sermons. He thus points to a whole body of rabbinic texts that are to be understood, according to his theory, as a record of voices.[6] Although this approach to selected midrashic collections has been the subject of much debate since it was first presented about thirty years ago, it poses a fascinating counterpoint to the notion of the Jews as the "people of the book." It also serves to complicate the understanding that orality and textuality, or vernacular and literary culture, can be polarized. Baron's incorporation of sermons into her short fiction is a unique and effective way for her to gesture to traditional Jewish literary culture while acknowledging the complicated nuancing of speaking voices underlying that culture both historically and personally.

The Hebrew title of Baron's story, "Abandoned Wife," can be literally translated as "anchored woman" or a wife whose husband has disappeared without two witnesses to attest to his death.[7] Because there is no way to obtain a writ of divorce from someone who cannot be located or whose death cannot be confirmed, the disappeared man leaves behind an "anchored woman," a woman who is considered forever married to someone absent. She cannot claim the privileges of a married woman or a divorcée, and is left in limbo for the rest of her life, unable to remarry, unable to collect the financial stipulations spelled out in her marriage contract in the event of death or divorce. The *agunah,* or anchored wife, has long been depicted in the rabbinic imagination as the figure of the Jewish people in exile, abandoned by God. Those readers untrained in the conventions of rabbinic parables are likely to encounter the agunah in the discourse of exile, of destruction, of longing, and not to understand its basis in real Jewish women's experience.

In Baron's "Abandoned Wife," a sermon unites men and women in an ostensibly democratic intellectual environment but polarizes them through the different ways that they apprehend the same oral communication. The sermon in this story serves as a version of "calling across" the partition of intellectual polarization. A "real" agunah listens to a sermon and identifies completely with the plight of a metaphoric agunah woven into a hermeneutic rubric that is almost totally inaccessible to her.

"Abandoned Wife" can be divided into four parts. In the first, we are introduced to a poor Lithuanian shtetl in the late afternoon on a winter's day, to an itinerant preacher, and to the synagogue he visits to preach a sermon between afternoon and evening services. In the second, we are transported into the world of the synagogue, specifically into the men's section, where we hear the words of the preacher from the men's perspective. In the third part of the story, a woman's perspective on the same sermon grows out of the silence with which the second part of the story concludes, as all the men wait expectantly for the preacher to elaborate on a parable presented in the sermon. Finally, we exit the synagogue and escort the only woman present for the sermon in the women's section back to her house. We begin outside the synagogue and end outside the synagogue, but we have two separate sermon experiences within the synagogue itself.

In the sermon, mythical figures come to life, and traditional texts are not only orally performed but essentially perform themselves by becoming the first active agents in the story. The narrative voice merges with the voice of the preacher, the voice of the preacher with that of the prophet Jeremiah, the Jewish historical past with that of the present. In order to illustrate the confluence of the narrator's voice with the voice of the preacher and the biblical characters, I shall quote the sermon from the men's perspective in its entirety:

> David the King comes, peace be upon him, and "appears" in the tractate *Brakhot*, he and his sweet harp, playing by itself.[8] "Wake up, my glory, the harp and the lyre: I will awake the dawn.[9] He is strengthened like a lion, gets up before dawn and pours out his prayers.[10]
>
> Aaron the priest comes, pure, pursuer of peace,[11] with his flowering staff, the almond staff,[12] and Jeremiah bent beneath the burden of sorrow, he whose entrails contracted[13] and whose eyes were darkened by tears, and he will seek out a resting place in the desert.[14]
>
> The congregation of Israel is living in agony, wounded, debilitated, and tortured: "every head is sick, and every heart faint."[15] Every day, new decrees are issued. "We are pursued to our necks: All our enemies have opened their mouths against us.[16] The excited Jew takes out his handkerchief and wipes his face. The fat murderous image of the Cossack, raiding and wrecking the stores, hovers before the congregants. They can almost hear the drunken sound of the non-Jews, and the riots on the market days—their day of distress.
>
> But that is nothing: Not for eternity will God abandon us, will he for-

get us, the holy one of Israel. "Fear not, Jacob, nor be dismayed, Israel, because I am with you,"[17] says the prophet persuasively in a moist, weepy voice. The darkness beyond the windows lightens and does not trouble one so much anymore. Exile is bitter, after all, and difficult, but fleeting, like a tabernacle in a garden, like a temporary dwelling place. And those who speak on our behalf do not stay silent:

From the Cave of the *Makhpelah* Abraham Our Father comes, and stands, protecting his sons, and begging for pity. After him, Isaac with his great fear appears, and Jacob, the master of small things. There is hope, there is hope. . . . Moses Our Leader shudders and speaks in a trembling voice. Is it possible? And even King David does not stay silent. If need be, Rachel Our Mother will appear on our behalf.[18]

Cloaked in light and wrapped in mourning, even from a distance she stretches out her merciful motherly hands. Weeping bitterly as she walks, she tears at the heavens with her exhortations until even The Holy One, Blessed Be He, cannot restrain himself any longer. He flees, as it were, into the corner, and weeps like a small boy.

Throughout this sermon, biblical texts are quoted verbatim, whereas rabbinic texts are explicitly cited but not quoted. Further along, textual citation of the biblical sources and explicit reference to Talmudic sources cease. By the time we arrive at a lengthy midrash about Jeremiah, the textual quality of the sermon has drifted off, as quotations of biblical texts and citations of rabbinic ones fall away and the orality of the moment triumphs. The sermon takes on a lyrical life of its own, and the voice of the preacher disappears, leaving the omniscient narrator full control over the pastiche of biblical and rabbinic texts.

When we arrive at the parable, identified by the narrator as *ikar ha-davar,* or "the essence of the sermon," however, we are no longer swimming in a sea of disjointed allusions to different well-known biblical figures. Instead, we are presented with a continuous narrative, the narrative of the abandoned queen:

And here we arrive at the essence of the sermon—The explanation and the illustration—The parable. Like the soft and delicate daughter[19] of a queen who married a king—her husband adored her, gave her beautiful tapestries and royal mantles and precious stones and diamonds. He even makes her a golden dress, called by women today a "Rotunda." But after a short time, the king grew angry at her, and took away her tapestries, her crown, and her clothes, left her and fled to far away lands.[20]

And her neighbors gathered together and came to her, shaking their heads and saying: Woe unto this pathetic woman—what her husband has done to her. And she herself sits desolate, wild-haired, lamenting and weeping at night about her destiny, weeping until her eye-lashes fall out. . . . The preacher lowers his voice and leans on the podium. The congregation beneath him crowds together and draws closer to him. All around, there is silence, and arrested breath.[21]

A parable consists of two parts fitting together like the pieces of a puzzle—the abstracted tale (the *mashal*) and its application (the *nimshal*).[22] In "Abandoned Wife," just as we arrive at the application, the narrator introduces an encompassing silence: "All around there is silence and arrested breath." The silence here seems to function as something of a literary "postscript" to the narrative text. The only one not silent—the one who speaks the silence—is the narrator. Out of this reverberating silence, in anticipation of the resolution of the parable, the woman featured in the third and fourth parts of the story emerges: "Up in the women's section, it is nearly dark. Only three or four rays of light make it through the lattice and splash diagonally onto the wall, the stove and the charity box." This shift into the women's section takes us backward in time, backward in the text, into the dim corner of the women's section of the synagogue. It is as if the sermon had not yet begun, though we have already read a transcription of it. A bit further along we are told that the woman cannot understand the sermon preceding the parable: "The scriptural sentences, and the rabbinic phrases are opaque, and do not suit her brain, like the dry pieces of bread in her husband's house that scratch her toothless gums. But that doesn't matter: The stocking and the packet of threads are with her, here in her hands, and she stands in the meantime, knitting." At this point we realize that the only way to understand the sermon is to perceive it from both sides of the synagogue. The expressive rather than grammatical syntax, the staccato interruptions of convoluted speech in the sermon, and the dissolution of the preacher himself into a netherworld of unconnected quotations and atomized fantasies reflect the perception of the men, many of whom are comfortable with the abstract because of their greater familiarity with traditional Jewish hermeneutics and who do not need to be oriented to the sermon through clear citations and syntax. However, the woman, listening from the women's section of the synagogue, cannot understand the logic of the sources that are being articulated in the sermon. She knits during the sermon that we, as readers, have just witnessed. She catches up to us belatedly, at the critical juncture of the parable, after we have already heard it: "Yet behold, the preacher fixed his *talit,* groaned and leaned against the podium. He arrived at the main point, at the parable—and the wool sock slipped out of her hand together with the coiled yarn."[23] "Groaned," "leaned," and "arrived" are in the past tense, reminding us that it has already happened, simultaneously with the telling of the parable in the previous section. By reiterating the phrase "the essence of the sermon," the narrator indicates that the two sides of the partition cannot be represented simultaneously because there is such a radical difference in the way the sermon is perceived by the people on each side. The phrase "the essence of the sermon" leads us back to the same moment prior to the telling of the parable that we saw from the men's perspective, creating a break in the temporal flow of the story.[24]

Finally, the parable is presented from the woman's point of view in an impressionistic synopsis as opposed to the narrative one that we read earlier: "Poor, distraught, woe is her and woe is her life—she shakes her aging head back and forth. A bitter-salty gall rises in her throat, a portion of the tears of the abandoned princess. And from her eyes all the worldly sorrows of the scorned woman shine out. And in the meantime, the preacher continues on."[25] The woman in the synagogue, the woman in the parable, the preacher, and the narrator converge here. When the passage opens with the idiomatic phrase "woe is her and woe is her life," we are pressed to understand who is the subject of the third-person reference and who is speaking. The third-person subject could refer either to the woman in the synagogue or to the abandoned princess of the parable, whereas the speaker could be either the narrator referring to the princess or to the woman, the preacher referring to the princess, the woman referring to the princess or to herself, or the princess referring to herself. The polyphony of voices in the parable, as perceived by the woman, allows for osmosis from the universe of the sermon to the osmosis of the parable and finally to that of the woman in the women's section. The woman becomes the princess as we witness an embodiment of a real woman's experience within the symbolic landscape of rabbinic tropes. The narrator relinquishes her control, taking it out of the preacher's hand as well, giving the woman in the woman's section the authority to animate, through her own identification with the princess, the experience of the princess. The princess consequently comes to life in a way that she does not when she is perceived from the men's section. In a sense, the woman in the women's section authors the parable for us, becoming, if only for a moment, the authoritative voice of the text. Our attention is drawn to the margins of the sermon experience, to the perspective of the listener without any scholarly background.

As the fourth part begins, we return to the women's section, and observe in great detail the woman's departure from the synagogue, her walk home, and her preparations for sleep. In her house, all of our senses are engaged: we smell rotting potatoes, feel the chill, see the darkness, and hear the woman speak in the only speech, aside from the sermon, in the story: " 'Raphael,' she reaches toward him with a thin hand, 'you understood the sermon in the synagogue: What happened to her, to the *agunah* in the end? Did her husband return to her?' No answer came. The old man was not asleep, but he would not answer." The woman, who for a brief moment took control of the story, animating the princess at the heart of the sermon and becoming, in turn, animated by her identification with her, asks her husband about the fate of the princess because she cannot understand the function of the parable. For her, the parable stands on its own and needs no contextualization, no justification.[26] It is important to note, however, that the woman acquires a voice and states her ignorance in one and the same breath. We are left with the woman's articulated confusion as the denouement of the sermon.

There are at least two ways to read the husband's silence. On the one hand, this woman's husband does not answer and never will answer *(aneh lo ya'aneh)* because he is not there. When she turns away, after receiving no response to her question, she does not turn "away" from Raphael. Rather, she turns "toward the wall, the window." Perhaps this woman is an actual agunah, not a symbolic agunah like the Jewish people in exile, or a princess in a midrashic parable. She does not understand the allegory because, for her, abandonment is not a trope; it is her life—her poverty, her loneliness, the smell and the chill of an empty house that she can never really claim as her own as long as she lives in the shadow of her husband's absence. Alternatively, the woman's unresponsive husband could actually be present, but depriving his intellectually curious wife of the answer to her query. He does not want to go to the trouble of helping his wife understand the nature of allegory in general and the particular applicability of this allegory to the situation of the Jewish people in exile.[27]

Baron's narrator straddles the synagogue partition dividing the women's section from the men's, adeptly manipulating the literary and linguistic tools of traditional male scholarship while seeing into the deepest recesses of the women's section. The narrator, entering the male textual world in order to weave a sermon for the itinerant preacher, enters the female world of the body with equal attention. The passage in which the voices of the preacher, the narrator, and the woman merge, when the fate of the queen is lamented, situated as it is before the hermeneutic denouement of the sermon (the presentation of the parable's application), is central to our understanding of the story as a confrontation between the world of speech and the world of silence, between the oral presentation of the textually erudite and the aural reception of the uneducated.

The passage in which the voices of the preacher, the narrator, and the woman merge keeps us from polarizing the men's section and the women's section of the synagogue in the same way that we must be wary of polarizing the oral and the written forces in a linguistic universe.[28] Baron's presentation of a sermon in "Abandoned Wife," perceived from the men's and women's points of view and negotiated by a narrator and a preacher, serves to blur the clear demarcation of oral and written texts. Here we have an oral presentation of literary traditions presented in a literary text and perceived, alternately, from the point of view of a male population familiar with its literary resonances and from the point of view of a woman unfamiliar with it. In experimenting with different strategies for the representation of an oral voice within a literary text, Baron taps into an indigenous Jewish institution, the sermon, that weds the oral voice and the written text. She complicates that marriage, however, by proposing an alternative voice for the preacher. The merging of the narrator in the story with the preacher, alongside the merging of the two with the woman, shifts the hermeneutics of sermon delivery into the domain of the person who did not learn traditional Jewish textual culture from the books out of which it has been traditionally understood to arise. Rather, textual culture seems to grow, in Baron's story, out of a primary oral experience of narrative fabrics, transposed into a modern narrative text and then rethematized as an oral performance.

The parable in the sermon is understood on its most literal level by the woman listening to it, and the narrator, merging with the woman in a moment of narrated monologue, collaborates with her. At the same time, the narrator has become indistinguishable from the preacher, blending her narration with the sermon as it is perceived by the men. By weaving together the voices of the narrator of "Abandoned Wife" with the preacher, the narrator demonstrates an erudite understanding of the nature of parables and of the seminal allegories of Jewish experience. As such, the narrator has the capacity to create real abandoned wives, or *agunot*, in the process of elaborating on allegorical ones.

The parable chosen by the preacher as the "essence of the sermon" is based on a parable in the midrashic commentary on the book of Lamentations, *Lamentations Rabbah*, chapter three. In commenting on the verse in chapter three, verse 21, of the book of Lamentations: "This I recall to my mind, therefore I have hope," the midrash says:

> Rabbi Abba Bar Kahana said: This is like a king who married a woman and wrote her a generous marriage contract, offering her (in writing) many houses, and jewels, and silver, and gold. Then he left her for many years

and went off to distant lands. Her woman neighbors teased her saying "your husband will not return to you. Go find yourself another husband." She wept and sighed and then she would go inside and look at her contract and sigh again, relieved. After a long time the king came back and said "I am shocked that you waited for me all these years." She replied, "If it weren't for the marriage contract you had written me, my neighbors would long ago have led me astray." Thus the nations tease Israel saying, "Your God isn't coming back to you. Come to us and we'll give you bathhouses and mills and officers." The children of Israel went into their synagogues and study houses and read in the Torah, "For I will turn myself to you and make you fruitful and multiply you, and establish my covenant with you. . . . And I will set my temple among you and my soul shall not abhor you." (Leviticus 26: 9–11) And when they read this, they are comforted. In the future, when redemption comes The Holy One Blessed Be He says to the Children of Israel, "Children, I am shocked that you waited for me all these years." And they reply, "If it were not for the Torah which you gave us, and not for the fact that we turned to it when we went into synagogues and study houses, and read 'I shall not abhor you' the nations of the world would have led us astray." As it is written, "If your Torah had not been my delight, I would have perished in my affliction" (Psalms 119: 92).[29]

In her selection of this parable as the basis of the one presented in "Abandoned Wife," Baron taps into several intriguing phenomena in the structure of rabbinic parables in general and this one in particular. As has been pointed out by Alan Mintz, the application of this parable "begins its explanation some point after its beginning."[30] The fact of the children of Israel's abandonment is assumed in the application to be parallel to the wife's abandonment in the parable, but it is not reiterated. Instead of articulating God's abandonment of the children of Israel, the application starts from the point at which the nations try to seduce Israel away from God without delving into the act of abandonment. Mintz further points to the fact that the application is temporally unaligned with the parable itself. The redemption of the wife, or her husband's return, takes place within the present of the parable. But the return of God takes place only in some deferred, imagined future.

Baron constructs her story as something of a modern-day variation on the parable of the abandoned wife. She presents the parable virtually in its traditional form, but she forestalls the presentation of the expected application. Instead, the rest of Baron's narrative serves as the parable's application. There is no resolution in the present, no return of the prodigal husband in the here and now. Baron's application is more desperate than the traditional application, however, because the deferred redemption is not articulated as a possibility in the future. Rather, the ambiguities of the text leave even the assumed future possibility of return open to conjecture.

Baron's reconstruction of the traditional parable draws attention to a fascinating discrepancy between the two major sources upon which she bases the itinerant preacher's parable. I chose to base my translation of the midrash from *Lamentations Rabbah* on the Buber edition as opposed to the Vilna edition because in the Buber edition, the textuality of the king's promise to his wife is overdetermined in a way that it is not in the Vilna edition. The Buber edition reads (as translated above): "This is like a king who married a woman and wrote her a generous marriage contract, offering her, in writing . . ." The Vilna edition is presented with a subtle difference: "This is like a king who married a noblewoman and wrote her a generous marriage contract, saying . . ."

In the Buber edition, the verb "he wrote" is reiterated. In the Vilna edition, the verb "saying" replaces the second "he wrote." The Vilna formulation is quite typical, even in English—"the king wrote his wife a contract saying . . ." The Buber formulation is somewhat more awkward, and thus draws attention to its redundancy—"the king wrote his wife a contract, writing . . ." The Buber edition leaves the reader with a real sense that the king and his bride have had no human contact beyond the contractual. He writes her a contract, then he leaves her. At least in the Vilna edition, the reader gets a sense that the written contract represents a human relationship in which some kind of exchange, no matter how limited, has taken place beyond the text. In both editions, the marital promises may very well not have been fulfilled before the king left his wife for distant lands, but in the Buber edition the confinement of those promises to the textual contract is much more palpably felt.

The parable at the heart of Dvora Baron's fictional sermon does not present this nuanced distinction between speech and text. Rather, the king in Baron's parable is fond of his spouse and gives her many treasures as a sign of his affection before he leaves her. In Baron's sermon, there is no writing of a marriage contract or promise of goods made in text alone yet left unfulfilled. The woman listening to the sermon goes home, demonstrating that she, like the woman in the parable she has just heard, has seen some of the standard terms and conditions of her marriage contract fulfilled—her husband has provided her with a dwelling place. But he will not provide her with an answer to her question about the parable—either through his absence or through his reticence—raising the specter of the text's unfulfilled promises once again. The woman is offered a text, orally, in the guise of a sermon. Ostensibly, she, like the men in the men's section, is granted equal access to the words of the Torah, to the discourse of exile and redemption so widespread within rabbinic literature and the culture of the eastern European community. Yet the textual contract granted the old woman from the pulpit is never fulfilled because she cannot understand the hermeneutic assumptions underlying the text, and no one is willing to teach them to her. The preacher physically abandons the podium before explicating the parable, and her husband abandons her, either physically or intellectually, before he can help her understand it.

In the ambiguity of her resolution, Baron may very well be reproducing the allegorical norm of the parable, allowing us to wonder whether the woman is a real agunah or a figural one. At the same time, Baron's literal fleshing out of the traditional application, her depiction of the physical squalor, hunger, and loneliness that characterize the woman's life, regardless of whether she is an actual agunah, embodies the mythical subject of the traditional parable and makes her seem like a real woman. Baron reconfigures the trope of the abandoned wife, forcing us to recognize the parable's antecedent as a real woman, if not also a real agunah.

Baron's simultaneous adoption and reconfiguration of the trope of the abandoned wife is similar to the multivalent way in which S. Y. Agnon adopts and reconfigures the same trope in his 1908 signature story

"Agunot" (Abandoned Wives). At the end of Agnon's story, the term "agunah" is used to denote a state of existential loneliness caused by inappropriate and ineffective love matches. The rabbi who takes responsibility for the unhappy fate of the couple in the story leaves Israel to "repair *agunot*": "The Rabbi stopped crying and understood the plain meaning of the events. He took himself in hand, got dressed, took his walking stick and his rucksack and called to his wife saying, 'my daughter, don't seek me out. I must go into exile in order to repair *agunot*.' He kissed the mezuzah and left. They sought him out but did not find him."[31]

There is only one real agunah in Agnon's story—the rabbi's wife. But by calling the story "Agunot" in the plural, Agnon draws attention away from the single "actual" agunah buried in the next-to-last paragraph. Like Baron, Agnon here taps into a conceptual discrepancy that is inherent in the traditional trope of the abandoned wife as an allegory of the Jewish people in exile. In the parable from *Lamentations Rabbah*, the king is the one who goes off to distant lands and the queen is the one who stays put, "at home" or in the homeland, as the case may be. The Jewish people in exile are traditionally likened to the abandoned wife, however, and not to the abandoning husband. Agnon plays with this discrepancy, leaving the actual agunah in the homeland and taking the seeker of metaphysical agunot away into exile.

In the continuation of the story, the rabbi is described as wandering around Europe in search of Ben-Uri, the artist in exile. He visits synagogues, trying to lure young artisans back to Palestine with him. Like the itinerant preacher in Baron's story, Agnon's rabbi in exile wears a rucksack and carries a stick. The stick and the rucksack signal the fact that the rabbi in Agnon's story, the creator of a true abandoned wife in his quest to rectify allegorical abandoned wives, may be the very same figure who goes from shtetl to shtetl in Baron's fictional universe, telling the parable of the agunah as a description of the Jewish people in exile.

At the end of Agnon's story, various conjectures are made as to the location of the rabbi at the time of the story's telling. The narrator concludes, "Only God has all the solutions," echoing the indeterminacy at the end of Baron's story. Both Baron and Agnon challenge the allegorical norm of the parable of the abandoned wife. But Agnon, essentially, continues to propagate the abstraction of the agunah, having the rabbi abandon his wife as he seeks out metaphysical agunot. Baron challenges that disjuncture, insisting on the ultimate embodiment of the agunah as a real woman.

In "Abandoned Wife" the two sides of the partition distinguish textual access on the basis of gender, whereas in Baron's "Family" a synagogue scene pits two women on one side of a partition against one another with a parable. The female protagonist of "Family," named Dina like the female protagonist of Agnon's "Agunot," has not borne her husband, Barukh, any children after ten years of marriage. Barukh's aunt Batyah is described as "the daughter of an itinerant preacher, one of those they called a 'foot soldier of the Torah'—a poor man who had no money for a dowry, but he did come from a learned lineage, and he had a powerful gift for midrashic interpretation, and his daughter had learned from him to speak with rhetorical flourishes."[32] Although the entire community is cognizant of the fact that Dina and Barukh have been childless for the number of years necessary to warrant a divorce by Jewish law, no one has acted on this information, most notably not the rabbi. Batyah, feeling particularly authoritative because of her textual heritage, decides to take matters into her own hands. She approaches the rabbi and, in conversations that are undisclosed in the story itself, convinces him of the necessity for Dina and Barukh to be divorced. In synagogue one day, she tells a parable about a fruitless tree standing among fruit trees that is chopped down for its nonproductivity. Dina, unlike the woman in "Abandoned Wife" who does not understand the structure of parables, realizes that she is the application of this parable; she is the tree that is meant to be cut down, ousted from the community of productive women. Like the woman in "Abandoned Wife," however, Dina is helpless to extricate herself from her own allegorization. Ultimately, Dina and Barukh are forced to divorce, but by a twist of luck, or law, their certificate of divorce is declared invalid, and they remain married, conceiving a son soon thereafter. In this scenario, rabbinic authority is the saving grace, and a textually adept woman is the threat to family happiness.

In both "Family" and "Abandoned Wife," parables are articulated at the expense of "real" women with real dilemmas. In both cases, the educated woman, presumably the narrator of "Abandoned Wife" and the itinerant preacher's daughter in "Family," seems to betray the women trapped on their side of the synagogue partition. Baron's biblical and rabbinic erudition, particularly in the context of the dramatic representation of sermons, sheds light on her own ambivalent stance vis-à-vis the perception that men's and women's systems of understanding and bodies of knowledge are diametrically opposed. In claiming those very texts she is supposed not to have had access to, Baron seems, in some cases, to be reifying the binary opposition between male and female intellectual worlds. She is, as it were, "adopting" the language of men by traversing the partition between the men's and women's sections of the synagogue, taking control of the texts that are confined to the male side and displaying her ability to inhabit that side, as her voice merges with the voice of the preacher. However, under closer scrutiny, Baron's simultaneous adoption and rejection of certain tropes—such as the agunah—subverts the polarization of male and female knowledge. She "steals the language" and takes it back to the other side of the synagogue, forcing it to confront its own allegorical subject, and making it, to some degree, women's own.[33] In so doing, Baron creates a successful vernacular literary texture—weaving a woman's unique auditory experience of Torah text study into an oral literary voice.

5

❦

Burying the Books

The Intertextual Imperative

Can a nation deny its language?—Jacob Zerubavel, "Issues of the Day" (1914)

We had to betray Yiddish even though we paid for this as for any betrayal. —Rachel Katznelson-Shazar, "Language Insomnia" (1918)

He spoke of the time of the redemption when all the dead would rise to life; at that time, he recalled, the sacred fragments that they were burying now would also rise. "And I will open your graves and I will lift you up and I will bring you unto the Land of Israel."—Dvora Baron, "Burying the Books" (1922)

INTERTEXTUALITY—allusions within a literary text to other texts— was the basis, as we have explored, of the construction of a secular Hebrew literature during the period of the modern Hebrew renaissance. In most cases, intertextuality was not a stylistic choice, but a stylistic imperative. Without a cultural context for spoken Hebrew, without a wealth of secular models or precedents, Hebrew authors had no recourse but to utilize the Jewish textual tradition—from the Bible, the midrash, the Talmud—to forge a modern literary corpus. Intertextuality in this vein was a double-edged sword. On the one hand, the Hebrew textual tradition is rich and ramified, so writers groping for linguistic and stylistic models did not have far to go. On the other hand, the intertextual styles that developed throughout the period of the Haskalah and the renaissance were, in and of themselves, the ground for generations of reactionary approaches to modern Hebrew literary production.

99

Abramowitz, as we know, developed the nusah in response to the earlier Haskalah biblical pastiche, or melitsah style, in which undifferentiated chunks of the Bible were strung together to express radically unbiblical themes such as epic romance or modern nationalistic sentiments. The anti-nusah writers, in their turn, such as Berdischevsky and Brenner, struggled to break out of what they considered the rather cumbersome display of transhistorical Hebrew stylistic virtuosity of the nusah—the melding together of all different historical types of Hebrew for vernacular effect. The types of intertexts and intertextual styles an author chose to use affiliated that author with a Hebrew stylistic "school" and became the grounds for canonic evaluations and judgments. If an author were to paraphrase the Bible throughout one's literary corpus and steer clear of rabbinic literature, for instance, he or she ran the risk of being considered a throwback to the Haskalah patterns of melitsah pastiche. If an author were to heavily utilize rabbinic language replete with Aramaic legalisms, then he or she may have been automatically affiliated with the nusah writings of Abramowitz and his cohort. Intertextual choices were, in other words, markers of generational affiliation as well as educational background. Baron's intertextual choices become an important means of assessing her "intimations of difference"—her attempts to affiliate herself with her peers even while marking the differences that set her apart and freed her, in many ways, from the tyranny of canon formation.

Through her choice of primarily rabbinic and biblical allusions, Baron demonstrates the ways in which she constructs Hebrew texts out of the same intertextual materials as her male colleagues; Baron uses erudite narrators like the one in "Abandoned Wife" to articulate her "similarity" to her writing peers. But in several of her stories, Baron gives us intimations of intertextual "difference" as well. Moving beyond Baron's insistence that she uses the *same* texts in the *same* ways as do her peers writing during the modern Hebrew renaissance, here I investigate Baron's use of *different* texts. The intertextual imperatives of the modern Hebrew renaissance are implicitly challenged by Baron's presentation, in two stories titled "Genizah" (Burying the Books) (1909, 1922), of *tkhines* and the *Tzenerene*, traditional Yiddish religious texts generally associated with eastern European Jewish women.[1] At the same time, those imperatives are explicitly supported in the first story published by Baron after her arrival in Palestine, "be-Eizeh Olam?" (In What World?) (1911). The relationship between the purported language of Zionist homecoming (Hebrew) and the purported language of the eastern European diaspora (Yiddish) underpins this discussion of conflicting intertextual (and interlinguistic) impulses in Baron's work.

Tkhines, devotional prayers in Yiddish, were first published in the seventeenth century in both eastern and western Europe. They were written by men as well as women and were formulated piecemeal over many centuries to commemorate and meditate upon the experiences, generally women's, not usually mentioned in the traditional Hebrew liturgy. Tkhines were recited as women walked their sons to school for the first time, when they made candles for sacramental purposes on the eve of Yom Kippur, when they baked challah for the Sabbath, when they collected charity for the poor, when Shabbat candles were lit, when they were about to stand under the marriage canopy or to immerse themselves in the mikvah, among countless other personal or communal acts performed by women during their lifetimes. Different collections of tkhines include different prayers and are written in very different styles. Many are written simply and are devoid of complex biblical or mystical references. Others are far more complex and allusive and reflect a substantial amount of scholarship in their composition.[2]

To illustrate the structure and function of different varieties of tkhines, I will briefly invoke two. The first is the introductory segment of a lengthy, erudite tkhine said to have been authored by "the *Rebbetzin* Seril, daughter of the well-known Rabbi Yankev Segal of Dubno, wife of the great and learned and profoundly wise Rabbi Mordkhe Katz Rappaport." This tkhine is recited during the penitentiary month of Elul preceding the Jewish New Year: " 'Please God. I have trusted in your great mercy and I entreat you.' I beseech you. God, I trust in Your compassion and I ask that You hear the bitter prayer of my broken heart and answer my plea. As it is written in Your holy *Toyre* [Torah]: 'Before they will call, I shall reply.' "[3] In contrast to this tkhine, modeled upon and incorporating the traditional Hebrew penitentiary prayers, we find in many collections of tkhines meditations such as the following, which is titled "Women Who Have Bad Luck with Children Should Recite This *Tkhine*": "I come to You and beg You, dear God, quickly remove from me the pain that I carry in my heart because of the bad luck I have had with my children. I beg you, dear God, act towards me as a father to a child, and keep your anger far from me. Let all my children live and may no child die, that we may live to raise them to Torah, to the Marriage Canopy [*Huppah*], and to Good Deeds [*Ma'asim Tovim*] with Fear of God [*Yiras Shomayim*]. Amen."[4] This tkhine has no pretense of erudition.

Unlike tkhines, written by a wide variety of people (male and female, known and anonymous) in a wide range of registers, the *Tzenerene* is a homiletic work written by a known author (Rabbi Yaakov ben Yitzhak Ashkenazi of Yanov) and divided according to the weekly synagogue readings of the Bible.[5] Its title is derived from Song of Songs 3:11 in which the young girls of Zion are told to "go out [*tzena*] and see [*urena*]." First published in Lublin in 1622, the *Tzenerene* has been called, by Chone Shmeruk, "the most popular book of Yiddish literature."[6] It was reissued in updated Yiddish at least 128 times before 1928 and was thus linguistically and contextually adaptive.[7] Haym Soloveitchik has described the *Tzenerene* as "far more than simply an amplified translation of the Torah." According to him, "Its cumulative impact on the religious outlook and spirituality of East European Jewry was incalculable." Yosef Svirski, in an autobiographical essay on Jewish life in Vilna, has described the *Tzenerene*'s role in his childhood home in the following way: "Our mothers used to sit on every Sabbath after their afternoon nap and read it aloud, chanting with emphasis. And we children would listen sometimes to hear the beautiful parables and the words of explanation, which the author would quote in the names of the commentators on the Torah." The *Tzenerene,* we thus see, served as the textual blueprint for a weekly household drama of Torah discourse. Women read it aloud, becoming introduced to traditional commentators and exegetical techniques and, indirectly, introducing their children—boys and girls—to them as well. Cynthia Ozick goes so far as to designate the *Tzenerene* the first and most uninhibited work of "art" in the Yiddish literary canon. She calls the *Tzenerene* "the work of a single teeming, twinkling, original, joyfully pious mind. . . . [I]t is an amalgam of enormous erudition and an energetic poetic imagination." Why then, she asks, did Rabbi Yaakov ben Yitzhak Ashkenazi of Yanov write this work "for women"? She proposes an answer that she calls, "deliciously intoxicating." "Where else," she speculates, "should he, could he, turn for the expression of the mandate of the storyteller's imagination?" [8]

Women's proficiencies and their advantages over men in traditional Jewish scholarly society are rarely discussed. Iris Parush has pointed out, however, that boys were taught the five books of Moses from an antiquated, interlinear Hebrew and Yiddish primer; they were, essentially, taught a language they did not know (Hebrew) in a language they did not know (Old Yiddish). Also, boys were taught the text of the Bible in a formalist, Socratic (or, in Jewish terminology, *pilpulistic*) fashion from a very young age. Although they became able to parrot and recite the words of the biblical text in a performative manner, their comprehension was limited at best. Girls, on the other hand, learned the five books of Moses informally via the Yiddish *Tzenerene* written in a constantly adaptive dialect. Thus, comprehension, and not inculcation or rote instruction, was the goal of an encounter with the *Tzenerene*. Furthermore, whereas those individuals who studied the Torah via the *Tzenerene* studied it in accordance with the weekly synagogue cycle of Torah readings, the ones who learned it out of order, beginning with the book of Leviticus (as was the custom in boys' heders), rarely, if ever, made it through the entire Torah text before graduating to the next stage of their schooling. [9] Those individuals who read the *Tzenerene*, even if they did not complete each week's entry, got a good sense of the narrative and thematic totality of the five books of Moses simply by virtue of reading it in order week after week. In contrast, after boys moved beyond the *humish heder*, the class where they studied the five books and the basic liturgy, their only exposure to the Bible was on the basis of the Talmud's system of internal citation. [10] Although according to Jewish law one is required to review the Torah portion three times each week, *shnayim mikra, ehad targum* (twice in Hebrew and once in Aramaic), it was not the same as doing it in Yiddish, the daily language of its students.

Jeremy Dauber argues that it is important not to regard the *Tzenerene* as the European Jewish "Bible for Dummies" during the seventeenth through the twentieth centuries because it takes at least a superficial acquaintance with rabbinic logic and with midrashic hermeneutics to be able to follow the *Tzenerene*'s line of reasoning. To illustrate this point, let us consider the opening passage of the *Tzenerene*:

> *In the Beginning God Created the Heaven and the Earth:* At the original creation of heaven and earth, the land was desolate and empty, and God's holy throne was suspended over the water (1:1). Why did the Torah commence with the letter *beis*? To show us that just as the letter *beis* is closed on three sides and open on the fourth, so God enclosed the world on three sides, while the northern side remained open. Another reason is that the letter *beis* stands for the word *berakhah* ("blessing," beginning with the letter *beis*), while the aleph (the first letter of the alphabet) represents *arur* ("cursed," beginning with an aleph). Not wishing to begin His Torah with the letter of a curse, the Almighty started with the *beis*. Upset, the aleph flew before God and complained that the Torah ought to begin with the first letter of the aleph-*beis* [alphabet]. God appeased the offended letter, assuring it that the Ten Commandments given on Mt. Sinai would begin with the word *anokhi* ("I"), which begins with an aleph.[11]

The *Tzenerene*, as we see here, opens with a meditation on the Hebrew letter *beth (beis* in its Yiddish pronunciation) and runs through a variety of explanations for why the Torah may have begun (in the word *Breshit* [In the Beginning]) with the second letter of the Hebrew alphabet as opposed to the first—an *aleph*. This argument presupposes knowledge of the Hebrew alphabet and of key words in Hebrew beginning with both an aleph and a beth *(arur, anokhi, berakhah)*. Furthermore, the exegetical technique employed here is philological—focused on the construction of the Torah's first word. Though one would expect the first discourse in the *Tzenerene* to be of a more thematic or even didactic turn, here we see an interpretation focused interestingly on the textual, and by extension literary, identity of the Torah. The notion that the world was created by God, as described in the first verse of the Torah, is deemed secondary to the fact that the account of God's creation of the world was written in the Hebrew language. Therefore, the first commentary presented in the *Tzenerene* is a kind of literary "metacommentary" on decisions pertaining to authorship, word choice, and letter choice.[12] Given these observations, I would argue in support of Dauber's claim, that, indeed, familiarity with the standard commentaries and hermeneutic practices is presumed in the *Tzenerene*. What Rabbi Yaakov ben Yitzhak Ashkenazi of Yanov chooses to focus upon reflects the expectation that his readership is not encountering the text of the Torah for the first and only time via the *Tzenerene*. Exposure to a discourse of Torah study—perhaps orally inflected—is understood beneath the surface of the text.

In reading Baron's work, therefore, it is necessary to consider not just what she did not learn as a matter of course because of her gender (or what she had to learn "through the back door," as it were) but also what she did learn. Although it would be impossible to argue that women were granted equal access to traditional texts, it is important to consider the texts and languages within traditional Jewish society to which women were granted access. Women's heightened sensitivity to the biblical narrative and to ethical literature, because both were widely available in Yiddish and were often read at home on the Sabbath, may be an important intertextual consideration when analyzing Baron's work. Whereas Baron's works have been considered, in our time as well as in her own time, anomalous by virtue of their scholarly erudition and the Hebrew in which they are written (given the gender of their author), how can we nuance this consideration? How can we read her work as a fascinating cross-linguistic testament not only to what women were not allowed to learn but also to what women were allowed to learn? Baron owes her greatest literary debt to rabbinic commentaries on the Hebrew Bible, texts normally associated with male literacy. But she also draws into her work strands from texts associated primarily with Jewish women.

"Burying the Books" was written in 1909 and substantially rewritten in 1922. Because it is among the only examples in Baron's work that refer to the Yiddish religious texts most widely read by European Jewish women, each of the two stories serves as a counterpoint to the displays of biblical and rabbinic erudition employed throughout the rest of her work. Both versions of Baron's "Burying the Books" deal with the burial of *shemot,* unusable holy texts. In the 1909 story, the female protagonist, rendered in a first-person voice, joins her brother in collecting for burial worn-out books from the family library. The brother of the protagonist rejects the mother's tear-stained, torn collection of tkhines as inappropriate for burial. He throws it aside, calling it a *smartut* (rag). The 1922 version of "Burying the Books" features an elderly woman, Mina, who attempts to bury her *Tzenerene* in the community *genizah,* or textual burial ground. Though the community children ridicule her and try to block her way to the grave, the community rabbi (the father of the female child protagonist) graciously accepts her offering.

Taken together, the two stories expose their readership to a range of Yiddish texts and attitudes toward them. In the earlier story, the tkhines are presented as the corpus that is dearest to the heart of the girl protagonist's mother, even as they are summarily rejected for burial in the holy textual burial ground by the protagonist's older brother. In the later story, we are introduced to the *Tzenerene* in the context of its acceptance for burial by the rabbinic figure overseeing the ritual of burying unusable holy books. Our first encounter with Yiddish religious texts—tkhines—in Baron's work, therefore, presents them to us as cultural, intellectual, and spiritual pariahs. Our second encounter—with the *Tzenerene*—is a bit more confused, as the children of the town implicitly reject the *Tzenerene,* calling it, as we will see, tkhines at first. When the *Tzenerene* is buried in this story, it joins the ranks of the more canonical Hebrew texts for which the grave was originally intended. But to what end? Let's take a look at excerpts from each story in order to understand the stakes of acceptance for or rejection from textual burial in Baron's literary world.

In the 1922 version of Baron's "Burying the Books," the owner of the *Tzenerene,* Mina, is introduced in the following scene:

> When she had finished putting on her satin dress which rustled with the sound of many distinguished generations of forebears, and when she had

finished putting on her tasseled headdress (without looking in the mirror because she had no mirror) she took out from under her floorboards—what a miserable life, the life of a woman on this earth—the packet of loose pages of the *Tzenerene*, the legacy of the mothers, and went out shutting the door behind her.

But her timing was without a doubt not very good. The synagogue *gabbai*, gussied up in his wool *kapota*, came out of the facing house—she could see him very clearly.[13] His sons carried a basket of *"shemot"* (whole folios of books) worn out by time.

She anxiously held onto the rope wrapped around the goat's horns and pulled him haltingly down the street with the package of *"shemot"* tucked under her arm, until she came to a well where she tied the end of the rope. Boys were crowding around her from all sides, so she recoiled, turning her face in the direction of the women's section.

But the children blocked her way in their eagerness to climb onto the goat. "Here's Mina with her *tkhine*," they said.[14]

The Yiddish text at the heart of this story seems to be somewhat indeterminate. Whereas Mina calls it, in her own idiom, the *Tzenerene yerushat imahot*, (the *Tzenerene*, legacy of the mothers), the omniscient narrator calls it *Shemot* (unusable holy texts), and the children, in ridiculing Mina, assume that it is a collection of tkhines. This last error reflects a hierarchical ranking of women's Yiddish liturgical texts in which tkhines are totally trivialized.[15]

Interestingly, in the later story, in contrast to the children who disparage the *Tzenerene* by calling it tkhines, the omniscient narrator of the story generalizes the *Tzenerene* to just *shemot*, not distinguishing it from the canonical Hebrew texts to be buried. As such, the *Tzenerene*, situated between tkhines and the generic shemot, seems to play the role of a changeling when considered along an undifferentiated continuum of "lowly" women's tkhines and generic men's shemot. Baron's ambivalent relationship with the *Tzenerene* as a middle ground between male and female textual worlds is akin to the narrator ambivalently located on both sides of the synagogue partition in "Abandoned Wife."

The conflicted presentation of the *Tzenerene* in the later text can be contrasted to a devastating depiction of the tkhines' rejection in the ear-

lier text. In the next-to-last scene the girl runs home to get the tkhines
that her brother, earlier, rejected for burial:

> My heart quakes, my brain reels in confusion. I force my way through the
> crowd and run home. I feel a stitch in my left side, I'm panting, dripping
> sweat, my curls blowing wildly in the wind—but I keep running. Here's
> her *tkhine* lying in the corner, its pages loose, covered with yellowish
> stains. . . . I grab it and race back to the graveyard. My father is still stand-
> ing there, face pale, eyes teary and lips moving. And now I'm the one who's
> right by the open grave.
> "Tzzzz!!!"
> The pages of the *tkhine* rustle as they touch the other worn books in
> the grave. And it seems to me that those torn holy books reproach the
> poor wretched *tkhine.*
> "Filthy r-r-r-rag! Get out of here! . . ."
> In another moment my brother has approached; peering into the
> grave, he glares at me, pulls the *tkhine* out, and tosses it aside—far, far
> away.[16]

Does the tkhine text itself, in the literary economy of the modern
Hebrew renaissance, cry out at the ostensible moment of burial, against
its identification as a "dead" text? Alternatively, is Baron, in her refusal to
bury the tkhines in this story, implying that the tkhines can never function as one of the texts that will facilitate the modern Hebrew renaissance through their utilization as the building blocks of vernacular
literature? Does she lament the impossibility of their burial (and their
subsequent "revival" in the culture of the modern Hebrew renaissance)
or celebrate it?

Critics have long argued over the terminology employed to characterize
the movement to transform Hebrew religious textual culture into a secular literary and speaking culture.[17] "Revival" implies life, death, and a return to life. But, as discussed in the Introduction, during the period of
the modern Hebrew renaissance, what was being revived? Hebrew,
within its eastern European internally bilingual milieu, was alive and

well.[18] It served as the language of books and correspondence within a culture where status and authority were granted, at least in theory, to the scholarly elite.[19] Hebrew was, indeed, not the language of speech, the language of play, the language of daily domestic or market affairs. But it was nevertheless present in the daily lives of the Jews, serving as the cornerstone of religious authority. It was only to those persons who considered texts dead that Hebrew was dead. Ironically, the rhetoric of textual death was most commonly found among those individuals who, themselves, were creators of texts—writers and ideologues of Jewish modernization. Throughout Chaim Nachman Bialik's essays on the revival of the Hebrew language, he employs a rhetoric of "life" for languages that exist in speech and "death" for languages confined to texts.[20]

Why are tattered, unusable editions of women's Yiddish religious texts not considered truly dead within the culture represented in Baron's "Genizah" stories? Is it because they were never truly alive and thus were ineligible for revival? Or is it because they never truly died? In the linguistic economy of the revival, if speech is living and text is dead, then Yiddish, which was considered the vernacular language of daily life, was never dead enough for burial, and in no need of revival.[21] Alternatively, perhaps life and death in the context of traditional *genizah* burial were measured wholly according to textual status. In the nineteenth century Yiddish was not considered by many, particularly within a religious milieu, to be a legitimate literary language. Thus, its texts were never quite "alive" and were not deemed worthy of burial. Even within a secular milieu, if one accepts Dan Miron's theory of "language as Caliban," Yiddish texts were considered by many to be strictly functional, used by Haskalah activists in order to reach and reform the Jewish masses.[22] Thus, as a vernacular language, Yiddish was still alive and could not be buried. As a literature, on the other hand, it had never, according to the later schema, been alive, and could not be revived.[23]

To push the conceit of textual life and death a step further, those persons who are functionally excommunicated from the society of living Jews are not allowed to be buried in the society of dead Jews, according to Jewish law; one who dies by one's own hand or chooses to disassociate oneself from the community through intermarriage or conversion cannot be buried among Jews.[24] The exclusion from burial of religious texts said to be used by at least half of the Jewish population implies a harsh value judgment. Those texts are in violation, it seems, of some basic tenet of Jewish community. Is the crime, within a gendered educational economy where women were not taught Hebrew, these texts' enabling women ("and men who are like women") to access the texts and traditions of the Jews? Was some fundamental understanding of educational exclusion and scholarly elitism violated in the creation of a Yiddish religious literature?[25]

A complicated network of the dead and the living begins to emerge in the period of the modern Hebrew renaissance. Hebrew religious texts were considered "dead" in the sense expressed in "Burying the Books" only until their next incarnation, as the building blocks for a secular literature and a speaking culture. The activists of the Hebrew revival were thus cast, in some sense, as the Messiah, actively rescuing the dead from their graves, bringing them back to their former state. How that redemption was to take place, what new form the old texts would take in a modern literature, how that modern literature would evolve into a speaking culture, remained to be seen.

Writers of the renaissance were quite conscious of the paradoxes inherent in trying to bring a literary language to vernacular life, both in text and in speech, when a vernacular language that was already becoming a literary language for all intents and purposes existed. In other words, Yiddish was becoming far more accepted as a literary language even as Hebrew renaissance activists were arguing for the political and cultural necessity of bringing Hebrew literary language into the vernacular realm.[26] Hebrew writers had, time and again, to confront the irony of their wanting to empower the Jewish masses by reinventing the Hebrew language while only the intellectual elite could really comprehend Hebrew beyond the prayer-book or cursory readings of the weekly Torah portion.

S. J. Abramowitz's Hebrew work serves as an excellent case in point. One of the unique and revolutionary aspects of his writings was his ironic treatment of his Hebrew endeavor within his own texts. Abramowitz challenges his own intertextual components by setting them into a rhetorical framework that declares itself "oral" even while drawing attention to its necessarily literary components.[27] Although the rhetorical strategies implemented by Abramowitz in order to render his texts "oral" seem to motivate the text, the text's orality is quite obviously produced by textual features. The linguistic levels of rabbinic and biblical literature merge in his texts in a way that reflects the fundamental tension beginning to be felt and expressed during the Haskalah between the scholarly language of the elite (Hebrew) and the oral language of the folk (Yiddish). Abramowitz makes his Hebrew texts "speak," acknowledging the distance between their scholarly textuality and the vernacular fiction that they are put to the task of creating.

In Abramowitz's time, at the end of the Haskalah and at the beginning of the Hebrew renaissance, Yiddish was considered the appropriate literary language for mass consumption, whereas modern Hebrew literature was understood to be the literary language for the very same elite male minority who could read traditional Hebrew scholarly texts. How was someone uneducated in the Bible and the Talmud supposed to understand a modern literature rendered in the language of the Bible and the Talmud? As a Haskalah ideologue (at least in the first part of his writing life), Abramowitz's own literary career expresses the struggle between the forces of Hebrew elitism and Yiddish folkism. Abramowitz wrote first in Hebrew, switched over to Yiddish for twenty-four years, and then went back to Hebrew with a series of short stories. Whereas Abramowitz's initial Hebrew publications, an essay and a novel, were rendered in classic Haskalah style (constituted by pastiches of biblical texts), with his return to Hebrew later in his career, the Hebrew nusah style (a fluid invocation of many different types of classical Hebrew texts) was born. Through the nusah, Abramowitz attempted to point to the dilemma he faced as a Hebrew writer during a populist moment in Jewish European history. He wanted to create a democratic literature, but in Hebrew he could do so only in the language of the elite. By placing the necessary textual tools in the mouth of a bathetic narrator named Mendele Mokher Sforim (from whence S. J. Abramowitz derived his pen name), he gave those texts a chance to reinvent themselves as populist. Of course, framing elitist texts as oral does not really render them accessible.

It simply creates a fiction of accessibility predicated on the assumption that the oral is popular.[28]

Dvora Baron, for her part, in alluding to Yiddish religious texts such as tkhines and the *Tzenerene* in "Burying the Books," may be undermining the assumption that one must necessarily utilize elitist Hebrew texts in order to approximate a vernacular language. To what extent, then, is Baron's thematization of the tkhines and the *Tzenerene* indicative of an allegiance to these texts as intertextual sources? She may thematize them, but she goes, it would seem, no further. Baron never depicts the contents of a woman's prayers. Neither does she explicitly employ the rhythms or the didacticism of the *Tzenerene*. So what does Baron accomplish in alluding categorically to these texts in her "Burying the Books" stories? Baron, I would argue, was attempting to circulate these texts, to name these texts for her generation in a cultural climate that had not only obliterated their validity but obliterated their memory as well.

The dramatic rejection in the earlier story of the tkhines for burial and the acceptance of the *Tzenerene* for burial in the later story force us to confront the possible valence of each outcome within Baron's literary universe. Does the tkhines' rejection from burial mark them as irreconcilably different from the other, male, texts in the grave? Or does the *Tzenerene*'s burial mark it as irreconcilably the same? Is burial, for that matter, desired or not desired in the literary economy of the modern Hebrew renaissance? In her later version of the story, the *Tzenerene*'s burial seems to signal the total end of an intertextual possibility in her work. It may be safe to say that Baron's elision of the different Yiddish women's texts in the later version of "Burying the Books" and her subsuming them both under the rubric of shemot are not simply a way of her leveling the playing field of Yiddish women's texts, and ultimately men's and women's religious texts. Rather, Baron may be gesturing toward her own silencing of those texts within her intertextual universe.

Baron's presentation of the tkhines and the *Tzenerene,* particularly in relation to the dead and dying Hebrew and Aramaic library awaiting burial in a traditional Jewish eastern European community, forces us to reassess the assumption of "revival" and "death" in the rhetoric of the modern Hebrew renaissance. She complicates the idealization implicit in the acceptance for burial of texts written in Hebrew and Aramaic, and the degradation implicit in the rejection from burial of texts written in Yiddish. The girl's insistence, in the first story, that her mother's tkhines be buried along with the more conventional shemot and the old woman's insistence, in the second story, that her *Tzenerene* be buried may, in fact, be Baron's way of gesturing to the death of Yiddish culture and the loss of women's voices with the birth of a modern Hebrew literary idiom. The "revival" of modern Hebrew is predicated, she indicates, on the death of a culture and tradition of Yiddish that is not simply the language of the masses, or the proletariat, but also the natural—literary as well as religious—language of Jewish women. As a Jewish woman writer, writing primarily in Hebrew, she plays with the complexities of her own involvement in insisting that Yiddish be buried alongside the traditional Hebrew canon in order to make way for a modern Hebrew literary idiom and culture. These stories are, in a sense, Baron's eulogy to a lost Yiddish culture.

Writing the two versions of "Burying the Books," as Baron was, across not only a thirteen-year period but also a great geographic divide—the 1909 story was written in eastern Europe and the 1922 version was written in Palestine—we are forced to consider the role of this geographic divide in her sense of Yiddish as a "lost" culture. The conflation of specific languages with regional thematics—of Hebrew with stories about life in Palestine and of Yiddish with stories about life in the diaspora—was a common, if not explicitly articulated, derivative of the Zionist nationalist ethos that dominated literary production on the new Yishuv. Yiddish was perceived by many ideologues of the second and third waves of immigrants to Palestine between 1904 and 1923 as a metonymy for eastern Europe and the old Yishuv (the Eastern European enclaves in Palestine composed of those individuals who had arrived with the first wave of immigrants from 1881 to 1903). However, the real Yiddish presence on the new Yishuv, as demonstrated by the number of Yiddish periodicals and newspapers still in circulation and the amount of Yiddish spoken on the streets and in homes, was substantial. Yael Chaver has argued that "the vehemence with which Yiddish was ostracized in the Yishuv seems to indicate the extent of the internal struggle, a situation whose implications and ramifications have still not been fully acknowledged or examined. The ambivalent position of *mame loshn,* the mother tongue, both beloved and rejected, may be said to have haunted the pre-statehood culture of Israel despite this culture's conscious allegiance to Hebrew and the eventual predominance of that language."[29]

As Chaver documents, even though by 1914 Hebrew was declared the language of instruction on the new Yishuv and by 1923 the British mandate authorities named Hebrew one of three "official" languages spoken in Palestine (alongside English and Arabic), Hebrew's adoption as the national Zionist language was still in question. Indeed, the "process of marginalizing Yiddish was part of the process of the hyper-masculinization of Hebrew," as demonstrated by the intense anxiety with which Yiddish was regarded as the "negation" of Hebrew and Zionism on the new Yishuv. In becoming a modern nation, the Jews of Palestine who had originated in eastern Europe were, according to the party line, obliged to "forget" their mother tongue. This forgetting was reinforced, in certain circles, as a form of coercion or terrorism. The Brigade of the Defenders of the Hebrew Language (Gedud Megine ha-Safah ha-Ivrit), for example—teenagers who used military tactics to "defend" Hebrew—carried out terrorist attacks against individuals and organizations that openly advocated for, or supported, Yiddish literature or speech on the new Yishuv and was known to have attacked Chaim Zhitolowsky, an outspoken Yiddishist, at a Tel Aviv speaking engagement in 1914.[30]

Baron's "In What World" (1911), her first story to be published after her arrival in Palestine, was one of two stories to be featured in the pilot issue of a short-lived Palestinian-based Zionist literary youth journal, *Moledet* (Motherland). Baron's story, along with one authored by the journal's editor, S. Ben Zion, was unequivocally rejected as "diasporic" by an anonymous reader: "[This story is] from the life of the diaspora, from the gloomy, painful life of the diaspora! For God's sake, when will this literature come to an end? We are sick of it! And why should [these stories] be directed toward our youth, in this new, vital country of ours?"[31]

"In What World?" is the story of a young Jewish girl, Rachel, from a midsize town in eastern Europe. After the death of her beloved rabbinic father, Rachel (an only child) and her mother become servants in the house of a wealthy local Jewish family. A neighbor, David, who is about her age and is also impoverished, befriends her, and together they build a fantasy world around David's imminent migration to Palestine where an uncle awaits him. Although fully expecting to emigrate with David, Rachel is, in fact, left behind when he finally does go. Rachel's mother subsequently dies, and Rachel focuses all her energy on waiting, alongside David's mother, for letters with a Palestinian postmark to arrive. "In What World?" posits multiple opposing worlds—Palestine and eastern Europe, fantasy and reality, the world of the young man who is able, independently, to emigrate to his fantasyland and the world of the young woman who is bound to eastern Europe by financial and familial constraints.

Apparently, Baron (according to her anonymous critic) refused to "relinquish" the shtetl, and in so doing, she refused to relinquish the diaspora even when she was writing on newly claimed native ground. She insisted on writing, even when she had resettled in Palestine, stories about young men and women in the diaspora—suffering from poverty, from intellectual and sexual frustration, and from spiritual malaise. These stories, although written in Hebrew and infused with Zionist longings, could (according to Baron's anonymous critic) have been written in Yiddish. They depict Yiddish-speaking worlds and the constellation of character traits and cultural values generally associated with Yiddish within the ideological landscape of the new Yishuv.

The erotic subtext of "In What World?" grants us a glimpse of the heterosexual ethos governing the relationship between Hebrew and Yiddish on the new Yishuv.[32] Descriptions of Baron's Zionist youth hold some fascinating clues for us as we try to decipher Baron's relationship to the Hebrew language as a woman and her relationship to Zionism as the "negation of the diaspora" and its attendant language, Yiddish. According to one acquaintance, during her sojourn in Mariampol (1906–1907) Baron would hold court on Friday nights in her rented room—lying in bed surrounded by male "students" where she would host a Hebrew conversational salon.[33] This scene of what I would call "Zionist erotics" was echoed in Baron's later years after her self-incarceration in her Tel Aviv apartment when she would receive individual guests—by invitation only—at her bedside. Baron's identity, in both scenarios, as a woman alone in a room of men, facilitating Hebrew culture, posits both her centrality to and her marginalization from the culture of Zionist nationalism. On the one hand, in Mariampol Baron was the Hebrew authority in the room, and it was by her invitation that the Hebrew salon was taking place. On the other hand, there do not seem to have been any other women with her there. Hebrew was, essentially, even with a woman as its arbiter, a masculine language.

The stunted and unfulfilled erotic connection between David and Rachel in "In What World?" over their mutual desire to emigrate to Palestine is fulfilled between other couples in later stories by Baron. Taken together at face value, these later stories posit a conjugal, heterosexual, prerequisite for Zionist fulfillment, as courtship and marriage anticipate "aliyah" or migration to Palestine. Baron's presentation of the Zionist dream as commensurate with the bourgeois and traditional Jewish fantasy of heterosexual union is rendered somewhat absurd in light of the image of Baron courting multitudes of men, from her bedside, both in her Zionist youth days and in her isolated adulthood in Tel Aviv after the death of her husband. I would conjecture, in fact, that in order to maintain the notion of Zionist fulfillment as a fulfillment of heterosexual conjugal fantasies, Baron needed, in Tel Aviv, to re-create the scene of her bedside youth gatherings in the Pale of Settlement—in isolation.

In testimonies of multiple women from the period of the second aliyah, collected in *The Plough Woman* by Baron's personal friend and the wife of the first president of Israel, Rachel Katznelson-Shazar, we read about women (such as Y. H. Brenner's own sister) who are rendered doubly superfluous in a culture where men could not find employment and many would-be pioneers found themselves in major cities, and back on the old Yishuv, resuming the bourgeois lifestyle they had left behind.[34] On settlements, many women refused to marry, and when they did, they wrote, in painful and stark terms, about their sense of profound disempowerment and social isolation. A sense of what I would call "familial paralysis" reigned inasmuch as the birth of a child decreed the death of a woman's chance at equality or "productive" labor within the agricultural collective.

The heteroerotic ties that bound women and men in equal measure to the Zionist cause in Baron's canonic works are, interestingly, rejected in "In What World?" The story negates Rachel and David's union with David's migration to Palestine and Rachel's abandonment. In so doing, Baron seems to be articulating a precocious awareness—given that the story was published within the first year of her arrival in Palestine—of the gendering not only of Zionist aspirations but also of Zionist fulfillment. There is, in effect, she says, no real hope of women's finding a place on the new Yishuv—one that can even approximate the fulfillment of the Zionist dream. Ultimately, it seems, the Zionist dream excludes women, rendering women who seek out heterosexual unions, marrying and bearing children, irrelevant and burdensome in many respects.

Baron's "Gilgulim" (Transformations) (1939), in fact, and her posthumous *The Exiles* articulate the sense of female disempowerment by women on the new Yishuv.[35] In *The Exiles,* a young woman, Ronia, is discouraged by a matron in her community from marrying a "political" man because, she is told, he will never come home and the needs of the settlement will take precedence over her own personal needs and the needs of the marriage.[36] In a similar vein, Gittel, the female protagonist of "Transformations," who, along with her fiancé, spearheads the Zionist movement in her small eastern European hometown, subsequently emigrating after her marriage, finds herself in a small cottage, doing domestic tasks alone for weeks on end as her husband runs around the country politically organizing his peers.[37] Yehudit Harari writes a poignant autobiographical account about a young woman—a teacher—in Neve Tzedek (where Baron also settled) who must give up her intense communal involvements and teaching commitments when she becomes pregnant with her first child.[38] In all these examples, we observe the initial advancement of a belief in the possibility of personal fulfillment, along the lines of the classic Zionist fairy tale of "boy meets girl, boy marries girl, boy and girl move to Palestine and fulfill their individual, communal, and historical destiny there." That fairy tale, however, is destroyed, when the girl is forcibly removed from the equation. The metonymic

gendering of Hebrew and Yiddish alongside Zionist homecoming and
European diaspora resonates, unsurprisingly, with the shattered dream
of conjugal, heterosexual fulfillment within a Palestinian landscape. Yiddish must be relinquished, in Palestine, in favor of Hebrew, just as
women must be relinquished as equal partners and nation builders in
favor of men.

Taken together, Baron's two versions of "Burying the Books" and "In
What World?" illuminate the complex discourse of "relinquishment" underlying the revival of modern Hebrew. Baron invokes Yiddish intertexts
but refuses to engage them in any serious textual way in "Burying the
Books." At the same time, she incorporates a *ma'aseh,* or rabbinic tale,
into "In What World?" declaring a different type of intertextual affiliation—one in which a text is not just marked but is actually woven linguistically as well as thematically into the fabric of the story. In the first
set of stories, she mentions the texts she refuses to engage within the
rhetorical fabric of her story as a form of commemoration, or as the sign
of a literary trace. In the second story, she affiliates herself with a discourse of rabbinics, of folktales, and of nationalism in her full intertextual deployment of a ma'aseh or rabbinic "tale."

Throughout this study, I have characterized Baron's different patterns of intertextual usage. To reiterate, briefly, biblical narratives in
Baron's works, particularly in her later works, provide physical embel-
lishment and psychological reflection. A good example can be found in
Baron's novella *The Exiles,* in which a mother teaches her daughter Jewish history from the Bible in a unique fashion: major historical events are
glossed over, while small details of daily living, the experience of wearing
new clothes, for example, or of children playing in freshly grown grass,
are represented fully; she elaborates on fictional details of the biblical
narrative while abbreviating the actual.[39] Baron's rabbinic intertextuality
is, on the other hand, frequently presented in such a way that the narrator poses as a rabbinic exegete, weaving rabbinic discursive language and
texts together. The rabbinic texts are not quoted as much as they are re-
configured within a new exigetical fabric mediated by the narrator. This

technique emphasizes the narrator's erudition, as Baron struggles to "prove" herself as an expert in texts associated almost exclusively with Jewish men.

In a similar way, the relationship between some of Baron's earlier and later stories could, in and of itself, be viewed as a complex web of intertextual reconfigurations and exegetical constructions. The later works, in other words, serve as not just revisions but also as commentaries on the earlier ones. According to her daughter and literary executor, Tziporah Aharonovitch, Baron called her earlier, uncollected works "rags," or *smartutim*. Aharonovitch elaborates, in her 1960 "Material for a Biography": "It is appropriate, here, to raise the issue of Dvora Baron's rejection of her youthful writings. She called them smartutim [rags] and was violently opposed to the publication of a story, or a paragraph from a story from those days. When she reviewed a list of works authored by her, arranged chronologically, she wrote the word *pasul* [invalid] beside them, as a kind of legacy for coming generations." [40]

Naomi Seidman has pointed to the coincidence between the rejection of the mother's tkhines (called "rags") in the 1909 "Burying the Books" and Baron's own textual "rags," as she herself referred to her earlier works:

> "Rags" echoing as it does the masculine assessment of the collection of Yiddish women's prayers in the first "Burying the Books" could signal the growing discomfort of a woman writer with her own proximity to feminine traditions and the distance of the later writer from these traditions. But we can also read Baron's calling her earliest stories rags as more evidence of her self-irony, not her self-denigration at all. Rags, after all, aside from their domestic usefulness, are often the raw material of women's bricolage, to reclaim Claude Levi Strauss's term for the female crafts. Baron's reworking of earlier material in her later work may be the perfect example of this feminine ingenuity in creating art from the discarded and outworn. [41]

Seidman, appropriately, points out Baron's consciousness of the uneasy relationship between the "Burying the Books" stories. In calling her earlier works rags, Baron may be focusing on the differences between the two stories, not in terms of the later one being more "legitimate" than the earlier one because of its style or its more subtle treatment of women's concerns. Rather, in Seidman's assessment Baron may use the term "smartutim" as a marker of her "feminine" style, or bricolage.

I would take this argument one step further. Baron's later works, the ones sanctioned by her and included in the collections published during her lifetime, are in many instances composites. As in the case of "Burying the Books," the later work can be read as a palimpsest that includes the earlier work but is in no way limited to a simple reworking of it. Baron's earlier texts could have been, as Seidman argues, the raw material for a sort of bricolage, a cobbling together of seemingly disparate materials into a folk-art form. But if that bricolage is pushed beyond Straussian readings of folk art into the realm of midrash, those early "rags" enable Baron to create a midrashic texture in her stories, to create midrash *on* her own stories. To some extent, her labeling of her early stories as rags enables Baron to participate more fully in the male intellectual hermeneutic endeavor of traditional Jewish textual culture, marking, in her distinction between versions of her own work, the similarity between her own writing and the traditional male culture out of which it arises. Thus, this story speaks its difference from men's literature in its exclusion from the burial in the textual burial ground. At the same time, in its "raggedness" as literary bricolage, or midrashic layering, it also posits its similarity to men's literature.

Baron's "midrashic" treatment of her earlier stories in some of her later ones is echoed in the way that she rewrites rabbinic "fairy tales" in works such as "In What World?" In invoking a familiar text with substantial emotional or thematic and linguistic alterations, Baron claims rabbinic fairy tales for herself. In so doing, Baron draws attention to the importance of the *ma'aseh* (the tale) and the *mashal* (the parable) in her own literary universe, as early literary models, and perhaps as bridges between tradition and modernity. The "tale" or the "parable" could be found in all genres of the national literatures that had been "recuperated" and constructed throughout Europe during the eighteenth and nineteenth centuries. Identifying these forms in rabbinic literature and using them as templates and themes for her own tales enabled her to participate in that discourse. Baron's intertextual allusion to a ma'aseh in a critical conversation between David and Rachel in "In What World?" wherein David vows to find Rachel wherever she may be and to wed her, love her, and provide for her is, in a sense, Baron's way of affiliating herself with a tradition of modern tellers of rabbinic folktales in her era. Bialik retells such folktales throughout his *Book of Legends* (1908–1912) and in a more expanded narrative form in his collection *And It Came to Pass* (1934). Alongside Bialik (and his coeditor, Yehoshua Hana Ravnitsky), M. Y. Berdischevsky, Louis Ginzburg, Saul Ginzburg and Peysakh Markesh, and Y. L Peretz also edited anthologies (in a variety of languages ranging from English to Yiddish, Russian, and German) of what they conceived of as traditional Jewish "folk" forms, gleaned either from rabbinic literature reimagined as ancient folklore, Hasidic tales, or oral traditions.[42] Baron, in invoking a "rabbinic fairy tale," or, as we will see, the *form* of a rabbinic fairy tale with her own content, is doing far more than demonstrating her rabbinic erudition. Rather, she is participating in a movement to rehabilitate traditional Jewish folk forms as modern European literature and, in so doing, to claim a place for modern Jewish literature in the panoply of modern literary expression. Moreover, she is recirculating literary forms and literary corpora that were long neglected in favor of more legalistic rabbinic texts within traditional Jewish society and biblical texts within the culture of the Haskalah.

Baron's reworking of the "tale" of a prince and his exiled beloved is an echo of a "tale" found in Buber's introduction to *Midrash Tanhumah*.[43] By looking at the original *Tanhumah Midrash* alongside Baron's interpretation, we will arrive at a better understanding of her commitment to keeping certain traditional texts and textual forms in intertextual "circulation"—or not—in the fiction of the modern Hebrew renaissance. The *Tanhumah* text reads:

There is a tale (ma'aseh) of Solomon the king who had a beautiful daughter, unrivaled by any maiden in the Land of Israel. He studied the constellations to see who she would marry and he saw that she was destined to marry a son of paupers, unrivaled in his poverty by any young man in The Land of Israel. What did her father do? He built a tall tower in the middle of the ocean and surrounded it from every perspective, took his daughter, and locked her inside the tower with seventy of his advisors from the elders of Israel. He did not make an opening in the tower, so that no one could enter, and he put many supplies inside it. He said, "Let's see how God handles this one."

A long time afterward, the girl's future husband, the poverty-stricken young man, embarked on a night journey. He was naked and barefoot, and hungry and had no place to sleep. He saw the carcass of an ox laid out on the ground and he slept between its ribs in order to protect him from the cold. A large bird who was also sleeping on the ox took the carcass and flew it up to the top of the princess's tower where he planned to eat it in the morning. When the princess left her room to take a walk on the roof, as she did every day, she saw the young man.

She said, "who are you and who brought you here?"

He said to her, "I am a poor Jew from Acre and a bird brought me here."

What did she do? She took him to her room and dressed him and washed him and anointed him. His appearance was so vastly improved by her ministrations that there was no other young man like him in beauty in all the borders of Israel. The princess loved him with all her heart and soul, and her soul became tied to his. The young man—quick witted, outspoken, and charming—was also a scribe.

One day she said to him, "Do you want to marry me?"

He said to her, "And who will give you away?"

What did he do? He squeezed out some blood and he wrote her a marriage contract and a dowry with his blood, and he married her and he said, "God is our witness, and the angels Mikhael and Gabriel are our witnesses." He came to her, in the way of men, and she became pregnant.

When the elders saw that she was pregnant, they said, "It seems to us that you are pregnant!"

She said, "Indeed."

And they said to her, "Who impregnated you?"

And she said, "Why do you want to know?"

They were terrified that Solomon would punish them so they sent for him. Solomon came on a boat and they said to him, "Our master, the king, such and such happened. Please don't torture us!"

When he heard what happened to his daughter and he asked her about it, she said, "God brought me a beautiful and kind young man, intelligent, a holy scribe." She called the young man and he came before the king and showed him the marriage contract he made for his daughter. The king asked him about his father and his mother and about his family and city of origin.

The king understood from the young man's answers that he was the one he had seen in the princess' horoscope and he was tremendously happy and he said, "Praise God who 'restores the lonely to their homes, sets free the imprisoned safe and sound.' "[44]

I have presented this "tale" in full because it serves as a crucial contrast to the "tale" that Baron writes as the emotional climax of "In What World?" Before we look at Baron's version, however, it is important to note that the *Tanhumah* tale, presented above, is a (roundabout) response to a passage from Psalms 68:7, quoted, as we saw, at the end of the narrative: "God restores the lonely to their homes, sets free the imprisoned safe and sound, while the rebellious must live in a parched land." Although taken in a traditional sense as a statement about exile and redemption wherein exile occurs to "the rebellious who must live in a parched land" and redemption takes place for "the lonely" and "the imprisoned" who are returned "to their homes," the tale explicitly articulates its locale as the "Land of Israel." The princess is the most beautiful "in all the Land of Israel," and her suitor (after he is cleaned up) is also named the most beautiful "in all the Land of Israel." Therefore, exile and redemption are taken here not in their most concrete sense—as exile to the diaspora and return to the Land of Israel. Indeed, exile is understood as a kind of mythical exile within the land itself.

Baron's variation on this tale, communicated from David to Rachel at the climax of "In What World?" reads as follows:

David told me a story (ma'aseh)—a tale of a prince who fell in love with the daughter of his nursemaid. He would visit with her every day and when the king found out about this, he exiled his son from the palace and locked the nursemaid and her daughter in a dark and sinister tower. What did the prince do? He withdrew to his house of prayer, contemplated his bitterness, wept and cried for three days and three nights that there be a miracle and he could grow wings. On the third day, in the evening, at the hour of mercy, the grace of God touched him and his wish was fulfilled— two large wings, white as snow, suddenly grew on his back—and that night he rose up and flew between the heavens and the earth—passing over rivers and oceans, cities and states—and his face and his heart were directed towards the high tower. He arrived there and stood at the window knocking with his finger—tap-tap.

"Who's there?"

"Little girl, my little girl, how your face shines!"

"My light is from the glow of your own face, my master the prince."

"Little girl, my little girl, what have you been doing this whole time?"

"I have been pulling my hair out, strand by strand, and have been weaving them into a tallis bag for you, my master, the prince."

"And what else have you done, my beautiful one?"

"I have been spinning fine delicate threads and have been weaving them, day and night, into a light blue huppah for us, my master the prince."

Immediately the prince embraced his lover and spread his radiant wings. He flapped them once or twice and the two of them were lifted together between heaven and earth, soaring and flying like heavenly angels until they landed on a large island which was like a garden inside the ocean. The prince intertwined the branches of a tree like a cradle, put his young woman inside it, and left.

"My beautiful young man, what are you doing?"

"I am collecting fine stones to build a palace for you."

"And what else are you doing?"

"I am hunting for the birds and animals I need to make a fine banquet in your honor."

And here I [Rachel] interrupted him: "And her mother, the nurse-maid, David?"[45]

As is self-evident, Baron has taken much license with the traditional tale. Most important is the fact that Rachel is focused upon the destiny of the nursemaid—clearly a stand-in for her own mother—and not the couple who serve as the conventional nucleus of the ma'aseh. Like the old woman in the woman's section in "Abandoned Wife" who is concerned about the plight of the king's wife beyond the constraints of the parable's application, so too, here, does Rachel express concerns that are not classically relevant within the hermeneutics of the story presented. Who cares what happens to the bride's mother in a fairy tale? Within the dualistic economy of exile and redemption that is usually expected in a narrative such as this one, the mother's presence in the tower serves as a harbinger for the further deconstruction of what one would expect in the denouement of the story. The theme of exile and redemption is almost entirely obliterated here, as the lovers do not return to the home of the king. Rather, they move to a deserted island where the prince builds the nursemaid's daughter a palace.

In response to Rachel's query about the fate of the nursemaid, David reassures her that she too will live in the palace with the young lovers. The next day, pleased with his answer, Rachel brings David a *tallis* bag (a bag in which to store his prayer shawl and phylacteries) that she has embroidered for him, a traditional sign of engagement. When David leaves Rachel behind to emigrate to Palestine, it is as if he has broken their engagement, and the fate of the nursemaid, the mother of the prince's beloved, is also left open-ended. What, indeed, happens to the nursemaid? Does she really come to live with her daughter and her husband on a deserted island? When David abandons Rachel, we understand that the nursemaid, as well, never really accompanied her daughter the way David promised she would. Implicit in the breakdown of David and Rachel's engagement, based on Rachel's interpretation of the tale, is a breakdown of Rachel's faith in a fluid osmosis between the literary and the lived. Rachel must relinquish her belief that David will return for her and that she is destined for better things than the poverty and loneliness of her existence in eastern Europe.

The modern Hebrew renaissance was a movement based on faith in continuity between the literary and the lived; Hebrew texts were viewed as instrumental to the "revival" of an ancient, dignified, nation. If secular literary expression in a religious scholarly tongue would magically usher in the creation of a vernacular language that could sustain a recuperated people in its transition to modernity, quite a lot of promises and assumptions "must be forgotten" in the process. In 1882, Ernest Renan argued that "the essence of a nation is that all individuals have many things in common, and also that they have forgotten many things."[46] This "imperative of forgetting," as pointed out by Yael Chaver, is exactly the dynamic played out in the princess's relinquishment of her mother when she is moved to a deserted island by her prince, in Rachel's relinquish-

ment of David as he moves to Palestine, and finally in Baron's relinquishment of her "mother tongue," Yiddish, and its accompanying texts. In invoking the tremendous loss suffered by Rachel when losing her future
husband to Palestine in "In What World?" and by failing to invoke Yiddish literature intertextually beyond its simple appearance as a subject in
her "Burying the Books" stories, Baron thematizes the "forgetting" that
underlies faith in the "revival" of a language and a culture. Baron has forgotten her Yiddish just as Rachel must forget David. But beneath the
lapse of memory lies a scar. That scar is the cry of the tkhines when they
are pitched from the grave of the Hebrew revival and of the *Tzenerene*
when it is acknowledged as "worthy" of burial but never deployed as an
intertext.

6

❧❦❧

Epilogue

Breaking Down the Door

If a mad lion were running through the street would not a sensible woman shut herself in?—1 Peter 5:8

The soul selects her own society / then shuts the door.—Emily Dickinson

BARON'S SELF-IMPOSED ISOLATION during thirty-three of the most crucial years of Israeli national formation—from 1923 until 1956—has recently become the object of Israeli popular interest. Not only did these years correspond with various political milestones on the way to the 1948 establishment of the State of Israel, but these were also the very years during which Hebrew actually blossomed into a vernacular language and writers became, for the first time, able to address a broad audience in a sufficiently developed Hebrew idiom. It seems quite strange that Dvora Baron, an ardent Zionist and a major writer of the modern Hebrew renaissance (not to mention the wife of one of the most influential public figures on the new Yishuv), would absent herself from the public life of the world she had, in part, ushered into existence.

In this study, I have not dwelled on the biographical facts of Baron's life—neither her family of origin nor her family in Israel. Baron's highly secretive nature, her severe isolation, and her daughter's jealous and complete control over Baron's personal documents have cast her biography into the deepest of shadows. Guessing about the motivations for Baron's lifestyle, for her extremely harsh rejection of her early works, and for her almost complete disregard of other literary women in the early years of the State of Israel has not been my goal here; I have resisted the sloppy correlation between Baron's work and her biography that inevitably results from too keen an interest in the pathologic contours of her later years.

Nevertheless, when lecturing on Baron, I have found that a primary interest of popular audiences is the mystery of Baron's last thirty-three years. Audiences want to know how she could spend the first thirty-six years of her life in the eye of the storm of Jewish modernization—acquiring a boy's orthodox Jewish education; leaving home at the age of fifteen to become a tutor, a writer, and a secular gymnasium student; emigrating to Palestine as a woman alone in the first decade of the twentieth century; becoming a mainstay of the literary and political establishment in prestatehood Palestine—and then spend the last thirty-three years of her life lying in bed and enlisting her only child, Tziporah, as a literary agent and housekeeper.

Baron's own explanations for her choices do not seem to satisfy the popular hunger for something racy, forbidden, and forbidding in her biography. She claimed to have contracted amoebic dysentery in Alexandria during the years of World War I when her family was exiled from Tel Aviv and never to have fully recovered her digestive faculties. Was this adequate cause for a total withdrawal from the world? She argued that her daughter, Tziporah, was kept home from school as a child and served as Baron's caregiver throughout her adult life because Tziporah was an epileptic who would suffer humiliation and rejection if she ever went out and tried to make a life for herself. Did Tziporah acquiesce willingly?

Each of these justifications could, certainly, contain a grain of truth. But they hold so much more. As the Hebrew in Baron's work becomes increasingly more archaic for a contemporary Israeli audience with every passing year, and as non-Israeli audiences become increasingly less likely to know enough Hebrew to read her work in the original, Baron's biography itself remains of interest. Indeed, in finding allusions to Baron in the popular Israeli press in the late 1980s and early 1990s—the years that correspond to the publication of Baron's biography by Nurit Govrin in 1988 and an "experimental biography" by Amia Lieblich in 1991—Baron's literary works seem to be of little or no importance in compari-

7. Mother and daughter, Dvora Baron and Tziporah Aharonovitch, Tel Aviv, 1935. *Courtesy of Gnazim Archive, Ramat Gan, Israel.*

son to Baron's mythology.[1] As I draw this exploration of Baron's responses to the imperatives of the modern Hebrew renaissance to a close, I feel compelled, finally, to discuss Baron's thirty-three-year withdrawal from society. Even so, it is important to keep in mind the limitations of ascribing psychological diagnoses to narrative choices and biographical idiosyncrasies to an entire creative oeuvre.

A variety of suggestions have been offered by literary critics, by journalists, and by psychologists for Baron's isolation. The 1921 Arab riots in Jaffa, in which Baron's good friend and compatriot Yosef Haim Brenner was murdered, coupled with Baron's receiving word of the death of her beloved brother Benjamin from typhoid fever while a doctor in the Russian army were, by some accounts, the reasons for Baron's retreat from society and the beginning of a protracted period of mourning and introspection.[2] Another explanation for Baron's isolation has been traced to her daughter's health. Instead of confining her epileptic daughter to the house and going out herself to live a public life, Baron was said to have confined herself to the house as a way of modeling the lifestyle that she believed her daughter needed to adopt in order to protect herself from the public humiliation of her illness; conscripting (or enslaving) her daughter into literary and household service was Baron's way of giving her daughter a sense of purpose in the absence of other prospects, as Baron conceived it.[3] Others have suggested that Baron isolated herself in order to facilitate her creative output and that, indeed, her most fully developed work was written after she disappeared from the streets of Tel Aviv.[4] Finally, Baron's sense of having abandoned her mother and her younger sister Chana in Europe (her other younger sister Tziporah drowned in young adulthood, and her older sister, Hayah Rivka, emigrated to Palestine before the establishment of the state) defeated her emotionally during the period between the two world wars, and certainly after World War II.

Baron's and her husband Yosef Aharonovitch's resignation from the labor Zionist newspaper *ha-Poel ha-Tsair* in 1922 after a public controversy over the continuing efficacy of its leadership apparently served as a natural point of departure from public life for Baron. Although Baron shut the door to her apartment and emerged only twice afterward—once to go down the steps of her building on the day of Aharonovitch's funeral in 1937 and once to enter the hospital for cataract surgery within months of her death in 1956—her husband, in contrast, became a founder of the Laborer's Bank (Bank ha-Poalim) and continued in his role as a public figure in Jewish Palestine until his death. Yosef and Dvora—in their separate responses to the collapse of their joint public endeavor as editors of *The Young Laborer*—exemplified the classical roles assigned to men and women in Western bourgeois cultures: Dvora withdrew into the private domain with a vengeance, and Yosef, according to Baron's own account, became completely swallowed up by his public role.

The contemporary Israeli author Amalya Kahana-Carmon (frequently designated Baron's literary inheritor) said in a 1988 conference organized to celebrate the one hundredth anniversary of Dvora Baron's birth that the literary universe of modern Israeli society can be understood in terms of public prayer and private prayer—or the individual prayers of traditional Jewish women as situated against the collective prayers of traditional Jewish men.[5] Men, according to Orthodox Jewish law, may gather to constitute a minyan, or a quorum of ten. As such, they can pray on behalf of one another and on behalf of women. Women, on the other hand, obligated to pray on only an individual basis and not counted in a communal quorum, cannot pray on one another's behalf and certainly not on behalf of the community. Thus, Kahana-Carmon's statement about women writers engaging in "individual" prayer as opposed to male writers engaging in "communal" prayer reflects a perception that women writers in Israeli society depict idiosyncratic "miniatures" of women's lives, whereas men represent the voices of the masses and the sensibilities of generations. Baron's withdrawal behind the door of her apartment could, indeed, be seen as both resistance and capitulation to the pressures placed upon her to write in a manner that was in keeping with the prevailing literary ideologies. If she were a man, she would have been expected to write about life in the settlements, the struggle to survive in Palestine, and the growing conflict between Arabs and Jews. Baron capitulated, in part, to this expectation, by withdrawing completely from the public eye because she was not employing the appropriate "communal" style. In so doing, she fulfilled the gendered expectations for a woman by writing in physical isolation and finding her signature voice in the process.

Perhaps it was Baron's very fulfillment of gendered expectations—through her physical isolation—that allowed her a place in the literary canon. Even though as a Hebrew writer she was expected to write about national concerns, as a woman writer she was expected to write about domestic ones. "Domestic" (or feminine) and "diaspora" in the ideological economy of the New Yishuv were, as I discussed in the last chapter, interchangeable. If Baron had continued in her public role as the editor of *The Young Laborer* while writing about eastern Europe, she might, indeed, have been too maverick for serious consideration by her peers. From behind the closed door of her apartment, Baron's difference could still be perceived as "intimations," not as declarations.

When is it appropriate to break down the door of Baron's Tel Aviv apartment? How do responsible critics discern which biographical information is relevant to a fair reading of Baron's work? Throughout this study, I have argued that Baron's literary affiliations, her invocation of the traditional education that enabled her to become a Hebrew writer, and her emergence from an educational system that under normal circumstances (had she not had a permissive father and a doting brother) would have excluded her from the ranks of Hebrew authorship and by extension from the canon of modern Hebrew letters are the only relevant biographical considerations in understanding her work. Even so, Baron's door has been "broken down" by a variety of different writers in recent years.

Interestingly, the name Baron can be read, if split into its component Hebrew parts, as *ba-aron,* or "in the closet." Baron's public presence, despite her assiduous attempt to maintain her privacy, has been largely facilitated in the course of the past two decades by the appearance of several (highly conjectural) creative works focused on her life that have, for all intents and purposes, forcibly removed her from her self-imposed "closet." Amia Lieblich's 1991 "experimental biography" of Dvora Baron, *Embroideries,* and a play by the popular contemporary writer Yehudit Katsir titled *Dvora Baron* (2000) have turned Baron into a female, if not feminist, Israeli pop icon.[6] Both works are wholly focused on the mystery of Baron's personal life in Israel. They guess at the motives for Baron's thirty-three-year self-incarceration in her Tel Aviv apartment on Oliphant Street, for her refusal to attend her own husband's funeral, and for her apparent subjugation and enslavement of her only daughter. More important, they emphasize the metaphoric potency of Baron's isolated home life, thereby raising the question of whether the "door" of Baron's apartment in Tel Aviv is, in any way, locked from the outside and not the inside, because of public perceptions of Baron's continuing "diasporic" identity through her narrative choices. In other words, to what extent do contemporary Israeli readers fail to read Baron's work within the international, multilinguistic trajectory of the modern Hebrew renaissance through their insistence on Baron's isolation within an Israeli context?

The setting of Katsir's *Dvora Baron,* first produced at Tel Aviv's ha-Bimah theater in 2000, is confined to a single room in Baron's apartment, with a large wooden wardrobe as its centerpiece. A wardrobe, in

Hebrew, as I pointed out earlier, is *aron*. It is also the word for the Torah ark in the synagogue and for a coffin. Baron's daughter, Tziporah, grows, in the course of the play, from a little girl to an embittered old maid. Baron's husband, Yosef Aharonovitch, dies in the course of the play, and Baron herself dies at the play's end. The wardrobe is at the stage's focal center. It stands dark and silent for most of the play, opens up infrequently to allow glimpses at another world—the world of landscapes and people left behind in eastern Europe with Baron's emigration to Palestine. Through the wardrobe Baron communes with her dead brother Benjamin. After Yosef's death he joins Benjamin in the wardrobe, and at the end of the play Baron herself abandons Tziporah, disappearing with her husband and her brother into the wardrobe's depths. By allowing us into Baron's apartment and placing the wardrobe with its view of Europe and of the next world at its center, Katsir facilitates a breaking down of Baron's door and places her within a landscape that straddles time and geography—the past and the present, pre-World War II eastern Europe and modern Israel.

Lieblich's book also posits a "breaking down" of the door of Baron's apartment in a series of twenty-four imagined "encounters" with Baron during the year before her death. Unlike Katsir, however, who uses the wardrobe to give us a sense that Baron's isolation was not total and that she led a rich life of communion with people and places beyond the new Yishuv and the confines of her Tel Aviv apartment, Leiblich sees no way out for Baron. In *Embroideries*, Leiblich is granted permission by the elderly Baron to visit her on a series of occasions, during which Baron and Leiblich "converse." As they talk, Leiblich attempts to elicit explanations from Baron for her unusual life choices.[7] In the twenty-third encounter, Leiblich shares research on famous "isolated" personalities, people who, like Baron, withdrew from society at the peak of their creative powers. Surprisingly, Leiblich does not mention the tradition of women artists writing in self-imposed isolation.

Emily Dickinson is the best known of these women, articulating in her poetry, "The soul selects her own society / then shuts the door." As Sandra Gilbert and Susan Gubar have pointed out, many women writers of the eighteenth and nineteenth centuries developed a rhetoric of "confinement" and enclosure in their literary works. Charlotte Brontë seems preoccupied with the image of the "haunted garret." Emily Brontë presents in her stories a variety of strangely morbid coffin-shaped beds. Ann Radcliffe's melodramatic dungeons find something of a corollary in Jane Austen's mirrored parlors, whereas Christina Rossetti valorizes the confinement of the convent.[8] In Leiblich's omission of the obvious (particularly Victorian) woman writers whose tradition Baron joined, she seems to be caught in a vortex of Baron's "Israeliness." Baron's locked front door in Tel Aviv is the symbol of the dead end toward which such an attitude leads. Understanding Baron's literary life in terms of the literary lives of other women and other traditions may, indeed, be a fruitful complement to the work that I have done here. Although I have focused on Baron's literary biography within the confines of the modern Hebrew renaissance, seeing her within an international tradition of literary "intimations" and of spiritual and cultural "isolation" may very well be an appropriate way to justify "breaking down" Baron's door.

The possibility of de-ghettoizing Baron is, interestingly, echoed in Baron's own decision to translate Flaubert's *Madame Bovary* (1932).[9] By translating that novel, she presented herself as a hebraizer of world literature and, from a different perspective, as a channel for the new Yishuv to alternative intellectual universes. Indeed, Baron did not translate a Russian novel, which was probably the mother tongue for most of her eastern European-born compatriots on the new Yishuv. Rather, she translated a novel from French—the language of the privileged and the educated in the eastern European Jewish community. In translating *Madame Bovary,* Baron was exchanging one variety of provincialism (her portraits of the shtetl) for another (Flaubert's portrait of the petite bourgeoisie in the French countryside), and one variety of conjugal angst (within the conventional world of Jewish law) with another (within the conventions of nineteenth-century bourgeois society). As such she was, perhaps, suggesting that provincialism and individual angst were not diasporic (or domestic) when taken beyond Zionist ideologies. They were art.[10]

In an obituary of Baron written on September 5, 1956, Shlomo Grozinski, a literary acquaintance of Baron's, recalls his first encounter with her work:

It was 1916 in New York. Just a few months earlier I had immigrated from my hometown in White Russia. I found the enormous city strange and depressing, the language impenetrable, the Jews there so different from those that I had known they were nearly unrecognizable. I kept them at a distance with a longing for what I had left on the other side of the ocean and specifically for the Hebrew library in my city where I spent many precious hours during my childhood. One day I left my parents house and for some reason was drawn to the large courtyard opposite. There I saw, poking out of a pile of paper, something in print that caught my eye. I picked up a worn out, water damaged edition of the journal *Moledet* [Motherland]. Thrilled about my unexpected discovery, I returned home. I lifted my eyes to the high tenement buildings surrounding me and wondered if there was someone on my own street who could read Hebrew, who could speak it. Would I be lucky enough to meet them? In this issue of *Moledet*, I read a story by Dvora Baron. I don't think it is collected in her books. But perhaps I am mistaken.[11]

The story Grozinski refers to is, perhaps, "In What World?" (1911), the first story published by Baron after her emigration to Palestine at the end of 1910 and the source of much controversy because of its perceived "diasporic" qualities.[12] "In What World?" serves here as the harbinger of hope for this new immigrant to New York, as the proof that there is a Hebrew culture waiting for him to discover in America.

The international flavor of the modern Hebrew renaissance was lost, in time, with the birth of the State of Israel. Because the Hebrew language and its literature came to be read as "Israeli," even anachronistically, the poetry and prose composed by individuals like Baron who wrote and lived at different stages of their literary careers in different countries came to be understood monolithically along a teleological trajectory headed, always, toward Israel. Baron, however, through her closed door in the heart of Tel Aviv, through her insistence on writing about eastern Europe, maintains, to this day, consciousness in her readers of her identity as a writer of the modern Hebrew renaissance, not as an Israeli writer.

My own position as a teacher and scholar of modern Jewish literature has been strongly impacted by my location in the United States.

Though versed in the discourse of Zionism, I am capable of seeing beyond it, in part because I did not grow up in its heartland. Israelis may be
distressed by Baron's isolation for the second half of her life because that
kind of behavior was wildly discouraged in the collective culture of Zionism. They attempt to break down her door, to see what kind of strange
psychological issues kept her from normalcy within the collective economy of the Zionist dream. But, in fact, Baron was not so different from
many successful artists who found their own idiosyncratic ways to maximize their work time and to minimize their distractions. Baron's intense
isolation from Israeli society, in other words, did not imply isolation
from the culture of the modern Hebrew renaissance or from other literary traditions. In this study I have not attempted to enter Baron's Tel Aviv
apartment. I am content to accept Baron's eccentric behavior while in-
vestigating the wide-open spaces of the literary universe she tried to create—across textual traditions, across genders, across geographic
divides—from within the confines of her own *dalet amot,* her own four
cubits.

Appendixes

Notes

Works Cited

Index

Two Translations and a Note

"In What World?" and "As a Driven Leaf"

"IN WHAT WORLD?" (1911) was written during what Nurit Govrin has called Baron's "first half," the period before Baron's isolation in her Tel Aviv apartment, whereas "As a Driven Leaf" (1949) was written during the "second half" of Baron's career, when her style became distinctly polished and far more ideologically circumspect. The differences between these two stories demonstrate not only the evolution of Baron's writing style but also the changing nature of the Hebrew language during the thirty-eight-year interval between them. Lexically, "In What World?" is somewhat impoverished, as evidenced by Baron's occasional surrender to cliché and truism. The later story, "As a Driven Leaf," is far more elegantly formulated; syntactically, the sentences contain many more dependent clauses, and the lexicon is richer and more natural.

I include these two stories here because they have never before been translated and they are rarely discussed in the critical literature on Dvora Baron. Because I focus on them in my book (particularly in Chapters 2 and 5), I thought that it would be useful for the English reader with little or no access to Baron's Hebrew originals to have recourse to these translations. Although these two stories are representative of two distinct stages of Baron's career—in the type of Hebrew employed and the affective resonance of each—the stories are very similar in their focus on young eastern European Jewish girls, on frustrated romance, on class inequity, and on ambivalence toward the dream of Zionist homecoming. It is important to consider these stories both on a continuum and across a great divide—from the beginning of Baron's sojourn in Palestine to her death in Tel Aviv, from the birth of a Hebrew vernacular prose to its successful implementation.

In my translation of "In What World?" I was often confronted with the dilemma of whether to preserve the rhythms of Baron's somewhat archaic Hebrew and awkward stylistic choices or whether to "smooth" the story out at certain critical junctures. Most of the time, I tried to preserve the original tone. "As a Driven Leaf" was easier to translate because I was not tempted to rewrite or embellish as much; the Hebrew was far more natural and could withstand translation into another cultural idiom better than its earlier counterpart. "As a Driven Leaf," the later of the two stories, appears here before the earlier story because I believe that it is a better story, and provides a stylistic context for the earlier "In What World?"

Indeed, translating and reading these two stories side by side may be the best demonstration both thematically and stylistically of Baron's difficult challenge within her generation as a modern writer of an archaic language and as a woman within a nearly exclusive cohort of men. In comparing these two stories, the evolution of Baron's Hebrew style and the muting of her feminist tonalities become obvious. In the first story, Baron's struggle for vocabulary and her unease with the rhythms of Hebrew syntax are apparent, while her articulation of the injustice of male and female opportunities for nationalist and ideological fulfillment is overt, and even overdrawn at times. Although in the later story the Hebrew is much more elegant and competent, its subtlety leaves something to be desired. It is, to my mind, entirely unclear what transpires between the protagonist and her employer's son, and also what happens, in the end, to the protagonist herself. Or perhaps one could argue that Baron's depiction of a community in Palestine that reproduces the class structure and the gender inequities of the European shtetl is all the stronger for the story's ambiguities.

Translation: "As a Driven Leaf" (1949)

The greengrocer from the southern neighborhood brought the girl to the house of Mrs. Pin, the widow. Of all the places where she herself had worked as a younger woman, this one seemed the most appropriate.

"Here you won't be mistreated," she explained to the frightened girl, a new arrival from her own village in Europe. "The customs here are just like those of the Sdoveski household back home where we come from, and the food is simple and homey: cutlets and vinegar and pickles."

She discussed the terms of employment with the widow, who agreed to all her conditions, and the very next day the girl was led up to the back veranda of the finely appointed house, where the elderly mistress, eating just then, welcomed her warmly.

"Go wash up and have a bite to eat," she said to the girl quite simply as she made room for her at the table.

The widow asked her if she wanted to rest a bit, but the girl wanted to start working immediately. After so many days of inactivity on the ship over, and her long rest in the house of the greengrocer (her neighbor from the old country), she was exhausted by her own idleness; she could even detect some dryness in the palms of her hands, from lack of use. The girl filled the water bucket with a thirsty gesture and started cleaning the house, which resembled the houses of the Sdoveskies, her employers back home. It had the same carpets and lacy curtains in the dining room, and the same beds with the high headboards in the bedroom. But she avoided looking into the mirror over the dressing table because of the dread that gripped her in the widow's private quarters.

They took their dinner on the back veranda overlooking the court-yard. As the elderly woman pushed first the salad bowl and then the butter dish toward the girl, she told her about all her sons scattered in cities across the ocean. Then she asked about the girl's mother, whom she had heard was alone, abandoned really, in a small out-of-the-way house over there, in one of the farthest corners of the shtetl. The girl, instead of answering, feigned cheerfulness. Her entire being, it seemed, had been hidden beneath a veil.

She completed her daily work in the kitchen quickly and according to the instructions that had been given to her; she closed the blinds in the dark dining room, and even fearlessly entered the bedroom in order to make up the old woman's bed. Only when her mistress, dressed in a nightgown, began to murmur her bedtime prayers—the verses of the *Shma*[1]—did the girl's bravery elude her, and the earth rolled beneath her, like the deck of a passenger liner.

A single thread stretched from the widow's sphere here to the small out-of-the-way house over there, in one of the farthest corners of the shtetl. And the barrenness all around both places had the same effect as the foggy mist that hung over the vast desolation of the ocean. At bedtime, when the girl took off her clothes, the veil she took such pains to wear in front of her employer came off as well.

The next morning the milkman woke her at the break of day, and the girl lit the gas stove and washed the pots, as her mistress had ordered her to do. Afterward she went out barefoot, dressed in just a thin robe that clung to her body. Her curls cascaded lazily down the curve of her strong neck, as she swept the path lined with cypress trees. The engineer's wife openly admired her, watching her from the balcony on the first floor of the building next door.

"What a beauty," said the woman to the cook standing beside her. But the cook, for lack of time, or perhaps because she didn't want to embarrass the girl, did not look at her. Only afterward, when she saw the girl beating the rugs with the palms of her hands, she instructed her to use a frying pan. She even went to get one for the girl and whacked the rug two or three times herself in order to demonstrate. As the dust rose, choking the two, they became friends.

The girl avoided the other women in the courtyard, feigning cheerfulness, thwarting any possibility of conversation when they fell upon her with questions. But she remained candid with the cook who worked at the engineer's house when they sat together on the bench beneath the poplar that evening. She shared the nickname by which she was known in the shtetl—Mirl—and she and the woman with the white hair and young eyes quickly became engaged in conversation.

The woman didn't say much about herself; she dismissed any inquiries with a hand gesture that indicated that what was done was done and wasn't worth discussing. But to the life story of the newcomer, nineteen years of age, she listened attentively, hanging on every word, as does someone who is following someone else to a new and unfamiliar place. She even helped her get through some of her more painful reminiscences by offering up some benign remarks to ease the sorrow and the longing—even her memory of the small out-of-the-way house over there, in one of the farthest corners of the shtetl, as it looked in the last hour of parting, when her mother, windblown in the fall gusts, clung to her.

It became clear in the course of that conversation that she had not initiated the "step" that landed her here. Rather, her mother, out of concern for her future, had made her do it. She had seen that the shtetl was emptying out, the boys learning agriculture and emigrating, and the girls doing the same. And when the "man from the settlement" had passed through and offered to accompany the girl on her trip (as a husband would accompany a wife), the woman agreed. She ran to the fabric stores and to the seamstresses and had the finest new clothes made because, as she said, "perhaps her luck will change." They heard, around that time, that Chava-Rachel, the shoemaker's daughter, had moved to Palestine with the pioneers and married a wealthy young man from a good family.

The girl herself, while all the arrangements were being made, felt as if she had been pushed aside, discarded. She didn't get involved, as if none of the hullabaloo had anything to do with her.

They had been renovating the dining room in the Sdoveski household, and although she no longer worked for them, the girl went to supervise the handling of the china. As she was moving the cups and plates about, she was told that everything was ready for her trip. The carriage came and she was taken, practically ripped, it seemed, from the arms of her mother.

The neighbors were the ones who separated them, pushing the girl and her trunk into the carriage. Like her trunk, she was subsequently transferred from carriage to train and from train to train for the rest of her trip to the ship.

She didn't have enough handkerchiefs to soak up all her tears, and the good man, her chaperone, took his out of his suitcase and offered it to her. He did this silently.

Over time she began to feel that she threw a pall on everything and everyone she encountered. When people saw her, they fell silent and often left the room. She understood that she had to pull herself together and even learned to feign cheerfulness. When she finally arrived at the ship, she pretended to be perfectly normal. Every day she waited impatiently for evening so she could throw off her veil. She would stand up and retreat to one of the corners where there was nothing but stars and night silence.

The young men on the ship sat together and sang while she sat alone, detached from the world, like a torn thread, or like the leaf she caught in her hand that had—as she sat now on the bench—drifted down from the crown of the poplar above her.

The white-haired woman murmured a few words of comfort into the void of the girl's pained silence after she had finished saying what needed to be said.

Death, she claimed, is the only thing that can separate people for eternity, not the distance that separates different times and different places. The path that led the girl here had not changed, and others, with her help, could follow the same path after her. Not a few parents had come after their children, even to other countries. All the more so, people come to this country to die even without the prospect of being met by children or acquaintances. The girl would get used to it here, grow accli-mated, and could save some money from her salary while her mother prepared to join her. The day would come when she would replace the sorrow of parting with the joy of reunion.

These sweet words entered the heart of the girl, and as long as these evening conversations continued, she felt less distressed, less uneasy.

She took care of all the housework alone now because with the arrival of fall, the widow's rheumatoid arthritis got worse and she spent most of the day dozing in her armchair. The girl dealt with all the merchants, oversaw the hired woman on laundry day, and even paid the baker and milkman's messenger boy. In her free time she knitted woolen sweaters for the women in the courtyard, work that was easy for her and was meant to bring in a little extra income, income she needed for her "plan."

She still dressed in her soft summer dress, with open sandals on her bare feet. She exuded warmth when she ran, her hair swinging, to the grocery, or when she swept away the rain water that had pooled on the balcony. And those who saw her bright, open face, her laughing eyes, be-came hopeful, breathed more easily, as if a gentle spring breeze had washed over them.

At the end of winter the youngest of the widow's sons, Borik, the one they called "the baby," and the one his mother missed especially much, came home from far away.

He arrived suddenly, unannounced, opened the front door with a key he had carried around in his pocket for a long time, and entered. The girl, that evening, told her friend about the meeting between the boy and his mother—how the sleeping woman had woken up and clung to him when he came in, calling him all kinds of strange names, and he had repeated a single word, over and over again, "mother," in a voice that seemed to have emerged straight from her—the girl's—heart.

From then on, the two of them—the girl and the woman—no longer had a free moment to continue their long conversations. Only in passing, by the communal pump, or by the laundry line, did they share a few terse words. It was easy to gather, though, that the girl was taking in everything she saw and heard.

She was amazed that the "half-dead" woman had come back to life with just a glance at her son. She brushed aside all her medicine bottles, put on her blonde wig, and became young again.

The old woman changed all the tablecloths and slipcovers by herself, and even started cooking again. She remembered exactly what kinds of food her son most enjoyed, and served them to him herself. When the girl saw how the mother stood before her son, gazing at him, like one blessing her Sabbath candles, or how he, manly as he was, would seat his mother in the rocking chair and rock her as they laughed together in one voice, her heart was filled with both joy and sadness.

The girl took her meals from that time on in the kitchen, in order to stay out of their way, and also because she was embarrassed to eat in front of them, even though he had simple habits and did not make any demands on her. He even stood up to help her when she had to lift something heavy. Once, when she was organizing his drawer in the bathroom, she cut herself on his razor, and he rushed over to bandage the wound. It amused her to see how frightened he was at the sight of the blood oozing slowly from her arm, as if she had never before been hurt in all the households (filled with knives no less sharp than his razor) where she had worked.

One of the many guests who came to call at the widow's during this period was Shifrin, the wealthy farmer from the neighboring settlement. On winter days he would park his car beside the front door, lift down a crate of oranges, and continue on his way down the boulevard. The girl, by order of her mistress, distributed the fruit to all the tenants—a full basket to each family, and only the bookkeeper's wife on the first floor, a native of the same settlement, knew that there was a link between this gift and the man's only daughter who was to inherit all of his wealth. An orange hue, remains of the fruit's peel, stained the garbage cans for days thereafter. The oranges were, after all, from among the finest.

When he had been doing this for some time, the car would stop and the man himself would come in carrying his box of oranges—tall, fit, and energetic, like one of the Sdoveskies the girl told her friend beside the laundry line. In his honor—the girl said—they made a fresh fruit salad, along with an omelet fixed according to the instructions of the doctor's wife on the second floor. By the time lunch was served, everything in the pantry and the ice box had found its way to the table—egg kichel, chopped herring, and chopped liver. He ate everything with gusto, leaving nothing on his plate. He spoke throughout the meal in a pressured way, as he demanded something from the old woman that she, apparently, couldn't give him, because she had to go get a handkerchief, into which she cried. Her son, who couldn't tolerate his mother's weeping, got up, left the courtyard, and leaned against the neighbor's fence.

The lemon and orange trees were in bloom then, in the garden, with their scents rising from them like a mist. He stood and watched until the two made up in the house, the table was set, and the guest washed his hands and sat down again.

The girl wanted to describe to her friend how they ate the special omelet afterward, but her mistress called her from the kitchen doorway to bring the linens in from the laundry line.

The days before Passover were burning hot. The fragrance of the citron trees hovered like white incense, and the purple clusters of lilacs on the nearby bush thickened and grew more abundant by the hour. New birds came from somewhere else and wove a sonorous tapestry in the hot, resonant air. Strawberries burned against the rich, deep background of cabbage leaves in the greengrocer's basket, and the women from the courtyard bought them: the bookkeeper's wife, the doctor's wife, and the girl's employer—the widow Pin.

They worked side by side "koshering" the house for the holiday. The girl had agreed to do the cleaning, and so she ran quickly with the necessary vessels to the communal pump while the engineer's wife—with her impeccable taste—looked on.

"Her hair waves like ripe sheaves of wheat," she said. "Her eyes are as blue as cornflowers, and what beautiful legs."

Indeed, the girl had very long, expressive, legs.

Around lunchtime, when she began washing the stairs, the "man from the settlement" appeared in the courtyard, her chaperone on the trip over, the one who called her "my wife" (even before their journey together had been decided upon). She grew sad whenever he stopped by, because just the sight of him made her remember the hour she had parted from her mother.

This time, he brought his brother who had not long before emigrated, like her, from her shtetl. He was a large young man with a childish face, and he stood shyly in the path. It was evident that the girl was embarrassed by her wet clothes and unkempt hair, and the man drew them together with a gesture, as if he wanted to introduce them. They were so adorable in their reluctance, the white-haired woman's young eyes filled with light, and she even considered whether the girl would change her "plan" to accommodate this new development. But the widow's son peeked out of the house just then:

His shirt sleeves were rolled up on his smooth arms, and his eyes, beneath his angry brow, burned like the cigarette in his mouth.

He is looking at the girl like a wolf at a sheep, said the engineer's wife, and with that, the light in the cook's eyes died out, and she became old, all at once.

Only four days remained until the holiday, and preparations in the courtyard intensified.

They washed the kitchen utensils at the pump, and every so often boys would ride up on their bicycles bringing deliveries of Matzo, other baked goods, or drinks. The strong scent of warm honey drifted out of the widow's kitchen one morning. They were making a beet jam with slivered almonds (according to the recipe of the bookkeeper's wife).

In the engineer's household, holiday preparations were not under way because they always went to their parents on the settlement, and the cook was already packing their suitcases. She did it listlessly because she didn't have the heart to leave, she said, and asked her mistress if she could stay behind. To the greengrocer, when she mourned with her much later, sitting on the bench beneath the poplar, she said that she already sensed something. Her heart had told her. But the engineer's wife wouldn't let her stay behind, under any circumstances, and so she packed her own suitcase as well. Before her departure, she found a moment here and a moment there to spend with the girl. She scrutinized her like one scrutinizes a piece of expensive fabric to make sure it hasn't been stained, and always found her perfectly happy: her face was cheerful, her beautiful hair was tidy, and she laughed.

On the last night, when she went out for a few minutes to meet her—to part from her—she was startled to see that something had happened to her—she had been "stained."

She sat with her on the bench under the poplar, as usual, but the girl was completely inaccessible—veiled, poisoned. Even so, her mouth was turned up, as if in a smile. Searching for something to talk about, the woman asked her how she planned to spend her free time during the holiday.

"He is buying me a ticket to see a play," the girl said.

"Who is?" the woman spluttered.

"Borik," she answered coldly.

After this there was nothing else to talk about. In her small room, later, the woman held her head in both hands, something she had never done before. She hasn't even written to her mother—she observed—she has forgotten her. And she has grown beautiful recently, blooming like the bushes and trees.

The next morning she departed—accompanied by the early song of the birds.

At the widow's house they also rose early. The old woman wanted to oversee the "koshering" of the stove by herself, while her son, as was his custom on Passover Eve when he was at home, helped exchange the Passover dishes for the non-Passover "leavened" ones.

With great agility, he climbed up and took the pots out of the storage closet high up, and the girl, a white apron tied around her waist (which only added to the light she exuded), brought the china down from the attic.

She carried it carefully, with a great sense of responsibility.

At moments, as she climbed down the steps, when she was most afraid of dropping her dishes, he would stretch his arms out to her, mischievously, as if about to gather her into himself, and his eyes, glowing like the cigarette in his mouth, made her feel ashamed. But downstairs, afterward, in the kitchen, he would be respectful and polite once again, and he would turn his head aside every time he exhaled smoke, because he knew that it made her dizzy.

At dusk, when he was already dressed for the holiday and smelled like cologne, he helped her set the table, and he brought her the pillows for the chair upon which he would recline during the seder. Afterward, as they read the Haggadah, he diligently filled her cup of wine and made her drink it down to the last drop.

As she served the food, she peeked out of the kitchen and saw the trees standing in a sort of holy silence, like the ones by her mother's house on evenings like this, and the houses surrounding them—as if they had rolled here from over there—were all illuminated. Her heart was suddenly gripped with grief, and she hurried to hide her face in the corner of her apron. He came over, as if to take something out to the table, and asked her why she was crying.

I don't know, it just happened—she explained, shamefaced, because she knew he couldn't stand weeping—it's because I'm so sad, so very sad.

Then he sang the funny songs at the end of the seder, using melodies from across the ocean. And after that, in the remaining light of the candles, he placed a book of photographs from far-away lands before her (after all, the friend with whom she spent most of her evenings wasn't here to entertain her), and leaned over her, breathing warmly on her bare neck. When she reached out to turn the page he asked to see the scar that remained from her encounter with his razor, and the sight of her own scar blurred before her, thickening and disappearing all at once.

She had lost her bearings like this also in childhood, when she walked over the rickety bridge on the count's property. The gardens surrounding her would intoxicate her with their delicate scents, even as dark and forbidding water swirled beneath her—and she would sway, helplessly unbalanced.

During the intermediate days of Passover she asked the greengrocer to tell her about Chava Rachel, the shoemaker's daughter who became a woman of means because of the man who fell in love with her. Because she had some leisure time during the holiday, the woman told the girl the story of the young servant girl who had become a moneyed matron in great detail:

She told her about what she served at meals, the types of servants she employed, about the shrubs at the entrance to her house trimmed to look like human figures, and the sound of the instruments always echoing in the rooms of her house, as if she hosted a perpetual wedding.

They scorned the greengrocer there, she said, but they liked her quality produce.

She dwelled, in her description, on the elderly mother, the shoemaker's wife, who now found pleasure in everything and whose life had been extended just from sheer enjoyment. From inside the kitchen, through the open doors, the greengrocer could see the old woman sometimes, stretched out on her bed with the high headboard, relaxing.

Finally, she asked the girl if she would join her for the last day of the holiday. The "man from the settlement" and his brother would be there, she told her joyfully and with a maternal glitter in her eye.

The girl promised to come, and on the last day of the holiday, a hot day, she set off, dressed for the occasion in her new summer dress with a thin, airy sweater draped over her shoulders. And every hot person she passed felt as if a refreshing breeze had washed over him.

Afterward, as darkness fell, she arrived at the bus stop, where she was told that there were no buses going south that evening, so she sat down on a bench to rest. She took a handkerchief out of her purse and fanned herself with it because of the heat, and even here passersby felt the refreshing coolness of her presence. Those who were born in that place regarded her with surprise and admiration, as if looking at a fine portrait.

Finally she stood up and began walking home.

Because her employers weren't at home when she left the house (they had gone out for holiday visits), she felt a distinct unease, which gradually turned into panic. She moved more quickly now, worried about something she could not identify. When she returned to the courtyard, the bookkeeper's wife threw her the keys from the first floor and told her that the widow and her son had just been picked up in a car and taken to the farmer's house on the settlement, where an engagement party was taking place.

The kind woman was about to tell her about the "arrangement" because she, having been born on the settlement, knew the family quite well. But the girl walked away from her before she could begin.

Like someone drowning who is looking for something to grasp hold of, she peeked for a moment at the apartment of the engineer where the blinds were drawn in all the windows. Afterward, she went into the kitchen, and by the dim light of a lantern, she gazed around the room, looking again for something to hold on to. In the end, she gave up and went into the bathroom with the lantern, and, finding the scar on the arm she had wounded a while back, she stabbed herself in the same spot with one of the razors that she took out of his drawer. The sobering pain that she caused herself overtook her memory of the earlier shock of pain and even blunted it.

Like the balance of a scale where first one side, and then the other, dips down—so too did her own sense of what she was doing move simultaneously, and equally, in two directions at once.

From among the linens her mother had sent with her for the day her "luck would change," she took out a towel and wrapped her wrist in it. Than she went outside and lay down on the bench outside, a place like the one on the ship where she had gone to be alone. There were only stars and night silence, and, like before, she felt herself floating in a gentle infinity, alone and severed forever like a leaf that has drifted off a tree.

The bookkeeper who returned home after midnight noticed her and called to his wife, and for a short time there was a hubbub in the courtyard.

They woke the doctor on the second floor and used the telephone. After that, the ambulance arrived, and the bench was emptied. And when the sun rose, order and quiet had been restored, as usual. Just beside the poplar, in the sand, there was a deep-red, bloody stain, like the first one that cried out to God when it was spilled on the earth. One of the tenants on the first floor came out and covered it up.

Translation: "In What World?" (1911)

I

Mother returns to the narrow room as if in search of something, and declares in a choked voice: "God help us, God help us . . ."

I rub my eyes with both hands and look over at the mountain of pillows and blankets in the other bed where Father lies ill. By the light of the lamp and the first glimmer of morning I see that his head is tilted backward and his eyes are wide open. His thin pale hands stretch before him, and as he gazes at me, his lips move . . .

"Father! Father!" I cry. Shaking with fear and love I jump out of bed, and reach out toward his darkening face. But Mother blocks my way.

"No, Racheli, let's go! We'll tear heaven with our voices! We'll prostrate ourselves before the Master of the Universe. Maybe he will have mercy . . ."

I am pulled into the shapeless chill of the morning, dragged behind my mother as my knees buckle and the soles of my feet search for firm ground. The tears are blinding.

Here is the house of study, with its holy stillness, its warm air infused with prayer and tears, Torah and mercy. Here is Father's desk, stacked high with books, beside the window; everything is covered in dust. Mother looks hungrily about her. And suddenly—God only knows what kind of idea has crept into her head—she stretches her hands toward the holy ark, lifts her eyes to heaven, and lets out a heart-rending cry:

"Torah, Torah! Beg God's mercy for this little child! Don't let her become an orphan."

The little child—that's me. Twelve years old, my father's only child.

I look down at my insubstantial body, my tattered clothes, my thin hands, and fall down, burying my face deep in the folds of my mother's dress, crying silently, voicelessly. My tears could melt the soul like wax in a flame.

Mother sits on a small stool, her head heavy, and her eyes red. The sky is growing dark, and the flame of a memorial candle dances on the windowsill.

Father has died.

Like the black wing of the angel of death, Mother's wide apron covers the mirror. Father's wine cup is on the shelf, alongside his ritual fringes and his silver watch, still ticking.

A neighbor stands near the stove, her arms crossed over her chest; what is the point of comforting us?

The grief is vast as an ocean. She just wants to explain that the little one won't, God forbid, be abandoned. We live among Jews, and a twelve-year-old girl can make her way—find a livelihood—even if it is just to rock a cradle in a wealthy household. Yes, she is talking about the orphan.

"The orphan," she says, and my eyes meet my mother's. How much sorrow and rage reside in that look? She shakes her head. Why won't she cry?

What to do? To go to her, and hold her head to my heart, stroking it with as much affection, as much compassion, as I can muster, and to say: "Don't worry, Mother, don't worry." Or maybe it would be better to stretch myself out on the ground, extending my arms and legs, to twitch like a slaughtered chicken and to scream out loud, to roar until the walls start to shake, until the ceiling, no—the whole house—collapses . . .

And the silence in the room is endless, even though Father's watch is still alive—ticking and ticking . . .

In the west the clouds drift away one by one, and a vivid red sky peeks out from beneath them. The windows of heaven are opened, and light pours down. Everything is illuminated. One pure spirit—Father's—hovers there. Can't it come down, reinhabit his body, return to us? On Shabbat he'll stroke my back, my forehead, my curls. The urn will bubble, and we will read together, sitting side by side . . . but the encroaching darkness casts a shadow, the heavens have grown dim, and the whole earth is wrapped in grief. Large, strange, black letters dance before my eyes:

". . . As the sun was about to set . . . a great dark dread descended upon him . . ." And an indistinct voice spoke out from the darkness: "Know that your children will be strangers in a strange land, and they will be enslaved and oppressed . . ."[2] And as if from a deep abyss the image of Abraham, our father, rises before my eyes—with his long, white beard, and his kind, worried face: "And they will be enslaved and oppressed . . ." Four hundred years of clay and bricks, beatings and whippings, endless labor until the slaves collapse, dead, into their deep dark graves. Father lies in one of those graves, wrapped in a *kittel* and a *tallis*.[3]

"Where is the orphan girl?"

The tearing of the mourners' garments . . . my dress is cut by a knife—kkkkrrrr.[4]

Hey! The knife punctures my chest, and tears open my heart . . .

"*Yisgadal ve-Yiskadash sheme Rabah . . .* "[5]

The shadows of the praying congregants sway, and my mother sits and cries in a corner. It seems to me that she can't possibly cry any more. She wails in a thin, inaudible voice so as not to disturb the congregation.

II

Mother is bent over as if carrying a heavy load, her back hunched beneath her blouse; her face is clouded over, and her forehead is lined.

"Mother!"

Instead of answering, she inclines her head, and looks out the window into the courtyard—"What's out there?"

Empty barrels are sunken into the snow, the wood shed is closed tight, angrily. Liza, the neighbor's daughter—a gymnasium student— sits on a small sled. She studies me for a moment, sticks her tongue out at me—as she always does—and goes back to sliding down a small hill of snow. I retreat to the corner between the bed and the stove with my Bible and throw myself into my reading. What could I possibly have to say to this well-dressed, stuck-up girl? I'm leaving this courtyard soon in any case—leaving the city altogether . . . I'll go far, far away to that big build-ing where the whistle blows, and travel through fields, hills and valleys, station after station—until I arrive in the big city with its tall buildings, streets, markets, and the gymnasium itself.

"Who are you, child? What do you want?"

"Me? I want to learn, to become educated, to become independent and support my mother."

"What about tuition?"

"Tuition? I'll help the teacher—lighting the stove, bringing water from the well, washing the floors—in exchange for lessons."

"Really? All right, then . . . sit here on the bench. Here are some books and a pad of paper. You say you have your own pencil? Good. Sit down and study."

The other students stare at me—my clothes are torn, my cheeks are hollow. But, no matter . . . the bell rings. The teacher—tall, handsome, gentle, with kind eyes asks:

"Rachel? Is there a Rachel here?"

My voice rings out clear and strong. Again, everyone stares—but this time in awe.

"Who is she?"

"Where did she come from?"

"How does she know so much?"

Silence . . . the teacher stands up, folds his hands behind his back, and walks through the aisles right up to me:

"You seem on track to go straight to the head of the class."

The head of the gymnasium class! My suffering, my hunger, my thirst, all fade into the ancient past . . .

Months pass; years go by. Two long braids hang down my back, and four languages dance on my tongue. As I walk, the hem of my skirt rus-tles; my hat is elegantly tilted.

"Rachel . . . Miss Rachel . . . Professor Rachel . . ."

In the morning I sit in my chair with my grade book open in front of me. How the little girls—my students—adore me! In the afternoon I carry numerous notebooks in my briefcase tucked under my arm. I hold the hem of my skirt in my hand, and my shoes squeak on the snow.

Creak . . . the door opens, and I am greeted by a pleasant warmth infused with the scent of delicious foods and my mother's voice. We sit down together and eat with pleasure:

"My darling daughter, the light of my life, it is because of you that I can now live at ease in such luxury—because of you . . ."

"Don't, Mother! I don't need your thanks . . . Who is that at the door?"

"Liza?! The schoolgirl who lived in the same courtyard as us many years ago?"

"Good heavens, how she's aged!"

"Pardon me . . ."

"Don't apologize! You aren't disturbing us at all, dear girl . . ."

She has one request for me. She needs my help . . .

"My help? I'm at your service . . . whatever you need, whatever you need . . ."

It would be better if I didn't remind her about how she used to stick her tongue out at me, not a word about that tongue . . .

The wind howls, and a wet chill permeates the room. We don't have even a single piece of straw to light the stove . . .

Our walls are bare. Only the corners are decorated—in spider webs. The furniture has disappeared. Even the copper pots are no longer on the shelf. My mother stands by the window, cutting fabric and biting her lower lip. Cutting is difficult for her, as if the fabric were hard as sheet iron.

"In wealthy households," she says to me, "the cook changes her apron several times a day. She wears one in the kitchen while she cooks and one to serve the tea in the dining room . . ."

"So?"

There are separate rooms for every single family member and employee, and even the cook has her own special room with a bed and a table. If she, the cook, has a child, for example, the child can live with her there . . .

And suddenly—her hands idle and drift down to the windowsill. The fabric and the scissors fall to the floor:

"Daughter, what would you say if we were to became employees in someone else's house?"

And she groans, bursting into sudden tears. She can't lie to me any longer . . . she can't. "We aren't going to relatives—we don't have any relatives, any acquaintances, no one, no one . . ."

Two neighbors help us pack the remnants of our worldly possessions into a basket and wrap me in my tattered coat.

"There, there . . . you'll live to walk her to the marriage canopy, God willing! Don't give in to your despair. If you kiss the mezuzah three times, God will come to your aid . . ."[6]

I look at our room for the last time: desolation and gloom. It seems to me that the black square on the back wall, a reminder of the destroyed temple, calls out in a small voice:

"Peace be with you!"

"Go in peace."

And a cold wind scatters the words to the winds.

Where are we going?

New streets, strange people who don't know me and don't even look at me, a pushing and shoving on the sidewalks—and I am posessed by a strange fear . . .

"Are you cold, my daughter?"

"Cold? No!"

The door of a large building opens up, and a throng of children armed with backpacks and briefcases pours out. They are all dressed in warm coats, their faces joyful, their eyes smiling—gymnasium students. Even Liza is here. She looks at me for a moment and then turns her face away. She won't stick her tongue out at me now, no . . . she bends toward another girl, shorter than her, with curly hair, whispers two or three words to her silently, and they both look at me and laugh.

Afterward, when we have arrived in the kitchen of the big strange house, mother is dressed in her new apron, and she has fed the wood into the stove, I see that little girl again, with her curly hair and her laughing eyes. She opens the door to the kitchen, looks at my mother, and afterward at me, and tries to flee. But her mother, our mistress, who is standing with us in the kitchen just then, places her hand on the girl's head and says,

"Don't be afraid, Lola, my darling. It's just the new servant's daughter ..."

"And she knows the Bible and all kinds of other books by heart," says my mother in friendship and good spirits as she places the frying pan on the stove. When she looks at the woman's face, however, she stops speaking abruptly.

The woman tells her that she should kindly keep in mind that we aren't really needed around here. We wouldn't be here if her mother-in-law had not insisted on a "kosher" cook for her meals.

The mother-in-law herself comes in. She is wrinkled and heavy and dressed in silks, with a black wig on her head. Expensive earrings dangle from her ears, and a precious necklace glistens on her throat.

"Don't mix the towels. The dairy pots are hung over here on the wall by themselves."

And her tongue clangs like the clapper of a bell, and saliva flies from her mouth as she speaks, as if she is spitting teeth. As she turns to go, she notices me:

"We don't need children getting in the way around here. Make sure she stays in her corner, cook!"

And my mother stirs the boiling soup in the pot, lifts up her apron, and buries her face in it ...

Silence. Outside, the sky is growing dark, and dusk overtakes the room. Cutlets sizzle on the stove, and the air is filled with the smell of hot oil.

Where should I go? Any minute that woman with the string of pearls and the showers of spit is liable to come through the door ... maybe I should go into that cabinet over there, beside the window, to curl up and wait?

An hour later I am sitting in a small, freezing attic room without a candle, shivering with my eyes closed, trying to imagine myself into another

place . . . a pleasant drawing room with flowers in crystal vases and thick rugs. Servants move about the soft couch upon which I lay.

"Rachel, Rachel, do you remember those terrible days when you were stuck in a dark room, hungry and thirsty and bitter and abandoned, and I, your mother, was in the kitchen with a face as black as the pot in which I cooked?"

There, in that strange house with those big glass windows and the crotchety mistress? Why would you want to remember that, dear mother? Wouldn't it be nicer to play something on the piano?

So I sit on the piano stool, and my fingers fly over the keys. A pleasant melody fills up the room, weeping for the father who cannot witness our pleasure, weeping but also comforting, spilling outside, outside . . . and in the garden groups of people gather about to listen, their hearts melting with pleasure:

"How she plays, oh, how she plays!"

From above, a young man looks out the second-story window opposite the house, a pale young man with a black shock of hair, and he feasts his eyes on me. I don't even know his name.

III

Through the window of our attic room we can see a small house, surrounded by snow, at the end of the block. This house has one small window out of which gazes the pale, pretty face of a thin boy. When I pass the window, I see the boy reading. Sometimes I see him sitting over his books, with his eyes wide open, looking out the window, lost in his thoughts, his hands motionless. His black hair peeks out from his cap, and he thinks and thinks. About what? About whom? Who is he?

When the sun sets, he usually leaves his spot. For a few moments he disappears into the darkness of the room, and afterward he appears outside wrapped in a thin coat, with books and notebooks tucked under his arm. Sometimes the door opens after him, and a woman cries out:

"David, David!" When she catches up to him, she unwraps the kerchief from around her own neck, folds it up and tucks it around the boy's neck inside his coat—despite his vociferous resistance. With remonstrations of love and devotion, she calms him down and sends him on his way. She must be his mother.

In the evening, when the candle is lit, they draw their curtains over their small window, and I am left inside my room, alone. Sounds and smells from the kitchen drift upward as hot foods bubble on the stove, and Mother bustles about, busy since early morning.

I put on my torn coat and go quietly outside, swallowed into the crowd of people on the sidewalk. Here, in between the tall buildings with the large windows, among the mass of well-dressed city folks, I seem to myself so small and weak—one light push, one breath, and I will fall, sprawling. No one will come to my aid; no one will stretch out his hand. What do they owe me? And why am I even walking around here? Where are my legs taking me? There are beautiful things in all the windows, but the wind blows viciously, cutting into my flesh, blowing my hair about. The men hold onto their collars, bracing themselves. The women bury their hands in their muffs to warm them as the streets ring with their laughter. And the door of the sausage shop opens and closes and opens again—emitting the hot spicy scent of smoked meat, roast geese, and pickles. I am cold and hungry. "David, David ..." Am I hearing her voice? But the door of the house is closed now, and our block is empty, completely empty.

I go back to our room; there is Mother, exhausted and spent, her face red from the heat and her eyes wet:

"You are practically frozen. Where were you? It's unseemly to wander the streets alone. I couldn't even save you a spoonful of hot food this time ..."

Those bits of food that Mother hides in her apron for me make me gag.

And when we lay in our rickety bed, I bury my face in my mother's breast and inhale the smell of onions and oil that she exudes. My mother's smell has changed ...

"Are you already asleep, Mama?"

No, she can't fall asleep. She lies for hours with her eyes wide open, thinking. ... and in the morning I see that her hair has grown even whiter.

The morning light shines through our window, and she is already on her feet. She is holding my only, threadbare, dress, turning it over and over and shaking her head:

"It can't be fixed anymore. . . . It can't be fixed."

In the afternoon my mother comes in with a strange gleam in her eye. She has managed to obtain a practically new linen dress for free. "Tonight they are celebrating Lola's birthday, and she has invited you. . . . What? You don't want to go? They'll play the piano, and there will be dancing. Do you see how the buttons sparkle on this dress? It even has beautiful button loops."

That evening, I am tempted by the sounds of the piano and the violin, and I go into the room where the electric lights illuminate all the beautiful china and the cheerful guests. I sit in a corner with my eyes on the ground. Lola's friends walk around on the soft carpets. They joke around, talk and laugh out loud. Just as long as no one sees me. . . . But Fetya, Lola's brother, takes an orange from the table and offers it to me.

"Why are you embarrassed, little girl?"

How does he know that I'm embarrassed? I'm too embarrassed even to flee. If only my mother would call me so that I could leave. But she is busy setting the tables. They are preparing to go to dinner. Now is my chance to slip out . . . but Mother calls me to help her set the table, and I run into Liza—the one who used to live next door. She stares directly at me as she narrows her eyes, and suddenly she turns to Lola, claps her hands, and shouts with pleasure:

"Lolka! Isn't that your summer dress! You gave your summer dress to the cook's daughter!?"

The cup I am holding slips out of my hand and shatters. I flee.

An hour later my mother comes into the dark room with a candle in her hand and finds me stretched out on the floor in my nightgown, shivering. And the dress? It is also on the floor. My mother picks it up and finds that it has been reduced to tattered and torn strips of fabric. My mother explodes . . .

"What have you done! Oh, what have you done, you thief!"

"I tore it because I wanted to!"

And my mother hits me . . . slaps my cheek, swats at my arms, pinches me, and shrieks in a choked voice until she bursts into tears and falls upon me, gathering me into herself, hugging me, her tears wetting my hair . . .

But a choking bitterness has taken shape within me:

"What am I doing here with this decrepit, skinny woman?"

We go to sleep. And I am leaving, fleeing, wandering outdoors, moving naked and barefoot, hungry and thirsty, through throngs of people in the marketplace.

IV

It is morning. I stand by the gate and look out onto the alley. The children are making snow creatures. Suddenly, behind me, I hear the sound of light, quick footsteps—David passes by, and then he turns to me and says:

"Do you live here in this attic?"

"My mother . . ."

"I see you sometimes. You come back late at night. Don't you have any books to read?"

"Just a Bible. And you?"

"Do you read Hebrew?"

"Father taught me."

"My mother says she knows your mother. She also knew your father. You used to live on the same street as the butcher, didn't you?"

That evening as I stand before the small mirror brushing my hair, I hear, again, the light, quick sound of his footsteps. This time they are on the stairs, and they are followed by a knock on the door.

"Who's there?"

"It's me. David."

He comes in, takes off his hat, and runs his hand through his hair.

"So . . ."

What can I say to him? I push the comb and the mirror aside, sit down, and say, "Sit."

"Is your name Rachel?"

"Rachel."

"Do you know who Rachel was?"

"The one buried on the way to Efrat?" [7]

"Have you seen a picture of the grave? If you come over I'll show you."

He takes a small book out of his pocket. "Do you want to read? I can bring you more Hebrew books, if you want . . ."

"I read this with my father once, but I can read it again. This is a story about life in the Land of Israel."

"Did you know that I am about to go there?"

"Where?"

"To the Land of Israel . . . can you believe it? I'm preparing to go. First I plan to study agronomy, then I will emigrate to work the soil. . . . I have an uncle in Petah Tikva . . . Do you know what Petah Tikva is? It's a settlement not far from Jaffa. Do you know where Jaffa is?"[8]

"Yes! Didn't Jonah throw himself off the ship there and get swallowed by the fish?"

My friend's cheeks have grown flushed, and he speaks excitedly . . .

"Listen to this—my cousin once rode on a donkey from Petah Tikva to Jaffa without a saddle, holding only a small switch in her hand . . . Come to our house, and you'll see the picture! She is so brave!"

My mother comes in, and David stands up with his hat in his hand.

"Stay longer, David," she says.

"No, I have to go to class! Good-bye!"

He leaves, and my mother sits on the edge of the bed, silent and thoughtful. I want to ask her about David and his mother, but she starts talking about something entirely different.

"I swear to God I can't take it anymore. From dawn until midnight hustle-bustle, stand, cook, fry, polish, scrub, serve, and cook again. My legs are swollen, my bones are broken—I have no more strength" . . . and her lips tremble and twist—a pathetic, broken, and depressed mother.

I offer her the bed, help her to take off her clothes, lay her down, and cover her with a blanket . . . she shudders, curls up, and closes her eyes. Her face is pale . . . so pale.

I sit down to read the book David brought me, but I can't . . . If only the good times I have desired for so long would come and my mother could stop working . . . I wouldn't let her lift even her little finger . . . like a queen sitting on a soft chaise longue wrapped in silks, bejeweled, and with a gold chain around her neck.

"Will you drink a cup of hot chocolate, Mama?"

"Chocolate? No."

"Then perhaps you would prefer some fried cherries?"

"No, my darling."

"Perhaps an orange dusted with sugar?"

And I ring the bell. The maid appears in the doorway:

"An orange with sugar."

"Right away, miss. But there is a gentleman waiting in the hallway. Can I let him in?"

A young man dressed in black enters.

"My God! It's David!"

"Just so, just so, Racheli. You have also grown, become beautiful. And your braids. . . . How is your mother? Ah yes, here she is."

"Let's sit down. Or maybe we should go out for a stroll in the garden? It is so pleasant to walk among the flowerbeds in the evening."

"Oh, I haven't enough time. I was just wondering if you would care to join me on my journey over there, to our land . . ."

He's going back to the Land of Israel?

"What a question!"

He has orchards and vineyards there, fields of wheat and a vegetable garden. . . . He has just returned to take me back. . . .

"So you'll come? Yes? Wonderful! Farewell until tomorrow."

"Farewell . . ."

Should I curtsey to him? No. I will stand, dignified, and offer him my hand.

And I take the small mirror, hang it on the wall, and stand up to it on my tiptoes, stretching out my right arm.

"Farewell, David!"

My mother, in the bed, turns over, opens her eyes, and looks at me in surprise.

David tells me a story about a prince who fell in love with the daughter of his nursemaid. He would visit with her every day, and when the king found out about this, he exiled his son from the palace and locked the nursemaid and her daughter in a dark and sinister tower. What did the prince do? He withdrew to his house of prayer, contemplated his bitterness, wept and cried for three days and three nights that there be a miracle and he could grow wings. On the third day, in the evening, at the hour of mercy, the grace of God touched him, and his wish was fulfilled—two large wings, white as snow, suddenly grew on his back. That night he rose up and flew between the heavens and the earth—passing over rivers and oceans, cities and states—and his face and his heart were directed toward the high tower. He arrived there and stood at the window knocking with his finger—tap-tap.

"Who's there?"

"Little girl, my little girl, how your face shines!"

"My light is from the glow of your own face, my master the prince."

"Little girl, my little girl, what have you been doing this whole time?"

"I have been pulling my hair out, strand by strand, and have been weaving them into a *tallis* bag for you, my master, the prince."

"And what else have you done, my beautiful one?"

"I have been spinning fine delicate threads and have been weaving them, day and night, into a light-blue wedding canopy for us, my master the prince."

Immediately the prince embraced his lover and spread his radiant wings. He flapped them once or twice, and the two of them were lifted together between heaven and earth, soaring and flying like heavenly angels until they landed on a large island that was like a garden inside the ocean. The prince intertwined the branches of a tree like a cradle, put his young woman inside it, and left.

"My beautiful young man, what are you doing?"

"I am collecting fine stones to build a palace for you."

"And what else are you doing?"

"I am hunting for the birds and animals I need to make a fine banquet in your honor."

And here I interrupt him: "And her mother, the nursemaid, David?"

"The nursemaid? The prince flew back and rescued her and settled her in the palace on a golden throne with silk pillows beneath her feet and golden tables laid before her. The prince and his bride served her themselves!"

"And the food they serve her—is it good?"

"Plump and juicy geese . . . food fit for a prince . . ."

After that Sabbath, when I saw David, I gave him a small *tefillin* bag that I had embroidered myself.[9]

At nightfall our attic room is cast in shadows, I throw my arms around my mother, kissing her and asking about the boy and his mother in the small house.

David, says my mother, is a genius. She remembers him as a small child with so many talents. He is just like his father, may he rest in peace.

"And what else do you know, Mother?"

"For God's sake, why are you smothering me with your hugs and kisses? Have you gone mad?"

V

David is fifteen years old: "The spitting image of his father," says his mother, "and he is already supporting us with private lessons . . . 'Go buy milk, Mother, and drink it. I'll pay the milkman.' With his teaching salary he wants to pay for it!" The wrinkles on her face smile together with her small, kind eyes:

"Do you see the books on the shelf? They are all his, bought with his own money. Also his notebooks—he writes quite a bit. He loves writing."

In a short time the house is filled with the vapors and scents of cooking and the cold winter air that David brings in from outside. His mother's work supplies—cigarette papers and packages of tobacco over which his mother sits stooped all day long, are pushed aside. She spreads a white cloth on the table, the copper utensils gleam, and the pickles give off a delicious fragrance.

"This time you cannot refuse. You must sit down and eat with us. We'll all eat from the same plate."

While David tells me about the new book he has taken out of the library, the old woman separates out hunks of meat from potatoes and pushes them over to us.

The food is delicious. And what will David's mother eat? Nothing

. . . Nevertheless, she recites the "Grace after Meals" with a slight flush creeping over her wrinkles, straightens and secures the knot of her kerchief on the nape of her neck, and returns to her work with a sense of well-being . . . labor does not appreciate idleness, she always says.

Embers are still burning in the stove, and the warmth of the room caresses the face and bathes the body in a pleasant, lazy way. David sits beside me on the couch, and tells me about his uncle in the Land of Israel (a land where there is no winter). This uncle was one of the early pioneers. He has already been there for twenty-five years. His grandfather, the uncle's father, was wealthy, landed, and there, above the bureau, hangs his picture. He wept like a baby when my uncle left on his journey. His old mother threw herself down on the ground in the front doorway and held her hands out to him: "Kill me instead! Don't leave me . . ."[10] He was the child of her old age. And what did he do? He stepped over her and left. His parents didn't send a penny to him over there, and he had many periods of hunger and thirst, homelessness and hard labor, fevers and glaucoma. And he—if only you could read his letters—they're over there in the bureau mixed together with Father's letters—"We will triumph," he wrote.

He speaks—David—intermittently and shivering slightly, looking over at the table where his mother sits. He lowers his voice and says: "Look, she's fallen asleep over her cigarettes. If we wake her, she'll go back to work. It would be better if we left."

We leave quietly, and David says: "My poor mother. She hasn't worked out in the open air in years. She has grown hunched and asthmatic."

"Are you cold?" he asks outside.

"And you?"

His right hand clutches my arm, and I cling to his sleeve.

"Watch out for that pile of snow."

"Careful, David, the ice is slippery."

We return from our stroll invigorated by the cold air and the warm conversation.

On the steps he takes my hand, squeezes it, and says: "Good night, Racheli!"

I sit in our freezing room for a long time without going to sleep. "Good night, Racheli." A special voice.

VI

Mother has been watching me carefully, and she looks worried. She brings me a bowl of soup from the kitchen and stands over me, begging me to eat it.

"Your face is getting thinner and thinner every day. . . . What's the matter? What's the matter?"

I escape her glance, go to the window, and open my French textbook.

There, beneath us, the trees are blooming, and the flowerbeds have burst into wild color. Fetya and Lola romp around together, laughing and shrieking. Lola holds onto her light summer dress, sits down on the swing. One push and the ribbons woven into her curls soar into the air, bright like the wings of a dove.

"Fetya, Fetya, careful!"

She flies up between the trees.

And there, beyond the garden, the little house with the worn-out roof and its single, dark, window:

"Be well, Rachel . . ."

It happened only a month earlier. A carriage stood in the middle of the block surrounded by his possessions. David fell on his mother's neck and kissed her:

"Don't cry, Mother, don't cry. . . . We'll see each other again soon, soon . . ."

He turned to me, held out his hand, and said:

"Be well, Rachel."

And nothing else. How many nights in the winter and the spring did we sit and talk, how many times did he bring me into his imaginary world? And he always said we would be together. We would learn together, travel to the Land of Israel together, and now—"Be well"—and he departed on his own. His uncle had sent for him.

Days pass and become weeks; weeks become a month. David has certainly arrived by now and is studying at the Hebrew Gymnasium—with his black curls and gentle eyes:

"Does anyone have an extra notebook? I forgot to bring my math notebook . . ."

"A notebook? Yes, I have an extra one . . ."

Thus says his cousin, dark haired and lovely, fifteen years old, just like him . . . and I start to pace the room with my book open in my hand. I know that it's ridiculous to waste my time on fantasies. What do I care about David and his cousin? What will happen to my French lessons?

"Nous parlons, vous parlez, ils parlent."

"To study, to study, to study. I will know French perfectly, and I'll also learn German and English. I will become educated, and I will master many languages . . . Here I am dressed all in black, my face pale and serious, and I stand on a stage, taller than any person in the audience, my voice is strong and pleasant, and I speak clearly and coherently in words that penetrate the hearts of the thousands of people standing before me, silent and amazed:

"Who is she?"

"The daughter of some teacher, I knew her father, he taught two or three boys for very little money . . . when her father died and her mother worked as a servant in a wealthy household, she rattled around in a freezing attic, hungry and dressed in rags—without parents and without teacher. But look what a little talent can do!"

And in the corner stands one man who can't keep his eyes off me. A young man with a beard and dark eyes—David.

I ask about his cousin. "She left the Land of Israel and married an Egyptian man . . ." If I would like, he can accompany me home, that is, back to my hotel . . .

And so, *"Nous parlons, vous parlez, ils parlent."*

Maybe it would be good for me to go outside for a moment, to breathe some fresh air. Just a little . . . to wrap myself in Mother's sweater and to stand at the end of the block . . .

The western clouds are illuminated with the red setting sun, and the trees in the garden stand silently, wrapped in shadows. The window of the small house is also shrouded in darkness, and inside it, beside the table, sits the old woman, cutting bits of paper and making cigarette wrappers. I'll go in and ask if David has left any books behind . . .

No! I might burst into tears . . . I am so terribly lonely.

VII

The broad heavens, a great ocean buffeted by waves, the ship sails . . . days and nights of travel, dizziness and nausea. But we are getting closer, closer to the port of Haifa. Just a bit longer. Here, we see the coast and its buildings . . . the final whistle of the boat . . . We are rocked in the waves, and David stands waiting, a distance away. The sun shines on him, and he is tall and strong—he waves his white handkerchief and smiles at me:

"Rachel, Rachel!" he cries out in a Sephardic accent . . . [11]

A small settlement. Evening. The skies are pure and deep. Children play in the paths, and the sound of Hebrew speech reverberates. Hebrew songs—mournful—can be heard in the vineyards, and I sit in the garden in front of my room, searching: David hasn't been here since morning. I understand that he doesn't have a lot of spare time, but isn't it vacation? I'll go try to find him . . . and here I am on the edge of the settlement, the window of his room is illuminated, and the curtain is slightly open. I go to him on tiptoe and see that he is lying prone in bed. His face is pale, and his eyes are halfway closed.

"David, are you sick? What's wrong?"

"Rachel? I waited for you all day, all day . . ."

"You're burning up, David! Here, I'll wet my kerchief and lay it on your forehead before I call the doctor . . ."

"Don't be silly, Racheli, just sit here beside me and I'll feel better. I just have a slight fever."

Dreams, dreams, dreams.

And when I awake, everything is so tiresome. I am broken and depressed, walking around the hospital, gazing at the closed doors:

Mother has been in there for a whole week, on one of the beds, her face burning, her eyes closed. From day to day her breathing becomes more labored, and her face changes from hour to hour.

"Mother, Mother, where will I go?"

Like Father on the night he died, she also throws her head back and stretches out her hands when I walk into the room. And when visiting hours are over, the nurse shows me to the door. It closes behind me, and I stand outside . . .

The bells at the top of the church ring in a sad, crass cadence. Ding, Dong, Ding . . . God help us, by this time tomorrow I may be walking behind her bier. And the nurses will hold me back, not allowing me to fall into the grave, into the arms of my mother.

"The orphan . . ."

One by one the mourners will go home, and I will be left alone in the din of evening sounds. And who will hold me? Who will share in my sorrow? Mother has died, and in the streets well-dressed strangers pass by, speaking, laughing, as if the world is running as it should and my mother is not buried in a dark grave, pale, cold, and dirty . . .

I press my head against the wall and bite my lips—how can I think this way?

In the meantime, night comes. A cold wind blows from the north and whips my hair up. The stores close one after the other, and the streets empty out. The whistle of the policeman sounds, and he comes over to me, tall and armed:

"Go home, little girl, you can't be out here alone at night."

Home.

I go into the small house without a greeting and with my head down. David's mother startles and stands up beside her packages of tobacco and her cigarette papers.

"What's happening over at the hospital?"

I collapse onto the couch, completely depleted.

I am creeping like a worm in a dark and narrow tunnel. There is no exit, and I am crushed, crushed, choked. . . . And I am carried by a cacophony of voices that are closing in on me: Who has died? Who has died? And who has thrown me into the river? A wide river with green banks and warm waves that wash over me, rinsing me, and I float on them. But I stop . . .

David's mother is speaking to me, and I can't understand her words until she says: "I received a letter from David, and he asked about you . . . Drink some milk, my darling." And I drink silently . . .

And Mother, Mother, where is she?

Why do you ask? She died during the time that I was laid up with a fever on the couch. But I knew it would happen that way . . .

VIII

Winter comes again, stormy, blinding, rainy days, mixed in with snow . . . and the rains stop, making way for blizzards. Snow covers the streets and the marketplace, the fields outside the city, and Mother's and Father's graves in the great cemetery. And David's mother sits bent over, armed with the materials of her trade, cutting paper into small strips, making tubes, and stuffing them with tobacco. And I sit and help her. We work together night and day; labor does not appreciate idleness.

Two months have passed without a letter or any other sign of David . . . and suddenly the old woman gets up and pulls a creased letter out of her prayer book, spreading it in front of me.

"Read it again, my daughter."

How many times have I read this letter? I read, and the old woman recites the words along with me. She knows the letter by heart:

"My dearest Mother," he writes, "here in our pleasant warm land you will rest from your labors . . . you will forget your suffering . . . you will become young again, believe me . . . Rachel will also find a job. She too will come . . ."

And the last coals are burning, and hissing in the stove, quietly, quietly. The woman returns to her work. The scissors squeak; labor does not appreciate idleness, and I join her . . .

Silence. The wind outside knocks on the door of the house . . . and images dance before my eyes: a settlement and orchards . . . I am picking giant oranges . . . David at the head of the hill stands on the ruins of an ancient castle, gazing at the flock of sheep spread throughout the valley . . .

"Why are you standing up suddenly, my daughter?" The old woman asks. "In what world are you?"

My God, my God! "In what world am I, and in what world will I be?"

Dvora Baron — A Bibliography of Primary and Secondary Works

Dvora Baron's Published Books

All of Baron's books, published both during her lifetime and posthumously, are listed here in chronological order, including small chapbooks, translations, and edited volumes. Individual Hebrew and Yiddish stories published early in Baron's career in periodicals but not in her collected works were edited and published in 1988 in book form by Nurit Govrin and Avner Holtzman, as enumerated below.

Liska: A Sketch [ליסקה : רשימה]. Odessa: Ahiasaf, 1911.

In What World? [ליסקה : רשימה]. New York: Bene ha-Am, 1917.

Stories [ספורים]. Tel Aviv: Davar, 1927.

> בראשית, גניזה, היום הראשון, חלומות, מצולה, בר אוז, עגונה, נכדים, בימות
> הסתיו, הניך, חתונה, על יד החלון, גרעינים, שומן, עגמת נפש, שפרה, טורקים,
> קצו של סנדר זיו

> (In the Beginning, Burying the Books, The First Day, Dreams, Depths, Duck, Abandoned Wife, Grandchildren, In the Fall, Henikh, Wedding, Beside the Window, Seeds, Fat, Distress, Shifrah, Turks, The End of Sender Ziv).

Burying the Books [גניזה]. Tel Aviv: Omanut, 1930.

Trifles [קטנות]. Tel Aviv: Omanut, 1933.

קטנות, רשע, משפחה

(Trifles, Evil, Family).

What Has Been [מה שהיה]. Tel Aviv: Davar, 1939.

בראשית, גניזה, היום הראשון, קטנות, חלומות, משפחה, רשע, מצולה, בר-אווז,
עגונה, נכדים, בימות הסתיו, על יד החלון, הניך, חתונה, גרעינים, שומן, עגמת
נפש, שפרה, תורכים, גלגולים, מה שהיה

(In the Beginning, Burying the Books, The First Day, Trifles, Dreams,
Family, Evil, Depths, Duck, Deserted Wife, Grandchildren, In the Fall, Be-
side the Window, Henikh, Wedding, Seeds, Fat, Distress, Shifrah, Turks,
Transformations, What Has Been).

For the Time Being [לעת עתה]. Tel Aviv: Am Oved, 1943.

דרך קוצים, כריתות, לעת עתה

(The Way of Thorns, Divorce, For the Time Being).

From There [משם]. Tel Aviv: Am Oved, 1946.

היום הראשון, גניזה, משפחה, דרך קוצים, הבת השנואה, עם הספר, משורר,
האמן, ריחשי לב, הבית, שעורים

(The First Day, Burying the Books, Family, The Way of Thorns, The Hated
Daughter, People of the Book, Poet, The Artist, Heart Murmurs, The
House, Lessons).

The Bricklayer [הלבן]. Tel Aviv: Am Oved, 1947.

פראדל, הלבן

(Fradel, The Bricklayer).

Sunbeams [שברירים]. Tel Aviv: Am Oved, 1949.

איש התוכחה, שברירים, פראדל, בית הקיץ, הלבן, תרמית, מתמיד, אמריקה,
זיוה, יום אחד של רמי, בעול, בני קדר

(The Reprimand Man, Sunbeams, Fradel, Summerhouse, The Bricklayer,
Deception, Since Forever, America, Ziva, A Day in Rami's Life, In the Yoke,
People of Kedar).

Tales [פרשיות]. Jerusalem: Mosad Bialik, 1951. Reprints, 1953, 1968, and
2000.

משפחה, קטנות, חלומות, דרך קוצים, פראדל, שברירים, מה שהיה, כריתות, איש
התוכחה, מסע, תרמית, בית קיץ, בכי, השעון, הלבן, בראשית, גניזה, היום
הראשון, רשע, מצולה, בר אוז, עגונה, נכדים, בשעת שממון, על יד החלון, הניד,
חתונה, עגמת נפש, שומן, גרעינים, שפרה, גלגולים, תורכים, בני-קדר, מתמיד,
אמריקה, לעת עתה, זיוה, יום אחד של רמי, בעול, כעלה נדף, הרמוניה, בלב הכרך

(Family, Trifles, Dreams, The Way of Thorns, Fradel, Sunbeams, What
Has Been, Divorce, Reprimand Man, A Journey, Deception, Summer
House, Weeping, The Watch, The Bricklayer, In the Beginning, Burying
the Books, The First Day, Evil, Depths, Duck, Abandoned Wife, Grand-
children, Depression, By the Window, Henikh, Wedding, Distress, Fat,
Seeds, Shifra, Transformation, Turks, People of Kedar, Since Forever,
America, For the Time Being, Ziva, A Day in Rami's Life, In the Yoke, As a
Driven Leaf, Harmony, In the Heart of the City).

Links [חוליות]. Tel Aviv: Am Oved, 1952.

כריתות, חלומות, תרמית, הלבן, מסע, שברירים, האמן, מדנים,אימים

(Divorce, Dreams, Deception, The Bricklayer, A Journey, Sunbeams, People of the Book, The Artist, Quarrel, Threats).

Since Yesterday [מאמש]. Tel Aviv: Am Oved, 1955.

מאמש, בצרור החיים, באור חרדות, כמו שהוא

(Since Yesterday, The Circle of Life, In Trembling Light, As He Is).

The Exiles [הגולים]. Tel Aviv: Am Oved, 1970.

מאמש, לעת עתה

(Since Yesterday, For the Time Being).

The Thorny Path and Other Stories. Translated by Joseph Shachter. Edited by Itzhak Hanoch. Jerusalem: Israel Universities Press, 1969.

(Family, Trifles, A Day in Rami's Life, What Has Been, Ziva, Wickedness, The Thorny Path, In the Bond of Life).

A Collection of Stories [ילקוט סיפורים]. Edited by Rivka Gorfein. Tel Aviv: Yahdav, 1969. Reprints, 1972, 1973, and 1981.

משפחה, פראדל, כריתות, היום הראשון, גניזה, שברירים, הלבן, איש התוכחה, גרעינים, אמריקה, זיוה

(Family, Fradel, Divorce, The First Day, Burying the Books, Sunbeams, The Bricklayer, The Reprimand Man, Seeds, America, Ziva).

Three Stories [שלושה ספורים]. Edited by Yafah Kamer. Jerusalem: The World Zionist Organization Division of Education and Culture in the Diaspora, 1975. Reprints, 1976 and 1984.

יום אחד של רמי, הלבן, שברירים

(A Day in Rami's Life, The Bricklayer, Sunbeams).

Early Tales [פרשיות מוקדמות]. Edited by Avner Holtzman and Nurit Govrin. Jerusalem: Mosad Bialik, 1988.

In Hebrew:

משיחות במרכבה, משיחות חסידים, סעודה שדודה: טרגיקומדיה בשני מחזות,
תמונות וצללים א, תמונות וצללים ב, מסיפורי קברן זקן, תמונות וצללים ג, שלש
אחיות, פרודים, טיול עברי, בלי קידוש, זוג מתקוטט, הרחמניה, בבית המשוגעים,
הארז הנפלא, בתוך החשכה, מיחוש, רוצח, התפרץ, קדישה, גניזה, עקיבקה נחש,
האוצר, פדקה, קרובה-רחוקה, ליזר-יוסל, הסבתא הניה, הקפות, דיר, הניד,
זוזיק, בחינות, אחות, על יד החלון, באיזה עולם, נכדים, ליסקה, פריל, עצבנות,
שוקולד, תכלת, עגמת נפש, שומן, קצו של סנדר זיו, פרוזדור, ממה שעבר: עגונה,
הסנדלר מזוזיקובקה, בץ, בסוף קיץ

(From Conversations on a Train, From Conversations with Hasidim, A
Plundered Meal: A Tragicomedy in Two Scenes, Portraits and Shadows I,
Portraits and Shadows II, From Stories of an Old Grave Digger, Portraits
and Shadows III, Three Sisters, Divorces, A Hebrew Trip, Without Kid-
dush, A Bickering Couple, The Compassionate Girl, In the Madhouse,
The Wondrous Cedar, In the Dark, Ache, Murderer, Outburst, A Female
Kaddish, Burying the Books, Sly Akavka, The Treasure, Fedka, A Distant
Relative, Leyzer Yosel, Grandmother Henya, Dancing, A Tenant, Henikh,
Jujik, Exams, Sister, By the Window, In What World? Grandchildren,
Liska, Pearl, Nerves, Chocolate, Blue, Anguish, Fat, The End of Sender Ziv,
Hallway, What Has Passed: Abandoned Wife, The Shoemaker from
Zhozhokovka, Mud, At the End of Summer).

In Yiddish:

בילדער פון לעבן א, בילדער פון לעבן ב, בילדער פון לעבן ג, טפרוקא (סקיצע), א
בת יחידה (פון מייו חברטעס כתבים), די באבע העניע, קדיש (פון מיינע קינדער
יארן), העניאך, פעדקא, אן אגמת נפש

(Pictures from Life, Tapruka [A Sketch], An Only Daughter [From My
Friend's Writings], Grandmother Henya, Kaddish [From My Childhood],
Henikh, Fekda, Anguish).

Divorce and Other Stories [כריתות וסיפורים אחרים]. Edited by Haim Beer.
Tel Aviv: Am Oved, 1997.

כריתות, מצולה, תרמית, בראשית, בר אוז

(Divorce, Depths, Deception, In the Beginning, Duck).

The First Day and Other Stories. Berkeley and Los Angeles: Univ. of California Press, 2001.

(In the Beginning, The First Day, Fradl, Bill of Divorcement [*sic*], Family, Deserted Wife, Shifra, Grandchildren, Ziva, Sister, Burying the Books, Kaddish, Bubbe Henya, An Only Daughter, Fedka, Aggravation, The End of Sender Ziv, Liska).

Fradel and Shifrah פראדל ושפרה . Tel Aviv: Bavel, 2001.

Translations and Edited Volumes by Dvora Baron

Flaubert, Gustave. *Madame Bovary.* Translated by Dvora Baron. Berlin: Stybel, 1932.

Aharonovitch, Yosef. *Collected Writings* [כתבי יוסף אהרונוביץ]. Edited by Eliezer Shohat and Dvora Baron. Tel Aviv: Am Oved, 1940.

Flaubert, Gustave. *Madame Bovary.* Translated by Dvora Baron. Tel Aviv: Merhavyah, 1957. Reprints, 1964, 1970, 1972, and 1981.

Monographs and Edited Volumes on Dvora Baron's Work

Aharonovitch, Tziporah, ed. *Agav Urkhah: Asufah me-ʿIzvonah, ʿal Dvora Baron umi-Svivah* (By the Way: Collected from the Archives, on Dvora Baron and Her Environment). Tel Aviv: Merhavya, 1960.

Amram, Maya. "Sogle Signon be-Sipurim ha-Yom ha-Rishon u-Ketanot li-Dvora Baron" (Stylistic Treasures in Baron's "The First Day and Trifles"). Master's thesis, Bar Ilan Univ., 1999.

Davidson, Charles Joseph. "A Literary Critique of the Writings of Deborah Baron." Rabbinic thesis, Hebrew Union College, 1958.

Gali, Aviva. *ha-Em veha-Bat: Mahazeh Bidyoni ʿal pi ʿUvdot me-Hayey ha-Soferet Dvora Baron* (Mother and Daughter: A Play Based on the Facts of Dvora Baron's Life). Tel Aviv: Y. Golan, 1995.

Govrin, Nurit. *Ma'agalim* (Circles). Ramat Gan: Masada, 1975.

———. *ha-Mahatsit ha-Rishonah: Dvora Baron, Hayehah va-Yetsiratah, 1887–1923* (The First Half: Dvora Baron, Her Life and Work, 1887–1923). Jerusalem: Mosad Bialik, 1988.

Jelen, Sheila, and Shachar Pinsker, eds. *Hebrew, Gender, and Modernity: Critical Responses to Dvora Baron's Fiction.* College Park: University Press of Maryland, 2007.

Katsir, Yehudit. *Dvora Baron: Mahazeh bi-Shtei Ma'arakhot* (Dvora Baron: A Play in Two Acts). In vol. 2 of *The New Anthology.* Israel: New Library, 2000.

Lieblich, Amia. *Conversations with Dvora: An Experimental Biography of the First Modern Hebrew Woman Writers.* Edited by Naomi Seidman and Chana Kronfeld. Translated by Naomi Seidman. Berkeley and Los Angeles: Univ. of California Press, 1997.

———. *Rekamot: Sihotai im Dvora Baron* (Embroideries: My Conversations with Dvora Baron). Jerusalem: Shocken, 1991.

Pagis, Ada, ed. *Dvora Baron: Mivhar Ma'amare Bikoret 'al Yetsiratah* (Dvora Baron: A Selection of Critical Essays on Her Literary Prose). Tel Aviv: Am Oved, 1974.

Seh-Lavan, Yosef. *Dvora Baron: ha-Ish va-Yetsirato* (Dvora Baron: The Man and His Works). Tel Aviv: Or Am, 1976.

Weinberger, Miriam. *Tashtiot min ha-Mesoret bi-Yestirat Dvora Baron* (Layers of Tradition in the Work of Dvora Baron). Ramat Gan: Bar Ilan Univ., 1986.

Scholarly Articles and Chapters on Dvora Baron

Scholarly essays on Dvora Baron published since the early 1970s are enumerated here. Most essays on Dvora Baron that appeared in the popular Israeli or pre-1948 Palestinian press are not included. A bibliography of selections from those works appears in Ada Pagis, ed., *Dvora Baron: A Selection of Critical Essays on Her Literary Prose* and in Nurit Govrin, *The First Half: Dvora Baron, Her Life and Work, 1887–1923.* A comprehensive, noncomputerized catalog of all newspaper, magazine, and scholarly articles on Dvora Baron from the beginning of her career until the present can be found at Genazim (Hebrew Writers' Archives) in Tel Aviv.

Adler, Ruth. "Dvora Baron: Daughter of the Shtetl." In *Women of the Word: Jewish Women and Jewish Writing*, 91–110. Detroit: Wayne State Univ. Press, 1994.

———. "The Rabbi's Daughter as Author: Dvora Baron Views the Rituals and Customs of a Lithuanian Shtetl." *World Congress of Jewish Studies* 11, no. C3 (1994): 53–60.

Agmon-Frukhtman, Maya. "Shinuye Seder ba-Mishpat u-Mivne Extrapozitsiyah be-Sipurehah shel Dvora Baron" (Syntactic Changes and Extrapositional Structures in the Stories of Dvora Baron). *Sefer Shabtiel* (in Hebrew) (1989): 160–68.

Barash, Asher. "ha-Meshoreret ba-Prozah" (The Poetess in Prose). In *Dvora Baron: A Selection of Critical Essays on Her Literary Prose* (in Hebrew), edited by Ada Pagis, 46–47. Tel Aviv: Am Oved, 1974.

Barzel, Hillel. "Mif'alah ha-Sifruti shel Dvora Baron" (The Literary Endeavor of Dvora Baron). In *Dvora Baron: A Selection of Critical Essays on Her Literary Prose* (in Hebrew), edited by Ada Pagis, 102–8. Tel Aviv: Am Oved, 1974.

Ben Mordechai, Yitzhak. "'Al Kahal ve-Kehilah be-Sipurehah shel Dvora Baron" (On Community and Communality in the Stories of Dvora Baron). *Eshel Beersheva* (in Hebrew) 3 (1986): 317–31.

———. "be-En Hesed uve-En Rahamim: 'Iyun be-Sipur Shavririm li-Dvora Baron" (Without Kindness and Without Mercy: A Study of "Sunbeams" by Dvora Baron). In *A Volume in Honor of Yitzhak Bakon* (in Hebrew), edited by Aharon Komem, 203–14. Beersheva: Ben Gurion Univ. of the Negev, 1992.

Ben Tzvi Sa'ar, Rivka. "be-Aspeklaryah shel Za'iruyot" (Through the Lens of Small Things). In *Dvora Baron: A Selection of Critical Essays on Her Literary Prose* (in Hebrew), edited by Ada Pagis, 143–48. Tel Aviv: Am Oved, 1974.

Bernstein, Marc. "Midrash and Marginality: The 'Agunot' of S. Y. Agnon and Devorah Baron." *Hebrew Studies* 42 (2001): 7–58.

Birati, Rachel. "The Shtetl as Depicted in the Writing of I. L. Peretz,

Sholem Aleichem and Dvora Baron." *Australian Journal of Jewish Studies* 10, no. 1–2 (1996): 45–64.

Cohen, Israel. "Dvora Baron." In *Dvora Baron: A Selection of Critical Essays on Her Literary Prose* (in Hebrew), edited by Ada Pagis, 71–79. Tel Aviv: Am Oved, 1974.

Cohen, Tova. "ha-Im Nignezah ha-Genizah? Makom ha-Sipur Genizah be-Nusaho ha-Sheni be-Hitpathut Toda'atah ha-Feministit shel Dvora Baron" (Was "Burying the Books" Buried? The Place of the Newer "Burying the Books" in the Feminist Consciousness of Dvora Baron). In *From Centers to Center* (in Hebrew), edited by Avner Holtzman, 240–61. Tel Aviv: Tel Aviv University, 2005.

Feingold, Ben-Ami. "ha-'Ayarah be-Sipure Dvora Baron: Ben Mitos le-Historyah" (The Shtetl in Dvora Baron's Stories: Between Myth and History). In *From Vilna to Jerusalem: The Culture of Eastern European Jewry, Presented to Professor Shmuel Wersses* (in Hebrew), edited by David Asaf, 449–66. Jerusalem: Magnes, 2002.

———. "Dvora Baron ke-Soferet Eretz Yisra'elit" (Dvora Baron as an Israeli Author). *'Al ha-Mishmar* (in Hebrew) (Oct. 30, 1981): 6.

———. "Dvora Baron ke-Soferet Feministit" (Dvora Baron as a Feminist Author). *Sadan* (in Hebrew) 4 (1999): 323–51.

———. "Genizah shel Dvora Baron" (Dvora Baron's "Burying the Books"). *ha-Sifrut* (in Hebrew) 21 (1975): 144–52.

———. "'Yom Ehad Shel Rami' u-Motiv ha-Mas'a be-Sipureha shel Dvora Baron" ("A Day for Rami" and the Journey Motif in Dvora Baron's Stories). *Moznayim* (in Hebrew) 50, no. 5–6 (1980): 399–404.

Fichman, Jacob. "Dvora Baron." In *Dvora Baron: A Selection of Critical Essays on Her Literary Prose* (in Hebrew), edited by Ada Pagis, 48–70. Tel Aviv: Am Oved, 1974.

Gilboa, Menuchah. "Dvora Baron: meha-Mahalakh he-Hadash el mi-Hutsah lo" (Dvora Baron: From Within the 'New Way' to Outside It). *Mehut* (in Hebrew) 1, no. 6 (1989): 56–62.

———. "ha-Mishpahah ha-Yehudit be-Asplekaryah shel ha-Sifrut ha-'Ivrit ha-Hadashah: Yitzhak Leibush Peretz u-Dvora Baron" (The Jewish Family in Modern Hebrew Literature: Yitzhak Leibush Peretz and Dvora Baron). In *The Jewish Family in Our Time: Essays and Analyses* (in Hebrew), 132–44. Tel Aviv: Committee on the Culture of the Jewish Family, 1979.

Goldberg, Leah. "*Parshiyot* li-Dvora Baron" (*Tales* by Dvora Baron). In *Dvora Baron: A Selection of Critical Essays on Her Literary Prose* (in Hebrew), edited by Ada Pagis, 93–101. Tel Aviv: Am Oved, 1974.

Goodman, Zilla Jane. "Traced in Ink: Women's Lives in 'Qotzo shel Yud' by Yalag and 'Mishpachah' by D. Baron." In *Gender and Judaism: The Transformation of Tradition,* edited by T. M. Rudavsky, 191–207. New York: New York Univ. Press, 1995.

Govrin, Nurit. "Ben Ason li-Yeshuah: Pesilato shel Get be-Sifrut ha-'Ivrit" (Between Tragedy and Salvation: The Nullification of the Writ of Divorce in Hebrew Literature: Yalag, Agnon, Baron, Burla). *Re'eh* (in Hebrew) 1 (1996): 28–40.

———. "Dvora Baron—mi-Gilui le-khisui: 'al Sipure ha-Reshit shel Dvora Baron" (Dvora Baron—from Revealed to Hidden: On Dvora Baron's Early Stories). *bi-Tsaron* (in Hebrew) 24–25 (1985): 56–62.

———. "Reshitah shel Dvora Baron" (Dvora Baron's Beginnings). In *Dvora Baron: A Selection of Critical Essays on Her Literary Prose* (in Hebrew), edited by Ada Pagis, 149–81. Tel Aviv: Am Oved, 1974.

———. "Tokhakhah mi-Golah" (A Reprimand from Exile). *Yeda Am* (in Hebrew) 20 (2002): 47–48.

———. "ha-Zeman veha-Makom be-Limud ha-Sifrut" (Time and Place in Literary Study). *Kivunim Hadashim* (in Hebrew) 8 (2003): 122–34.

Jelen, Sheila. "All Writers Are Jews, All Jews Are Men." In *Hebrew, Gender, and Modernity: Critical Responses to Dvora Baron's Fiction.* College Park: University Press of Maryland, 2007.

———. "She Sermonizes in Wool and Flax: Dvora Baron's Literary Vernacular." *Prooftexts* 23, no. 2 (2003): 182–209.

Kariv, Abraham. "Bat Lita" (A Lithuanian Daughter). In *Dvora Baron: A Selection of Critical Essays on Her Literary Prose* (in Hebrew), edited by Ada Pagis, 139–42. Tel Aviv: Am Oved, 1974.

Katznelson-Shazar, Rachel. "Dvora Baron." In *Dvora Baron: A Selection of Critical Essays on Her Literary Prose* (in Hebrew), edited by Ada Pagis, 33–45. Tel Aviv: Am Oved, 1974.

Keshet, Yeshurun. "'al Dvora Baron" (On Dvora Baron). In *Dvora Baron: A Selection of Critical Essays on Her Literary Prose* (in Hebrew), edited by Ada Pagis, 80–92. Tel Aviv: Am Oved, 1974.

Kimhi, Dov. "Dvora Baron." In *Dvora Baron: A Selection of Critical Essays on Her Literary Prose* (in Hebrew), edited by Ada Pagis, 23–26. Tel Aviv: Am Oved, 1974.

Komem, Aharon. "ha-Ishah ha-Sotah veha-Ba'al ha-Karnan: Dvora Baron, Agnon, Baschevis Singer" (The Adulterous Woman and the Cuckold Husband: Dvora Baron, S. Y. Agnon and Baschevis Singer). In *Studies on Agnon* (in Hebrew), edited by Hillel Weiss and Hillel Barzel, 237–52. Ramat Gan: Bar Ilan Univ., 1994.

Lahover, P. "Dvora Baron." In *Dvora Baron: A Selection of Critical Essays on Her Literary Prose* (in Hebrew), edited by Ada Pagis, 27–29. Tel Aviv: Am Oved, 1974.

Lerner, Anne Lapidus. "Lost Childhood in East European Hebrew Literature." In *The Jewish Family: Metaphor and Memory,* edited by David Kraemer, 95–112. New York: Oxford University Press, 1989.

Lichtenbaum, Y. "Dvora Baron." In *Dvora Baron: A Selection of Critical Essays on Her Literary Prose* (in Hebrew), edited by Ada Pagis, 30–32. Tel Aviv: Am Oved, 1974.

Lieblich, Amia. "'Al Melekhet ha-Biographyah" (On Biography). *Dvarim Ahadim* (in Hebrew) 2 (1997): 31–43.

———. "ha-Mukdam veha-Meuhar bi-Rekamot: 'al Biographiyut, Obyektiviut, Nashim, ve'al Dvora Baron, 1887–1956" (Temporal Order in Embroideries: On Biography, Objectivity, Women, and Dvora Baron, 1887–1956). *Alpayim* (in Hebrew) 8 (1994): 204–24.

Lipsker, Avidov. "Mah Nivat ba-Mishkefet she-Einah Mekatseret et ha-Reiyah? Ha-Tahbir ha-Realisti be-Sipure Dvora Baron" (What Can Be Seen Through Binoculars That Does Not Bring the World Closer? Realist Syntax in Dvora Baron's Stories). *Dapim la-Mehkar ba-Sifrut* (in Hebrew) 8 (1992): 270–84.

———. "Tsamarot shel Hazayah" Signon Impressionisti bi-Leshonam shel Gnessin, Baron, Kimhi, va-Yizhar" (The Height of Fantasy: Impressionist Style in the Language of Gnessin, Baron, Kimhi, and Yizhar). *Bikoret u-Farshanut* (in Hebrew) 29 (1993): 121–42.

Lubin, Orly. "Derekh Kotsim: ha-Mered ha-Samui shel ha-Guf ha-Meshutak" (The Way of Thorns: The Silent Rebellion of the Paralyzed Body). In *Can You Hear My Voice? Representations of Women in Israeli Culture* (in Hebrew), 199–212. Jerusalem: ha-Kibutz ha-Meuhad, 2001.

———. "Zutot mi-Mitbahah shel Nehamah: Le'umiyut Alternativit beha-Goim shel Dvora Baron" (Tidbits from Nechama's Kitchen: Alternative Nationalism in Dvora Baron's 'The Exiles'). *Teoriah u-Vikoret* (in Hebrew) 7 (1995): 159–75.

Meged, Aharon. "Kolah ve-'Olamah shel Dvora Baron" (The Voice and World of Dvora Baron). In *For the Love of Authors* (in Hebrew), edited by Israel Aliraz, 87–101. Tel Aviv: Dvir, 1984.

Miron, Dan. "Perakim 'al Yetsiratah shel Dvora Baron" (On Dvora Baron's Work). In *Dvora Baron: A Selection of Critical Essays on Her Literary Prose* (in Hebrew), edited by Ada Pagis, 117–30. Tel Aviv: Am Oved, 1974.

Pagis, Ada. "Yestiratah shel Dvora Baron be-'Einey ha-Bikoret" (Dvora Baron's Work in the Eyes of the Critics). In *Dvora Baron: A Selection of Critical Essays on Her Literary Prose* (in Hebrew), edited by Ada Pagis, 7–22. Tel Aviv: Am Oved, 1974.

Pinsker, Shachar. "Unraveling the Yarn: Intertexuality, Gender, and Cultural Critique in the Stories of Dvora Baron." In *Hebrew, Gender, and Modernity: Critical Responses to Dvora Baron's Fiction,* edited by Sheila Jelen and Shachar Pinsker. College Park: University Press of Maryland, 2007.

Rovner, T. "Madanim u-Fius" (War and Peace). In *Dvora Baron: A Selection of Critical Essays on Her Literary Prose* (in Hebrew), edited by Ada Pagis, 131–38. Tel Aviv: Am Oved, 1974.

Schweid, Eli. "Hidat ha-Retsifut" (The Riddle of Continuity). In *Dvora Baron: A Selection of Critical Essays on Her Literary Prose* (in Hebrew), edited by Ada Pagis, 109–16. Tel Aviv: Am Oved, 1974.

Seidman, Naomi. "Baron in the Closet: An Epistemology of the Women's Section." In *A Marriage Made in Heaven: The Sexual Politics of Hebrew and Yiddish,* 67–101. Berkeley and Los Angeles: Univ. of California Press, 1997.

Shavitzky, Ziva. "Dvora Baron and the Marginalized Voice." *Australian Journal of Jewish Studies* 18 (2004): 125–36.

Weinberger, Miriam. "Hashpa'at Darkhe ha-Sipur ha-Mikrai 'al 'Itsuvo shel ha-Sipur ha-Baroni" (The Influence of the Biblical Text on the Baronian Story). *Alon la-Moreh le-Sifrut* (in Hebrew) 12 (1991).

———. "Mekomah shel Eretz Yisrael be-Yetsirat Dvora Baron" (The Place of the Land of Israeli in the Work of Dvora Baron). *be-Emet* (in Hebrew) 4–5 (1991): 61–76.

Zierler, Wendy. "'In What World?' Devorah Baron's Fiction of Exile." *Prooftexts* 19, no. 2 (1999): 127–50.

———. "The Rabbi's Daughter In and Out of the Kitchen: Feminist Literary Negotiations." *Nashim* 5 (2002): 83–104.

———. "Staring at the Bookcase: Daughters, Knowledge, and the Fiction of Devorah Baron." In *Hebrew, Gender, and Modernity: Critical Responses to Dvora Baron's Fiction,* edited by Sheila Jelen and and Shachar Pinsker. College Park: University Press of Maryland, 2007.

Notes

A Critical Preface

1. Dvora Baron, "Fradel," in *The First Day and Other Stories*, 33.

2. A shtetl is a provincial community of Jews coexisting with non-Jews. There were four mass migrations *(aliyot)* to Palestine in the late nineteenth and early twentieth centuries. The "second aliyah" took place from 1904 to 1914 in the wake of the Kishinev and other pogroms in 1903 and the failed Russian Revolution of 1905.

3. The former is a purportedly ethnographic study of the shtetl, conducted after the Holocaust in the early 1950s, through interviews primarily with people in the United States who had emigrated from the shtetl years before. They recalled the shtetl through a haze of nostalgia and grief, and the ethnographers of the study themselves acknowledge that they are depicting the shtetl in the broadest of possible strokes, painting a "general" portrait, not a specific one. Heschel's work, in a similar vein, is a philosophical meditation on the essential theological and psychological spirit of the shtetl and, though breathtakingly beautiful, is certainly not equal to the task of a historical or ethnographic definition.

4. Baron, "Fradel," in *First Day*, 42–43.

5. Baron shares her birthplace with the enormously influential twentieth-century Jewish legal authority Rabbi Moshe Feinstein (1895–1986) who also was born in Ouzda and has been identified as the community rabbi's child. Since Baron's father died in 1908, it is possible that Rabbi Feinstein's father was the next community rabbi. All biographical and bibliographical information on Baron is drawn from Nurit Govrin, *ha-Mahatsit ha-Rishonah: Dvora Baron, Hayehah va-Yetsiratah (1887–1923)* (The First Half: Dvora Baron, Her Life and Work [1887–1923]). Govrin's exhaustive research on Baron and her willingness to discuss my work have been immeasurably valuable.

6. Their names are not recorded in Govrin's account.

7. Baron's father was not opposed to Baron's exposure to Haskalah texts. His students attest to the fact that he spent several hours every night, after everyone else had gone to bed, reading the same literature that his son introduced to his daughter.

8. Baron, "mi-Sihot ba-Merkavah" (From Conversations on a Train), *ha-Melitz* (in

187

Hebrew) (Apr. 10, 1902): 2; Baron, "mi-Sihot Hassidim" (From Conversations of Hassidim), *ha-Melitz* (in Hebrew) (Apr. 14, 1902): 2; "Bilder Fun Lebn" (Pictures from Life) *Der Tog* (in Yiddish) (Feb. 22, 1904): 1. These stories are collected in Baron, *Parshiyot Mukdamot* (Early Tales), 341–44.

9. Moshe Ben Eliezer (1880–1940) and Dvora Baron were engaged for five years, from 1904 to 1909. He emigrated to France and then to the United States around the same time that Baron emigrated to Palestine. Govrin, *ha-Mahatsit ha-Rishonah*, 44.

10. Her older sister, Hayah Rivka, had joined Dvora in Palestine, and her younger sister Tziporah had drowned as a young woman under questionable circumstances.

11. Govrin, *ha-Mahatsit ha-Rishonah*, 309–10. Additional collections of Baron's work published in Hebrew during her lifetime and posthumously include: *Sipurim* (Stories); *Mah she-Hayah* (What Has Been); *mi-Sham* (From There); *ha-Laban* (The Bricklayer); *Shavririm* (Sunbeams); *Parshiyot* (Tales) (1951); *Huliyot* (Links); *me-Emesh* (From Yesterday); *Yalkut Sipurim* (Collected Stories); and *ha-Golim* (The Exiles). Baron's stories have been anthologized in both Hebrew and English, and two English collections of her stories have been published: *The Thorny Path and Other Stories* and *The First Day and Other Stories*. Also, the following stories by Baron appear in English anthologies: "Burying the Books," in *The Plough Woman: Records of the Pioneer Women of Palestine, a Critical Edition,* translated and edited by Mark A. Raider and Miriam B. Raider-Roth; "Sunbeams," in *The Oxford Book of Hebrew Short Stories,* edited by Glenda Abramson; "Fradel," in *Stories Form* [sic] *Women Writers of Israel;* and "Kaddish" and "Bubbe Henya," in *Beautiful as the Moon, Radiant as the Stars: Jewish Women in Yiddish Stories, an Anthology.*

Introduction: Intimations and Imperatives—A Biography Through the Looking Glass

1. Baron, "The First Day," in *First Day,* 19–20.

2. Cited in Govrin, *ha-Mahatsit ha-Rishonah*, 25. The letter is from August 20, 1960. In it, Baron's daughter asks a nephew to correspond with Harari and demand a correction in her book *Ishah ve-'Em be-Yisrael: mi-Tekufat ha-Tanakh 'ad Shnat ha-'Asor li-Medinat Yisrael* (Woman and Mother in Israel: From Biblical Times until the First Decade of the State of Israel).

3. James Olney, "Autobiography and the Cultural Moment," 9.

4. Celeste Schenck, "All of a Piece: Women's Poetry and Autobiography," 285; Jacques Derrida, "The Law of Genre," 221, quoted in ibid., 285; Nancy K. Miller, "Women's Autobiography in France," 59. She refers specifically to Jean Larnac's early study of women's literature in France, *Histoire de la literature feminine.*

5. Virginia Woolf, *A Room of One's Own,* 35.

6. Lily Rattok, foreword to *Small Change: A Collection of Stories,* by Yehudit Hendel, xiii.

7. For a synopsis of the theoretical, ideological, and historical orientation of "New Historicism," see Catherine Gallagher and Stephen Greenblatt, *Practicing New Historicism.*

8. In May 1921 Brenner was killed in anti-Jewish Arab riots in Jaffa. Zohar Shavit provides a model for viewing literary establishments as markers of literary movements in prestatehood Palestine in his *Hayim ha-Sifrutiim be-Eretz Yisrael, 1910–1933* (Literary Life in the Land of Israel, 1910–1933). Joseph Hayyim Brenner was known both among his peers and by literary critics as Y. H. Brenner; similarly, we have Ch. N. Bialik, M. Y. Berdischevsky, and U. N. Gnessin, writers from the same period.

9. For a discussion of the link between language and nationalism, see Benedict Anderson, *Imagined Communities;* and Regina Bendix, *In Search of Authenticity: The Formation of Folklore Studies.*

10. The modern Hebrew renaissance of the late nineteenth and early twentieth centuries can be traced back as early as 1782 with the founding of the Society for the Advancement of the Hebrew Language in Koenigsburg, Germany. Shmuel Feiner, "Towards a Historical Definition of the Haskalah," 187.

11. Other maskilim such as Zev Bukhner, Shalom ha-Cohen, David Zamosh, M. A. Guenzberg, and Meir ha-Levi Letris demonstrated their commitment to transforming the Hebrew language into a vernacular tongue in their compilation of model letters in Hebrew *(Brieven Shtellers)* to encourage correspondence in Hebrew as opposed to Yiddish, German, or any of the other vernacular languages used by Jews during the period of the Enlightenment. Moshe Peli, "Tehiyat ha-Lashon Hahelah ba-Haskalah: *ha-Measef,* Ktav ha-'et ha-'Ivri ha-Rishon, ke-Makhshir le-Hidush ha-Safah" (The Revival of Hebrew Began During the Enlightenment: *ha-Measef,* the First Hebrew Journal as a Tool of the Revival).

12. Eliezer Ben Yehudah (1858–1922) has been considered the "father" of the revival of modern Hebrew in his active modeling of and agitation for the exclusive use of Hebrew in the Jewish community in Palestine. His own wife was forbidden to sing their child lullabies in Russian, and he was relentless in his insistence on the centrality of the vernacularization of Hebrew to the revitalization of modern Jewry.

13. Gershom Scholem, *von Berlin nach Jerusalem* (From Berlin to Jerusalem), 188; Bialik cited in Benjamin Harshav, *Language in Time of Revolution,* 86.

14. Dan Miron cites this correspondence in *Bodedim be-Moadam: le-Diyuknah shel ha-Republikah ha-Sifrutit ha-Ivrit bi-Tehilat ha-Meah ha-Esrim* (When Loners Come Together: A Portrait of Hebrew Literature at the Turn of the Twentieth Century), 50. In particular, see a letter from Brenner to Berdischevsky, dated March 21, 1908, in S. Bartonov, ed., *M. Y. Berdischevsky and Y. H. Brenner: Halifat Igrot, 5667–5681* (M. Y. Berdischevsky and Y. H. Brenner: Correspondence, 5667–5681), 45–47.

15. Eliezer Goelman, "ha-Me'avak Neged 'Ivrit ke-Safah Meduberet" (The Struggle against Hebrew as a Spoken Tongue), 141–45.

16. Ibid.

17. The major canon-making works of these particular authors are: Joseph Klausner, *Historyah shel ha-Sifrut ha-'Ivrit ha-Hadashah* (The History of Modern Hebrew Literature); Fishel Lahover, *Toldot ha-Sifrut ha-'Ivrit ha-Hadashah* (The History of Modern Hebrew Literature); Gershon Shaked, *ha-Siporet ha-Ivrit,* (Hebrew Literature), vol. 1, *ha-Golah* (The Exile); and Miron, *Bodedim be-Moadam.*

18. See Alan Mintz, *"Banished from Their Father's Table": Loss of Faith and Hebrew Autobiography.*

19. Chava Weissler, *Voices of the Matriarchs: Listening to the Prayers of Early Modern Jewish Women,* 52; Weissler, "For Women and for Men Who Are Like Women: The Construction of Gender in Yiddish Devotional Literature."

20. Letter from Y. L. Gordon to Mrs. Shana Wolf of Grodno, dated Nov. 26, 1881, collected in Y. L. Gordon, *Mikhtave Yehudah Leib Gordon* (Letters of Yehudah Leib Gordon), 5, cited in Iris Parush, *Reading Jewish Women: Marginality and Modernization in Nineteenth-Century Eastern European Jewish Society,* 239n54.

21. Y. L. Gordon, *Kitve Yehudah Leib Gordon (Prozah)* (Collected Works of Yehudah Leib Gordon [Prose]), 325.

22. For a tragicomic depiction of this phenomenon, see Chaim Nachman Bialik, "Big Harry," in *Random Harvest: The Novellas of Bialik.* In Hebrew, the story is titled "Aryeh Ba'al Guf" and can be found in Chaim Nachman Bialik, *Kol Kitve Chaim Nachman Bialik* (Collected Works of Chaim Nachman Bialik). For an exposition on the possibility of, but difficulties inherent in, overcoming class boundaries via scholarship, see Shaul Stampfer, "Heder Study, Knowledge of Torah and the Maintenance of Social Stratification in Traditional East European Jewish Society," 271–89.

23. The laws creating *agunot,* for example, have long been the subject of contention in the legal community. The *agunah* is an "abandoned wife" who cannot remarry either until her husband presents her, willingly, with a writ of divorce (a *get*) or until two witnesses to his death can be located.

24. Shaul Stampfer, "Gender Differentiation and Education of the Jewish Woman in Nineteenth-Century Eastern Europe," 187–206.

25. Eliyana R. Adler, "Educational Options for Jewish Girls in Nineteenth Century Europe." For a fictional account of a girl studying Hebrew formally both with a tutor and in a school, see S. Y. Agnon, "In the Prime of Her Life." Also, for an autobiographical account of the first female Hebrew teacher in Poland, see Puah Rakovsky, *My Life as a Radical Jewish Woman: Memoirs of a Zionist Feminist in Poland.*

26. Liliane Weissberg has written about Jewish women's literary salons in Germany. See "Bodies in Pain: Reflections on the Berlin Jewish Salon."

27. The most notorious account of this can be found in Solomon Maimon's autobiography, originally written in German. For an English translation, see *Solomon Maimon: An Autobiography.*

28. For a fictional account of this dilemma in English translation, see M. Y. Berdis-chevsky, "Without Hope," in *Oxford Book,* ed. Abramson, 28–39.

29. Y. L. Gordon expressed the noble sentiment toward women that permeated the Jewish Enlightenment in his poem "The Tip of the *Yod*": "Who can know your life? / In darkness you came and in darkness you will go. . . . / How mournful your heart, Jewish woman." See Gordon, *Kitve Yehudah Leib Gordon (Shirah)* (Collected Works of Yehudah Leib Gordon [Poetry]).

30. Shmuel Feiner, "ha-Ishah ha-Yehudiyah ha-Modernit: Mikrah Mivhan ba-Ya-hase ha-Haskalah veha-Modernah" (The Modern Jewish Woman: A Test Case in the In-tersection of Modernity and the Enlightenment).

31. Eliyana Adler, "Women's Education in the Pages of the Russian Jewish Press."

32. Robert Alter, *The Invention of Hebrew Prose,* 9.

33. E. Adler, "Women's Education," 125; and Parush, *Reading Jewish Women,* 224.

34. Parush, *Reading Jewish Women,* 224.

35. E. Adler, "Women's Education," 125.

36. Editorial by Avraham bar Gottlober in *ha-Boker Or* (Morning Light) (1877), quoted in Parush, *Reading Jewish Women,* 209; n. 7.

37. Gottlober, *ha-Boker Or* (Morning Light) (1869), quoted in Parush, *Reading Jewish Women,* 299. ˙

38. In a survey of the attitude toward Hebrew of major personalities from the period of the Jewish Enlightenment, Azriel Shohat discusses the intense commitment to the He-brew language expressed by the first editor of the major Hebrew language journal *ha-Measef,* Isaac Euchel. In correspondence with the important poet and activist Shalom ha-Cohen, who wanted Euchel to restart *ha-Measef* after its not being published for two years, Euchel refused to take on the task of editor in chief for a second term. His justifica-tion was that, "in contrast to the young men who established *ha-Measef,* the next genera-tion of young activists was not in the least bit concerned with the Hebrew language." Thus, we see that the Hebrew language did not always benefit from the devotion of the Haskalah's champions. It was often the recipient of much negative attention, not posi-tive, as different generations of maskilim struggled to define themselves vis-à-vis the shifting winds of Hebrew's popularity or perceived importance in the ideologies of the era. Shohat, "Yehasam shel Maskilim be-Rusyah el Lashon ha-'Ivrit" (The Relationship of Russian Enlighteners to the Hebrew Language), 358–59.

39. Barukh Ben Yehudah, "Dvora Madrikhat Noar" (Dvora, a Youth Counselor), 213.

40. Letter from Leib Fink to Dvora Baron, document no. 79754 in the Baron file, Genazim, Tel-Aviv, Israel, cited in Govrin, *ha-Mahatsit ha-Rishonah,* 114–17.

41. This is not to say that simply because etymologically and morphologically the English word for "authorship" is not gendered that the institution of authorship is not

gendered in English. However, the gender-marked nature of authorship is, tellingly, more transparent, and perhaps more insurmountable in Hebrew, than in English, as reflected in the grammatical psychology of the Hebrew language itself.

42. Govrin, in her comprehensive biography of Baron, attests to this appellation by calling the first subsection of the first chapter of her study "Bat ha-Rav" (The Rabbi's Daughter), in *ha-Mahatsit ha-Rishonah,* 23. See also Wendy Zierler's essay on several modern Hebrew women writers, including Baron: "The Rabbi's Daughter In and Out of the Kitchen: Feminist Literary Negotiations," in *And Rachel Stole the Idols: The Emergence of Modern Hebrew Women's Writing,* 251–72.

43. Baron was married to Yosef Aharonovitch, the editor of the important labor Zionist newspaper the *Young Laborer,* and she served as the paper's literary editor from the time of her immigration to Palestine in 1910 until 1923, when they both resigned from the paper. Aharonovitch died in 1932. Govrin, *ha-Mahatsit ha-Rishonah,* 11–22.

44. Yeshurun Keshet, "'Al Dvora Baron," 80; Rachel Katznelson-Shazar, "Dvora Baron," 33; Baron, *First Day,* back cover.

45. Morpurgo was the only woman writer acknowledged in Joseph Klausner's seminal history of modern Hebrew literature, *Historyah shel ha-Sifrut ha-'Ivrit ha-Hadashah* (38–49). For a more recent analysis of Morpurgo's work, see Yaffa Berlovich, "Rachel Morpurgo: ha-Teshukah el ha-Mavet, ha-Teshukah el ha-Shir; la-Tivah shel ha-Meshoreret ha-'Ivrit ha-Rishonah ba-'Et ha-Hadashah" (Rachel Morpurgo: The Desire for Death, the Desire for Poetry; Understanding the First Modern Hebrew Woman Poet in the Modern Period), 11–40. Also, for an overview of women's writing in Hebrew, from Morpurgo through the middle of the twentieth century, see Zierler, *Rachel Stole the Idols,* 15–36.

46. Chava Shapira, whose pseudonym was Em Kol Hai (Mother of All Living Things), published her first collection of stories, titled *Collected Stories,* in 1908. The eminent critic David Frischmann would not write a review of her work. As a way of acknowledging her introductory remarks in which she laments the absence of women in Hebrew literary production, he derogatorily remarks that criticism of her work is best left to women. Parush, *Reading Jewish Women,* 231–32.

47. Lili Rattok, *ha-Kol he-Aher: Siporet Nashim 'Ivrit* (The Other Voice: Women's Fiction in Hebrew), 352.

48. Sarah Feige Meinkin Foner, *Beged Bogdim: Sipur mi-Yeme Shimon ha-Kohen* (The Garment of a Traitor: A Tale from the Days of Simon the Hight Priest); Foner, *Ahavat Yesharim o ha-Mishpahot ha-Murdafot: Sipur min ha-'Et ha-Hadashah* (The Love of the Righteous or the Pursued Families: A Modern Tale); Foner, *mi-Zikhronot Yeme Yalduti o Mar'eh ha-'Ir Dvinsk* (Memoirs of a Childhood or a Portrait of Dvinsk). Also see Foner, *A Woman's Voice: Sarah Foner, Hebrew Author of the Haskalah.* Also, for biographical information, see Zierler, *Rachel Stole the Idols,* 29–33.

49. For historical definitions of the different aliyot, see Harshav, *Language in Revo-*

lution, xi. Also, on the achievements of Ben Yehudah, see Reuven Sivan, *The Revival of the Hebrew Language,* 9–11. For challenges to the claim that Ben Yehudah singularly enacted the Hebrew revival in Palestine through his establishment of the Hebrew Language Committee and his own domestic commitment to spoken Hebrew, see Harshav, *Language in Revolution,* 84–85; and M. Z. Kaderi, " 'Iyun be-Toldot ha-Lashon ha-'Ivrit ha-Modernit" (A Study of the Evolution of Modern Hebrew).

50. Nurit Govrin, "Nashim be-'Itonot ha-'Ivrit: ha-Hathalot" (Women in Hebrew Journalism: The Beginnings).

51. Y. L. Gordon, *Tsror Igrot Yalag el Miryam Markel Mozesohn* (Collected Letters of Yalag to Miriam Markel Mosesohn).

52. On Miriam Markel Mosesohn and her relationship to Y. L. Gordon, see Carole B. Balin, *To Reveal Our Hearts: Jewish Women Writers in Tsarist Russia,* 13–50.

1. All Writers Are Jews, All Jews Are Men: The Autobiographical Imperative

1. Simon Halkin, *Mavo le-Sifrut ha-Ivrit: Reshimot lefi hartsaotav bi-Shnat 5712* (Introduction to Hebrew Fiction: Lecture Notes from 1952). For a synopsis of Halkin's typology of the different "tlushim," see Nurit Govrin, *Alienation and Regeneration,* 20–30.

2. On Halkin's use of this phrase, see Miron, *Bodedim be-Moadam,* 9. Also see Govrin, *Alienation and Regeneration,* 12. The first story to designate the talush as a character "type" was Y. D. Berkowitz (1885–1967), in "Talush" (1904). In the story a young physician, Doctor Veinik, who has left his impoverished family behind in order to seek an education and a professional career, becomes integrated into the Jewish middle class. He finds that he no longer has a "home" to which he can return now that he has achieved his professional goals and attained the social rank he has long aspired toward. He is called to his dying brother's bedside and is shocked by the squalor he sees—a squalor he cannot in any way ameliorate. At the same time, he accompanies the daughter of a colleague to the theater and is disgusted by the vapidity of her conversation and her concerns. His own sense of himself is completely "uprooted"—caught between cultures and sensibilities. Berkowitz's "Talush" names a phenomenon, or a character type, that had already come to be identified as the biography of a literary generation. Berkowitz, "Talush," in *Sipurim* (Stories), 1–18.

3. See, for example, Joseph Hayyim Brenner, *Breakdown and Bereavement: A Novel;* or S. Y. Agnon, *Only Yesterday.*

4. Zygmunt Bauman, "Allosemitism: Premodern, Modern, Postmodern," 149–50.

5. Daniel Boyarin and Jonathan Boyarin, "Diaspora: Generation and the Ground of Jewish Identity," 697.

6. Bauman, "Allosemitism," 151.

7. Ibid.

8. Max Silverman, "Refiguring 'the Jew' in France," 198; Gillian Rose, *Judaism and Modernity: Philosophical Essays,* 200, 205.

9. Daniel Boyarin, *Unheroic Conduct: The Rise of Heterosexuality and the Invention of the Jewish Man.*

10. Friedrich Nietzsche similarly compares the adaptability of women and Jews in *Joyful Wisdom* (New York: Ungar, 1960). Quoted in Ritchie Robertson, "Historicizing Weininger: The Nineteenth Century German Image of the Feminized Jew," 27.

11. Robertson, "Historicizing Weininger," 31; Otto Rank, "The Essence of Judaism," quoted in Robertson, "Historicizing Weininger," 34.

12. Jean Franáois Lyotard, *Heidegger and "the jews,"* 3; Boyarin and Boyarin, "Diaspora," 700; Silverman, "Refiguring 'the Jew,'" 197.

13. Joseph Hayyim Brenner, "mi-Hirhure Sofer" (Musings of an Author), 241.

14. Dan Miron, *Imahot Meyasdot, Ahayot Horgot: Al shte hathalot ba-Shirah ha-Erets Yisraelit ha-Modernit* (Founding Mothers, Adopted Sisters: Two Beginnings for Modern Palestinian-Jewish Poetry).

15. See Michael Gluzman, *The Politics of Canonicity: Lines of Resistance in Modernist Hebrew Poetry.*

16. M. Y. Berdischevsky, *Urvah Parah* (A Raven Flies), 69.

17. Bialik's poems "ha-Matmid" (The Diligent One), "El ha-Tsipur" (To the Bird), and "Al Saf Bet ha-Midrash" (On the Threshold of the House of Study) all allude, in various ways, to the plight of the "eternal student" who longs to escape the house of study but cannot. See Bialik, *Kol Kitve,* 73–78, 1, 6.

18. Baron, "Behinot" (Exams), in *Parshiyot Mukdamot,* 499.

19. Baron, *Parshiyot Mukdamot,* 492–95.

20. Shmuel Wersses, "Portrait of the Maskil as a Young Man," 128.

21. Georges Gusdorf, "Conditions and Limits of Autobiography," 29–30.

22. Ibid., 33.

23. Carolyn G. Heilbrun, "Non-Autobiographies of 'Privileged' Women: England and America," 66.

24. Balin, *To Reveal Our Hearts,* 18–19.

25. Baron, *Parshiyot Mukdamot,* 492–93.

26. Baron, *First Day,* 203; Baron, *Parshiyot Mukdamot,* 593.

27. Baron, *Parshiyot Mukdamot,* 598.

28. Baron, *First Day,* 206; Baron, *Parshiyot Mukdamot,* 595.

29. Henry James, preface to *The Ambassadors,* 11.

30. Baron, *Parshiyot Mukdamot,* 599; Linda S. Kauffman, *Discourses of Desire: Gender, Genre, and Epistolary Fictions,* 22, 24.

31. Baron, *Parshiyot Mukdamot,* 603.

32. Ibid., 592.

33. Ibid., 599–600.

34. The literal definition of "preterite" in the *OED* is "expressing past action or state." In literary terminology it indicates the expression of a past action or state in the

present flow of the literary moment. For a more elaborate presentation of the place of the preterite in narratological terms, see Kate Hamburger, *The Logic of Literature.*

35. Baron, *First Day,* 208; Baron, *Parshiyot Mukdamot,* 596.

36. Baron, *First Day,* 218; Baron, *Parshiyot Mukdamot,* 602.

37. Baron, *Parshiyot Mukdamot,* 597.

2. Strange Sympathy: The Talush Imperative

1. Shaked, *ha-Siporet ha-Ivrit,* 454; Y. Uvasi, "Dvora Baron," 224.

2. Ruth Adler, "Dvora Baron: Daughter of the Shtetl," 91–109.

3. Baron, "What Has Been," in *Thorny Path,* 77; Baron, "Mah she-Hayah," in *Parshiyot* (1968), 126.

4. Baron, *Thorny Path,* 89–90; Baron, *Parshiyot* (1968), 135.

5. Baron, "Mishpahah" (Family), in *Parshiyot* (1968), 32.

6. Baron, "Mah she-Hayah," in *Parshiyot* (1968), 153.

7. Dan Miron, "The Literary Image of the Shtetl," in *The Literary Image of the Shtetl and Other Studies of Modern Jewish Literary Imagination,* 1–48.

8. Baron's first published collection was, as detailed earlier, *Sipurim* (1927).

9. Y. Uvasi, "Dvora Baron," 223. The Hebrew word for shtetl, incidentally, is *ayarah,* a feminine noun.

10. Yitzhak Ogen, "Dvora Baron," 147.

11. Nancy Armstrong, *Fiction in the Age of Photography: The Legacy of British Realism,* 1–31.

12. Susan Bordo, *Unbearable Weight: Feminism, Western Culture, and the Body,* 139–86.

13. Dov Sadan, *'Al Sifrutenu* (On Our Literature), 11–12.

14. Sidra DeKoven Ezrahi, "When Exiles Return: Jerusalem as Topos of the Mind and Soil," 39; Ezrahi, *Booking Passage: Exile and Homecoming in the Modern Jewish Imagination;* George Steiner, "Our Homeland, the Text."

15. Ezrahi, "When Exiles Return," 49.

16. David Bergelson (1884–1952) was born into a Hasidic family near Uman in the Ukraine. His earliest writings were in Hebrew and Russian. He switched to Yiddish in 1907 and continued to write for the rest of his career in Yiddish. He published short stories and novels, most notably *Nokh alemen* (When All Is Said and Done) in 1913. He founded a literary society in 1912 in Kiev called the League for Jewish Culture along with Der Nister, Peretz Markish, David Hofstein, and Leib Kvitko. A strong supporter of communism in the 1920s, he was executed by Stalin in 1952 along with most of the surviving Yiddish writers living in the Soviet Union. See Golda Werman, introduction to *The Stories of David Bergelson: Yiddish Short Fiction from Russia,* xviii–xxiv.

17. In juxtaposing the talush and the *luftmensch,* it is important to consider the fact

that the classic shtetl texts tend to be Yiddish (with later Hebrew translations and adaptations, as in the case of Abramowitz's corpus), whereas the talush texts tend, as earlier discussed, to be identified with the Hebrew modernist tradition. The talush is identifiable in various Yiddish works such as those authored by Bergelson, but he is predominantly recognizable in the Hebrew works of the latter part of the modern Hebrew renaissance.

18. Baron, "Behinot," in *Parshiyot Mukdamot,* 492–93.

19. Mikhail Krutikov, "Berdichev in Russian Jewish Literary Imagination: From Israel Aksenfeld to Friedrich Gorenshtein," 95.

20. Ben Cion Pinchuk, "Jewish Discourse and the Shtetl," 176, 172, 170.

21. M. Gil, "Sipure Dvora Baron" (The Stories of Dvora Baron), 144.

22. Pinchuk, "Jewish Discourse," 176; Miron, *Literary Image,* xii.

23. S. Y. Pinles, "Mah she-Hayah" (What Has Been), 59. Pinles states this in reference to Frischmann's statement that "if, let us assume, a deluge comes, inundating and washing away from the face of the earth the Jewish ghetto and the Jewish life it contains, not leaving behind so much as a residue, a sign, except by sheer chance, Mendele's four major works as well as two or three shorter works, then, I doubt not, with these spared, the future scholar would be able to reconstruct the entire map of Jewish shtetl life in Russia of the first half of the nineteenth century in such a manner that not even one iota would be left out." See David Frischmann, "Mendele Mokher Sforim," 74, quoted in Miron, *Literary Image,* 7.

24. Baron, "What Has Been," in *Thorny Path,* 153.

25. On this rhetoric of strength, power, and the new Zionist (male, of course) Jewish body, see Anita Shapira, *Land and Power: The Zionist Resort to Force 1881–1948.* Also see Shapira, *Yehudim Hadashim Yehudim Yeshanim* (New Jews Old Jews).

26. See Joseph Hayyim Brenner, *ba-Horef* (In Winter), 175.

27. Georg Lukacs, *Studies in European Realism.*

28. Todd Hasak-Lowy, "Between Realism and Modernism: Brenner's Poetics of Fragmentation."

29. Joseph Hayyim Brenner, "ha-Genre ha-Eretz Yisre'eli ve-Avizarotav" (The Eretz Yisrael Genre and Its Accouterments), 268.

30. Baron, *Parshiyot* (1968), 546.

31. Ibid., 549–50.

32. Orly Lubin, "Zutot mi-Mitbaha shel Nehama: Leumiut Alternativit *ba-ha-Golim* shel Dvora Baron" (Tidbits from Nehama's Kitchen: Alternative Nationalism in Dvora Baron's *The Exiles*).

33. Baron, *ha-Golim,* 148.

3. Things as They Are: The Mimetic Imperative

1. Vivienne Silver-Brody, *Documenters of the Dream: Pioneer Jewish Photographers in the Land of Israel, 1890–1933,* 31.

2. See Ruth Oren, "Zionist Photography, 1910–1941: Constructing a Landscape"; Yeshayahu Nir, "Photographic Representation and Social Interaction: The Case of the Holy Land."

3. Baron, "In the Beginning," in *First Day,* 8; and Baron, "Bereshit," in *Parshiyot* (1968), 229.

4. Frischmann, "Mendele Mokher Sforim," 76.

5. A. L. Ben Avigdor, "Leah Mokheret ha-Dagim" (Leah the Fish Monger) (Warsaw, 1891), 1, quoted in Shaked, *ha-Siporet ha-Ivrit,* 223.

6. Tziporah Aharonovitch, ed., *Agav Urkha: me-Izvonah, 'al Dvora Baron ve-Svivotah* (By the Way: From the Archives on Dvora Baron and Her Context), 244.

7. Her first book was not published until 1927 in Jerusalem.

8. Joseph Hayyim Brenner, "mi-Sadeh ha-Sifrut" (From the Literary Field), 334–35.

9. Joseph Hayyim Brenner, *me-Emek Akur* (From a Barren Valley).

10. Ogen, "Dvora Baron," 147.

11. Baron, "Fradel," in *First Day,* 33; and in Baron, *Parshiyot* (1968), 102–3.

12. Baron, "The First Day," in *First Day,* 20; and "ha-Yom ha-Rishon," in Baron, *Parshiyot* (1968), 248.

13. Baron, "In the Beginning," in *First Day,* 6; and Baron, "Bereshit," in *Parshiyot* (1968), 227–28.

14. Baron, "In the Beginning," in *First Day,* 11; and Baron, "Bereshit," in *Parshiyot* (1968), 232.

15. Baron, "Mah she-Hayah," in *Parshiyot* (1968), 127.

16. Naomi Rosenblum, *A History of Women Photographers,* 41.

17. Victoria Olsen, *From Life: Julia Margaret Cameron and Victorian Photography,* 142.

18. The negative was the first photographic image, created as early as 1816 by Joseph Nicephore Niecpe, a French inventor. Using silver chloride, he figured out how to fix an image projected by what he called an "artificial eye" (a camera). The background was black, and the photographed images were white—just like the negatives from which we derive photographic images today. Niecpe could not determine, however, how to print a "positive" image from this photographic negative. In 1827 with the invention of a helio-graph, Niecpe managed to fix a positive image on a metal plate after an exposure of eight hours. William Henry Fox Talbot, around the same time, created paper negatives that facilitated the dissemination of many copies of the same image. The problem, however, with Talbot's calotypes was that the silver salts that fixed the image to the paper kept reacting to light, and the images he created could not be rendered permanent. As a corrective, in 1851 Frederick Scott Archer invented the wet collodion process wherein a glass negative produced a sharper, more permanent image than the paper calotype. Wet collodion negatives, however, had to be developed right away because they could not be worked with once they dried. In the 1870s, gelatin glass-plate negatives replaced collodion wet plates, enabling photographers to store their plates for an extended period. As

evidenced in this brief, unscientific account of the development of photographic technology, Daguerre, the figure generally associated with the birth of the photographic image, is missing. The famous daguerreotypes invented in 1839 by Daguerre created images that were irreproducible because they were based not on negatives, but on silver plate positives that skipped the negative stage. Olsen, *From Life*, 45–48.

19. Baron, *Parshiyot* (1968), 127, 180.

20. First published in 1952, the research for the book was conducted immediately after World War II, drawing to a conclusion in 1949. The original title of the book was *Life Is with People: The Jewish Little-Town in Eastern Europe*. With its reissue in the early 1960s, the subtitle was changed to *The Culture of the Shtetl*, thus effectively introducing the word "shtetl" into the vocabulary of American readers. David Roskies, "The Shtetl as Imagined Community," 6.

21. Mark Zborowski and Elizabeth Herzog, *Life Is with People: The Culture of the Shtetl*, 23.

22. Diane Roskies and David Roskies, *The Shtetl Book;* Roskies, "Shtetl as Imagined Community," 4, 8

23. Lucjan Dobroszycki and Barbara Kirschenblatt Gimblett, *Image Before My Eyes: A Photographic History of Jewish Life in Poland, 1864–1939*, 27.

24. Carol Zemel, "Imaging the Shtetl: Diaspora Culture, Photography and Eastern European Jews," 193–206.

25. Francis Galton, "Composite Portraits," 132, quoted in Daniel Novak, "A Model Jew: 'Literary Photographs' and the Jewish Body in *Daniel Deronda*," 58.

26. Alter Kacyzne, *Poyln: Jewish Life in the Old Country*, 27.

27. Ibid., 25.

28. Marianne Hirsch, *Family Frames: Photography, Narrative and Post-Memory*, 18.

29. Ibid.

30. Annette Kuhn, *Family Secrets: Acts of Memory and Imagination*, 157.

31. Baron, "What Has Been," in *Thorny Path*, 79; and Baron, "Mah she-Hayah," in *Parshiyot* (1968), 127.

32. Baron, *Parshiyot* (1968), 180.

33. Susan Sontag, *On Photography*, 64.

34. Walter Benjamin, "The Work of Art in the Age of Mechanical Reproduction," 236–37.

35. Martin W. Sandler, *Against the Odds: Women Pioneers in the First Hundred Years of Photography*, 3; Constance Sullivan, ed., *Women Photographers*, 12.

36. For a discussion of this polemic, see Hannan Hever, *Producing the Modern Hebrew Canon: Nation Building and Minority Discourse*, 13–18.

37. Pierre Bourdieu, *Photography: A Middle-Brow Art*, 7.

38. Ibid., 74.

39. Roland Barthes, *Camera Lucida: Reflections on Photography*, 70.

40. In fact, though women are excluded from Jewish communal life and are thus not obliged to follow most Jewish laws that are incumbent upon the individual Jew, the laws of family purity are one of three sets of laws that do pertain specifically, and exclusively, to women. The other two laws are the lighting of the Sabbath and holiday candles and the separation of a small bit of dough, called "hallah," when baking a certain amount of bread.

41. Baron, *Thorny Path,* 237; Baron, *Parshiyot* (1968), 84.

42. Baron, "The Thorny Path" in *Thorny Path,* 250; and Baron, *"Derekh Kotsim"* in *Parshiyot* (1968), 94; Benjamin, "Work of Art," 236.

43. Barthes, "To Write: An Intransitive Verb?" 18–20.

44. Donna Haraway, "The Persistence of Vision," 285.

4. She Sermonizes in Wool and Flax: The Vernacular Imperative

1. Moshe Gitlin, "bi-Neurehah: mi-Zikhronot ben Ir" (In Her Youth: Memories of a Neighbor), 208.

2. See "Mendele's Gurgling," in Sheila Jelen, "Writing from the Pulpit, Speaking from the Page: The Oral Voices of Modern Hebrew Fiction," 24–28. Also see Henry Louis Gates Jr., *The Signifying Monkey: A Theory of African-American Literary Criticism,* xxv–xxvi. Although Gates does not explicitly acknowledge it, his coining of the term "speakerly" is in dialogue with Roland Barthes's presentation of "readerly" and "writerly" texts in *S/Z.* See Roland Barthes, *S/Z,* 5.

3. Baron, "Mishpahah," in *Parshiyot* (1968), 11.

4. Agnon presents a lengthy one in *Only Yesterday;* Brenner depicts scholarly monologues in *Breakdown and Bereavement;* Haim Hazaz—a writer from a later generation—dedicates an entire story titled "ha-Drashah" (The Sermon) to the text of a modern secular sermon on a kibbutz.

5. In the Jerusalem Talmud, tractate Sotah 3:4, Rabbi Eliezer Ben Hyrcanus says: "The words of the Torah should be burnt rather than be taught to women."

6. See Joseph Heinemann, *Drashot ba-Tsibur bi-Tekufat ha-Talmud* (Public Sermons During the Period of the Talmud) and "Mesirat ha-'Agadot Ba'al Peh" (The Oral Transmission of Legends). For contenders to his theories, see Jacob Neusner, "The Oral Torah and Oral Tradition: Defining the Problematic," 59–78; and Yonah Frankel, *Darkhe ha-Agadah veha-Midrash.*

7. Baron's "Agunah" (Abandoned Wife) first appeared under the title "mi-mah she-'avar" (From What Has Passed), with "Agunah" as the subtitle. It is one of the few stories from Baron's "early period" (before 1923, as designated by Nurit Govrin) that she deemed good enough to publish in collected form. It first appeared in her 1927 volume and was subsequently republished in her 1939 and 1951 volumes. Naomi Seidman titles it "Deserted Wife" in its most readily available English translation.

8. Babylonian Talmud, tractate Berakhot 3b.

9. Ps. 57:9 and 108:3.

10. Babylonian Talmud, tractate Berakhot 3b and Eyn Yaakov 4.

11. Babylonian Talmud, tractate Sanhedrin 6b.

12. Num. 17:20–23.

13. Lam. 1:20.

14. Lam. Rabbah 1 and Yalkut Shimoni 1.

15. Isa. 1:5.

16. Lam. 5:5 and 3:46.

17. Jer. 30:10–11.

18. Jer. 31:14 and Gen. Rabbah 82.

19. Pesikta Rabati 20.

20. Lam. Rabbah 3.

21. Baron, "Agunah," in *Parshiyot* (1968), 301–3.

22. David Stern has termed the translation of *nimshal*, or resolution for a parable in midrashic literature, an "application." See Stern, *Parables in Midrash*, 8.

23. Baron, *Parshiyot* (1968), 303, 231. The woman's act of knitting through the preacher's sermons is more than a distraction from the performance of the sermon. In another story of Baron's, titled "Bereshit" (In the Beginning [1927]), the construction of sermons is developed in two conceits, surprising in their juxtaposition to each other. In the first, the father of the narrator, the community rabbi, embroiders sermons: "As he wove the threads of the sermon's embroidery, he strengthened it from time to time with proofs and evidence from various places." This conflation of what has traditionally been viewed as a woman's handicraft with a man's intellectual work lends an interesting dimension to our understanding of Baron's view of sermons. In "Agunah," embroidery and sermons seem initially to be deemed mutually incompatible, though, as we will see, the woman's point of view takes over the sermon and, to a certain degree, becomes responsible for its presentation to the reader.

24. The same phrase occurs in Baron's "Genizah" (Burying the Books). It seems to be a tool repeatedly used in Baron's sermon stories to provide an "in" for the narrator's voice. When the narrator tells us that we have arrived at the "essence of the sermon," we are reminded that the narrator is in control of the sermon's construction, or at least intimately connected to the sermon in such a way that he or she can parse the sermon for us as it unfolds.

25. Baron, *Parshiyot* (1968), 304.

26. Ibid., 306. Understanding the parable this way does not simply reflect ignorance of rabbinic hermeneutics on the woman's part. Rather, according to Shachar Pinsker, this understanding could reflect an alternative poetics, an alternative hermeneutic system. See Pinsker, "Old Wine in New Flasks."

27. Raphael's silence reflects the anxiety best expressed in the famous midrash about

the woman who goes to hear a sermon being given by Rabbi Meir on a Friday night. (The presence of the charity box of Rabbi Meir the Miracle Worker in the women's section also gestures toward this midrash.) While she is away, the Shabbat candles burn out, and when she returns home, her husband is so enraged that he throws her out of the house and tells her that she will not be allowed to come back until she spits in the eye of the rabbi whose sermon she attended. The rabbi, hearing about this, creates a situation in which she can spit in his eye for medicinal purposes without humiliating either herself or him, thereby enabling her to return to her husband. In this midrash, a woman seeking access to textual male culture through the medium of the sermon is punished for having "shirked" her God-given female responsibilities. An air of judgment, of anxiety over the possibility of women accessing that which is strictly male, also permeates the silence at the end of Baron's story. See Leviticus Rabbah, 9:9; and see Palestinian Talmud tractate Sota 1:4.

28. Brian Stock eloquently discusses the interplay between orality and textuality and how important it is to view them as diachronic, not synchronic, phenomena. He says that there is "no orality without implied textuality: no literacy without the primal force of the spoken word." See Stock, *Listening for the Text: On the Uses of the Past,* 4.

29. Lamentations Rabbah (Buber), chap. 3.

30. Alan Mintz, *Hurban: Responses to Catastrophe in Jewish Literature,* 80–83.

31. S. Y. Agnon, "Agunot," 315.

32. Baron, *First Day,* 77; and Baron, *Parshiyot* (1968), 26.

33. See Alicia Ostriker, *Stealing the Language: The Emergence of Women's Poetry in America.*

5. Burying the Books: The Intertextual Imperative

1. Other Yiddish works from the early modern period (such as *Bovo Bukk* [1507–1508] by Elia Levita and *Brantshpigl* [1602] by Eliahu Bakhur) were also associated primarily with Jewish women, but since Baron only mentions *tkhines* and *Tzenerene* here, those are the only two we will be discussing.

2. Chava Weissler illustrates the variety of *tkhines* beautifully when she compares two different *tkhines* to be recited on the occasion of baking hallah for the Sabbath. One draws upon obscure mystical traditions and reflects great erudition on the part of its author. One simply invokes a good angel to make sure the hallah rises nicely and tastes good. See Weissler, *Voices of the Matriarchs,* 32–33.

3. See Isa. 65:24. *"Tkhine* of the Matriarchs for the New Moon of Elul," in *The Merit of Our Mothers: A Bilingual Anthology of Women's Prayers,* edited by Tracy Guren Klirs, Faedra Lazar Weiss, and Barbary Selya, 46.

4. Ibid., *"Tkhine* of the Matriarchs," 116.

5. Weissler, *Voices of the Matriarchs,* 6; Chone Shmeruk, "Di Mizrah-Europesheh

Nusahaos fun der Tzenerene (1850–1786)" (The Eastern European Versions of the *Tzenerene* [1850–1786]), 320–36. Jeremy Dauber has observed that the earliest extant copy of the *Tzenerene* was published in 1622, but that volume refers to two earlier ones. Dauber, "A New Look at the *Tzenerene:* What Did it Take to Be an Uneducated Jew?"

6. Shmeruk, "Di Mizrah-Europesheh Nusahaos fun der Tzenerene," 195.

7. For background on the *Tzenerene,* see Chone Shmeruk, *Sifrut Yiddish ba-Polin: Mehkarim be-'Iyunim Histori'im* (Yiddish Literature in Poland: Studies and Historical Overviews), 147–64. See also Shmeruk, *Sifrut Yiddish: Perakim le-Toldotehah* (Yiddish Literature: Chapters in Its Evolution), chaps. 1–5. Quoted in Weissler, *Voices of the Matriarchs,* 193–94.

8. Haym Soloveitchik, "Rupture and Reconstruction: The Transformation of American Orthodoxy," 129; Yosef Svirsky, "Dapim Mitokh Pinkasai: Perakim mi-Tokh Sefer Zikhronotai mi-Yerushalayim" (Pages from My Notebooks: Chapters from My Jerusalem Memoirs), quoted and translated in Weissler, *Voices of the Matriarchs,* 207; Cynthia Ozick, "Notes Toward Finding the Right Question," 131.

9. On heder culture in medieval Europe, see Ivan Marcus, *Rituals of Childhood: Jewish Acculturation in Medieval Europe.* Although Marcus describes education during a period historically earlier than the period under discussion, the general institution remains the same. Also, for a rendition of the educational system in a more contemporary period, see Stampfer, "Heder Study," 271–89.

10. Iris Parush, *Reading Women: The Advantages of Marginality,* 65.

11. Yaakov ben Yitzhak Ashkenazi, *The Weekly Midrash: Tzenerene—the Classic Anthology of Torah Lore and Midrashic Commentary,* 17.

12. In a similar vein, the author of the *Tzenerene,* in choosing to share this midrash at its outset, bypasses the more standard commentary—that of Rashi (Rabenu Shlomo Yitzhaki, 1040–1105, Troyes)—which is automatically taught, in traditional communities, alongside the primary text of the Torah. Indeed, the author of the *Tzenerene* draws from the commentary of Hizkuni (Rabbi Hizkiyah ben Harav Manoah, sixteenth century, Venice), also a well-known commentator but not "standard" in the Bible edition (Mikraot Gedolot, or the Greatest Hits version) generally used for instruction.

13. A *gabbai* is the man in a traditional synagogue responsible for making sure the service (both prayer and Torah reading) goes smoothly. A *kapota* is a long black dress robe that Orthodox men in eastern Europe wore over their clothing on fancy occasions.

14. Baron, "Genizah," in *Parshiyot* (1968), 241.

15. Perhaps *tkhines'* lowly status, as reflected in the children's ridicule in the later story as well as in the brother's absolute refusal to consider burying the mother's *tkhines* in the earlier story, can be taken in the context of Yiddish texts written for "women and men who are like women." *Tkhines* from the nineteenth and early twentieth centuries were considered exclusively for women if only because, in general, they acknowledge life events experienced only by women. This belief, according to Chava Weissler, however, is

a misperception. She points out that harbingers of Yiddish *tkhines* written to commemorate women's life-cycle events and domestic rituals originated in the Galilean town of Safed, the home of Jewish mysticism, during the sixteenth century as pietistic Hebrew *tehinot,* or extraliturgical devotions. The introduction to an early collection of Yiddish *tkhines* in 1648, in fact, says that women wanted to participate in the recitation of Hebrew mystically based devotional prayers but needed to have them translated into Yiddish in order to do so. Thus, although by the nineteenth century in a non-Hassidic milieu Yiddish *tkhines* seem to have been exclusively associated with women, they were, at their inception, a mystical pietistic form originally authored in Hebrew and designated for men. Weissler, *Voices of the Matriarchs,* 12.

16. Baron, "Burying the Books," in *First Day,* 153.

17. See Iris Parush, "Mabat Aher 'al 'Hayey ha-'Ivrit ha-Metah': hav'arot ha-mekhuvanot bi-Leshon ha-'Ivrit be-Hevrah ha-Yehudit ha-Mizrah Iropit ba-Me'ah ha-19 ve-hashpa'atah 'al ha-Sifrut ha-'Ivrit ve-Kore'hah" (Another Look at the Life of Dead Hebrew: Deliberate Obstruction of the Hebrew Language in 19th Century Eastern European Jewish Society and Its Influence on Hebrew Literature and Its Readers).

18. Max Weinreich in a 1959 essay defines the relationship between Hebrew and Yiddish in eastern European Jewish society as a relationship of "internal bilingualism." The two languages play separate sociological roles within the community and can be distinguished by speech in the Yiddish domain and writing in the Hebrew domain. Weinreich, "Ineveynikste Tsvey Shpra'khikeyt In Ashkenaz Biz Der Haskoloh: faktn un bagrifn" (Internal Bilingualism in Ashkenaz until the Haskalah: Facts and Concepts). Quoted in Naomi Seidman, *A Marriage Made in Heaven: The Sexual Politics of Hebrew and Yiddish,* 1:139.

19. Of course, money held much sway within the traditional community as well. One could, however, climb the social ladder with scholarship and without money. Young promising scholars were often groomed by their penniless families to be "sponsored" by a family with money who would provide a bride and room and board for the furtherance of the young scholar's aspirations. This marriage of scholarship and money, its successes and its failures, has been amply documented in the literature of the turn of the century in Hebrew, English, and Yiddish. See, for example, Abraham Cahan, *The Rise of David Levinsky.*

20. See, for example, Chaim Nachman Bialik, "Hevle Lashon" (Language Pangs), 185.

21. In the space of the past half a century, that equation has changed significantly, and the language that has ceased to be used by the majority of Jews of European origin is now being called a "dead" language.

22. For a discussion of the choice to write in Yiddish over Hebrew during the period of the Jewish Enlightenment, see Dan Miron, "A Language as Caliban," in *A Traveler Disguised: The Rise of Modern Yiddish Fiction in the Nineteenth Century,* 35–66.

23. David Neal Miller points out that Yiddish only belatedly was able to articulate a literary tradition for itself. Miller, "Transgressing the Bounds: On the Origins of Yiddish Literature," 95.

24. See the Kitzur Shulhan Aruch, Law 201. In fact, many exceptions can be made to this rule. For example, if the suicide victim was mentally ill, or severely depressed, the suicide is not viewed as a violation of the law, "and you should live by them." Also, those deceased who are supposed to be buried a distance from other Jews do not have to be outside the graveyard, but only a legislated distance apart.

25. Chava Turniansky of the Hebrew University of Jerusalem is currently writing a monograph on the history and reception of Yiddish translations of the Bible. It provides an interesting case study of Yiddish as a channel for what was considered the most sacred of texts, and reactions to the use of the vernacular language for that purpose.

26. In the twentieth century, Yiddish literature was finally legitimated as a vehicle for contemporary Jewish bathos and comedy (as in the work of Sholem Aleichem at the end of the nineteenth century), as a fully realized modernist fictional idiom (as in the work of Y. L. Peretz and S. Ansky at the turn of the twentieth century), and finally as the tool for a wide range of poetic expression (as in the movement of the New York Yiddish poets during the 1920s and the 1930s).

27. For an example of this complex dynamic, see S. J. Abramowitz, "be-Seter Ra'am" (In the Secret Place of Thunder) (1886). Mendele, in this story, meditates at great length on his impulse to speak in *melitsah* style. He seems, in the Russian formalist sense, to be "laying bare his own device," pointing to the role of texts within even an orally configured rhetorical voice. Mendele creates a hall of mirrors in which his oral style and the written style in which his oral style is depicted reflect each other to construct a commentary on the oral performance of textual culture. Abramowitz, "be-Seter Ra'am," 12–13.

28. Even while working to render his texts oral, Abramowitz encodes consciousness of the fictionality of that orality, of the impossibility of creating a truly accessible oral text out of elite intertextual components. Both Chaim Nachman Bialik and S. Y. Agnon do the same thing throughout their corpora, expressing incredulity over the possibility of expecting that the Hebrew in which their texts are rendered is really the language of the discourses represented within the texts themselves. Bialik, in "Aryeh Ba'al Guf" (Brawny Aryeh) (1899), has his protagonist, in Hebrew, undermine the very Hebrew in which the text is rendered by expressing disdain for Hebrew and the cultural milieu with which it was associated. He claims, in Hebrew, not to know a word of Hebrew, and not to have any desire to learn it. In S. Y. Agnon's "Shvuat Emunim" (Betrothed) (1943), Shoshana, the main female protagonist, turns to Yaakov about fifty pages into the Hebrew story and asks him what language he is speaking to their carriage driver in Yafo. "Oh, Hebrew!" she says. "How quaint." See Bialik, "Brawny Aryeh"; and Agnon, "Shvuat Emunim."

29. Yael Chaver, *What Must Be Forgotten: The Survival of Yiddish in Zionist Palestine,* xxii.

30. Ibid., 15–16, 6, 18–19.

31. Nurit Govrin, *Dvash mi-Sel'a: Mehkarim be-Sifrut Eretz Yisrael* (Honey from a Rock: Studies in Israeli Literature), 302–3.

32. In her study of the sexual politics of Hebrew and Yiddish, Naomi Seidman introduces this approach to Hebrew and Yiddish as "gendered" and "sexualized" vis-à-vis one another during the period of the modern Hebrew renaissance. See Seidman, *Marriage Made in Heaven.*

33. Ben Yehudah, "Dvora Madrikhat Noar," 214.

34. See B. B. (Batya Brenner), "I Become a Worker," 65–85.

35. *ha-Golim* was published posthumously by Baron's daughter, Tziporah Aharonovitch, in 1970. It comprises two novellas: *le-Et Atah* (For the Time Being) and *me-Emesh* (Since Yesterday), which were originally published in 1962 and 1955, respectively.

36. Baron, *ha-Golim,* 174.

37. Baron, "Gilgulim" (Transformations), 400–411.

38. Yehudit Harari, "Huryah," 33–43.

39. Baron, *ha-Golim,* 33–34.

40. Baron and her daughter did, in fact, burn many of her earlier manuscripts, and archival material is virtually nonexistent beyond the publication correspondence for her later works. Because Baron's literary career spanned approximately fifty years and the circumstances of her evolution as a Hebrew writer have so many social and cultural implications, it has been the source of much scholarly frustration and disappointment that a more comprehensive examination of her manuscripts cannot be conducted. The shifts in Baron's treatment of women's issues, the evolution of her Hebrew style, the shifts in her intertextual preferences over the years, and her treatment of political Zionism before and after her emigration to Palestine are all issues that could best be explored in a comparative manner, through scrutiny of earlier and later manuscripts of the same stories as well as different ones. With the preservation, however, of all the original journals in which her early stories were published, though we may not have access to the process whereby many of her stories were transformed, or the decisions involved in the rejection of much of her early work, we are able, at least, to read the final versions of her earlier stories. Nurit Govrin has collected most of those stories in *Parshiyot Mukdamot.* Aharonovitch, "Homer la-Biographiah" (Biographical Materials), 9–10.

41. Seidman, *Marriage Made in Heaven,* 1:92.

42. Chaim Nachman Bialik and Yehoshua Hana Ravnitsky edited *The Book of Legends* between 1908 and 1912. Micha Yosef Berdischevsky published a series of anthologies, beginning in 1900 with an anthology of Hasidic tales. From 1903 to 1904, he edited *The Life of Moses, the Man of God,* a narrative composition on the life of Moses based on biblical and midrashic texts. In 1914 he published *From the Treasures of the Aggadah* and *Secrets and Legends.* Both represent the marriage of folk traditions, gleaned from tradi-

tional rabbinic texts, and modern narrative art. From 1913 to 1927 he published, in German, *The Legends of the Jews,* and from 1916 to 1923, he also published in German, *The Spring of Judah.* By compiling these works in German he attempted, according to Tziporah Kagan, to "place the legends of Israel among the other great collections of folk legends that were considered to be the timeless assets of the nations of the world." His most famous anthology was titled *Mimekor Yisrael* (From the Fount of Israel), which was published posthumously in 1939. This anthology contains about a thousand tales and fictional stories, presented as folktales. It gleans material from post-Talmudic sources through Hassidism. In *The Legends of the Jews (1909–1938),* Louis Ginzberg collected parables, maxims, and legends from rabbinic literature and wove them into a continuous narrative. Y. L. Peretz edited *Folkstimlekhe Geshicktes* (Folksy Tales) from 1903 to 1904, and in 1901 Saul Ginzburg and Peysakh Markesh published 376 Yiddish folksongs.

43. This same midrash is drawn upon by Bialik, too, in his story "Agadat Shloshah ve-'Arba'ah" (The Legend of the Three and Four.) Scholars of Bialik have dedicated much energy to tracking down Bialik's sources, both textual and oral, for this narrative. See Ephraim A. Auerbach, "'Agadat Shloshah ve-'Arba'ah'—Yetsirah Mekorit" ('The Legend of the Three and Four'—the Story and Its Sources); and A. M. Haberman, "Nusah Kadum shel Makor 'Agadat Shloshah ve-'Arba'ah' " (An Earlier Source for "The Legend of the Three and Four").

44. Ps. 68:7; Solomon Buber, ed., *Midrash Tanhumah,* "Introduction," Section 42, 136.

45. Baron, *Parshiyot Mukdamot,* 530–31.

46. Ernest Renan, "What Is a Nation?" 8–22.

6. Epilogue: Breaking Down the Door

1. Govrin, *ha-Mahatsit ha-Rishonah;* Amia Lieblich, *Rekamot: Sihotai im Dvora Baron* (Embroideries: My Conversations with Dvora Baron); Lieblich, *Conversations with Dvora: An Experimental Biography of the First Modern Hebrew Woman Writer.*

2. Billy Moskona-Lerman, "Malka ba-Armon Shahor" (Queen in a Black Palace).

3. Yael Fishbein, "Tfilat ha-Yahid u-Tefilat ha-Tsibur" (Private Prayer and Public Prayer).

4. As I have mentioned in the course of this study, many writers lost their wherewithal upon arrival in Palestine. After spending so much of their childhoods and early careers imagining a dramatic redemptive homecoming, they found instead, once they arrived, that they had left a cosmopolitan, variegated world in Europe behind for a dry, dusty, and defeating intellectual and political landscape. Baron may very well, in this view, have had enough of Palestine by 1923 and, having already established a family there, decided that her only recourse was to withdraw from it—into her apartment.

5. Amalya Kahana-Carmon, "The Song of the Bats in Flight," 235–48.

6. Yehudit Katsir, "Dvora Baron: Mahazeh bi-Shtei Ma'arakhot" (Dvora Baron: A Play in Two Acts), 542–96.

7. How does Lieblich write this strange dialogue? Baron's "voice" is drawn whole cloth from her fictional works. Lieblich's voice, on the other hand, is rendered in contemporary Hebrew and inserted primarily as a commentary on and a dialogic response to Baron's narratives.

8. Sandra Gilbert and Susan Gubar, *The Madwoman in the Attic: The Woman Writer and the Nineteenth-Century Literary Imagination,* 83.

9. Nurit Zarhi published a fictional account about Baron entitled "Madame Bovary in Neveh Tzedek" (Madame Bovary bi-Neveh Tzedek), in which Madame Bovary visits Dvora Baron in Neveh Tzedek. The disgust and compassion with which Baron beholds Madame Bovary are brilliantly indicative of Baron's own conflicted status as a woman caught up in a net of bourgeoisie expectations. This story also reflects Baron's continuing impact on contemporary Hebrew writers as a mythical figure and a model of sorts.

10. In fact, Baron's translation is still the translation of choice in contemporary Israel. A new, unabridged translation from the French by Irit Akravi seems not to have appeared until 1991. Between 1932 and 1991, Baron's was the only extant unabridged translation from the French.

11. Shlomo Grozinski, "Dvora Baron: he-Hayim ha-Mesuparim" (Dvora Baron: The Narrated Life).

12. Although Grozninski found it in 1916, he describes it as having been discarded in a trash pile outside in the courtyard of his building. We can assume, in the scene he describes, that the journal was at least several years old.

Appendix A. Two Translations and a Note: "In What World?" and "As a Driven Leaf"

1. The *Shma,* the "Hear O Israel" prayer, is recited several times a day in traditional Jewish culture, including bedtime.

2. Gen. 15:12.

3. A *kittel* is a white robe worn by men at their marriage, and on major Jewish holidays such as Passover and the Day of Atonement. They are also buried in it. A *tallis* is a prayer shawl.

4. According to Jewish law, the close relatives of the dead must go through a process of mourning that includes the ritualized tearing of the mourner's garments.

5. The mourner's Kaddish is recited, in traditional Jewish society, by the son of the dead, or by the closest male relative. Here, Rachel watches the congregants recite this prayer through a curtain because she cannot participate in communal prayer and cannot say the prayer for the dead over her father.

6. A mezuzah is a scroll containing the "Hear O Israel" prayer that is affixed to every doorway of a house.

7. Gen. 48:7.

8. Petah Tikva was the first modern agricultural settlement in Palestine.

9. This act is a traditional sign of engagement.

10. Num. 11:15.

11. As the Hebrew language was being revived, there was a movement to pronounce spoken Hebrew according to a "Sephardic" accentual system, with ultimate stresses as opposed to penultimate, and with pronounced gutturals. It was called Sephardic only in order to distinguish it from the eastern European "Ashkenazic" system in use for millennia. In reality, it would best be called a non-Ashkenazic system because there is no single distinctly Sephardic system. Rather, different accents evolved in different regions. There was, simply, strong resistance to Hebrew sounding "like" Yiddish in Ashkenazic mouths, so Ashkenzai pronunciation was demonized.

Works Cited

Aberbach, David. *Bialik*. New York: Grove Press, 1988.

Abramowitz, S. J. "be-Seter Ra'am" (In the Secret Place of Thunder). In *Kol Kitve Mendele Mokher Sforim* (Collected Works of Mendele Mokher Sfarim). Jerusalem: Moriah, 1911.

————. *Kol Kitve Mendele Mokher Sforim* (Collected Works of Mendele Mokher Sfarim). Tel Aviv: Dvir, 1956.

————. "Of Bygone Days." In *A Shtetl and Other Yiddish Novellas*, edited by Ruth Wisse. New York: Behrman House, 1973.

————. *Tales of Mendele the Book Peddler: Fishke the Lame and Benjamin the Third*. Edited by Dan Miron and Ken Frieden. Translated by Ted Gorelick and Hillel Halkin. New York: Schocken Books, 1996.

Abramson, Glenda, ed. *The Oxford Book of Hebrew Short Stories*. Oxford: Oxford Univ. Press, 1997.

Adler, Eliyana R. "Educational Options for Jewish Girls in Nineteenth Century Europe." In *Polin: Studies in Polish Jewry*, edited by Antony Polonsky. Oxford: Littman Library of Jewish Civilization, 2002.

————. "Women's Education in the Pages of the Russian Jewish Press." In *Jewish Women in Eastern Europe: Polin*, edited by Chaeran Freeze, Paula Hyman, and Antony Polonsky. London: Littman Library of Jewish Civilization, 2005.

Adler, Ruth. "Dvora Baron: Daughter of the Shtetl." In *Women of the Word: Jewish Women and Jewish Writing*, edited by Judith R. Baskin. Detroit: Wayne State Univ. Press, 1994.

Agnon, S. Y. "Agunot" (Abandoned Wives). In *Elu ve-Elu* (These and Those). Tel Aviv: Schocken, 1978.

———. "In the Prime of Her Life." In *Eight Great Hebrew Short Novels,* edited by Alan Lelchuk and Gershon Shaked. New York: New American Library, 1983.

———. *Only Yesterday.* Translated by Barbara Harshav. Princeton: Princeton Univ. Press, 2000.

———. "Shvuat Emunim." In *'Ad Henah* (Until Here). Jerusalem: Schocken, 1977.

Aharonovitch, Tziporah, ed. *Agav Urkha: me-Izvonah, 'al Dvora Baron ve-Svivotah* (By the Way: From the Archives on Dvora Baron and Her Context). Israel: Poalim, 1960.

———. "Homer la-Biographiah" (Biographical Materials). In *Agav Urkha: me-Izvonah, 'al Dvora Baron ve-Svivotah* (By the Way: From the Archives on Dvora Baron and Her Context), edited by Tziporah Aharonovitch. Israel: Poalim, 1960.

Alper, Rivka. "'Al Dvora Baron" (On Dvora Baron). In *Agav Urkha: me-Izvonah, 'al Dvora Baron ve-Svivotah* (By the Way: From the Archives on Dvora Baron and Her Context), edited by Tziporah Aharonovitch. Israel: Poalim, 1960.

Alter, Robert. *The Invention of Hebrew Prose.* Seattle: Univ. of Washington Press, 1988.

Anderson, Bendedict. *Imagined Communities.* London: Verso, 1983.

Anderson, George K. *The Legend of the Wandering Jew.* Providence: Brown Univ. Press, 1965.

Armstrong, Nancy. *Fiction in the Age of Photography: The Legacy of British Realism.* Cambridge: Harvard Univ. Press, 1999.

Ashkenazi, Yaakov ben Yitshak. *The Weekly Midrash: Tzenerene—the Classic Anthology of Torah Lore and Midrashic Commentary.* Translated by Miriam Stark Zakon. Brooklyn: Mesorah, 1994.

Auerbach, Ephraim A. "'Agadat Shloshah ve-Arba'ah'—Yetsirah Mekorit" ('The Legend of the Three and Four'—the Story and Its Sources). *Ha-Universitah* 18, no. 2 (June 1973): 58–71.

Balin, Carol B. *To Reveal Our Hearts: Jewish Women Writers in Tsarist Russia.* Cincinnati: Hebrew Union College Press, 2000.

Bark, Sandra, ed. *Beautiful as the Moon, Radiant as the Stars: Jewish Women in Yiddish Stories, an Anthology.* New York: Warner Books, 2003.

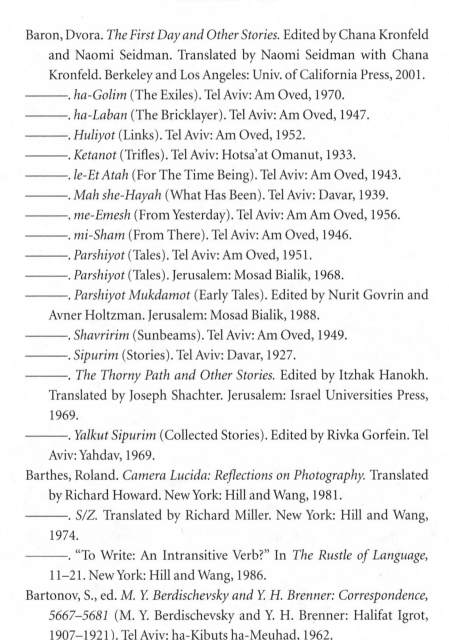

Baron, Dvora. *The First Day and Other Stories*. Edited by Chana Kronfeld and Naomi Seidman. Translated by Naomi Seidman with Chana Kronfeld. Berkeley and Los Angeles: Univ. of California Press, 2001.

———. *ha-Golim* (The Exiles). Tel Aviv: Am Oved, 1970.

———. *ha-Laban* (The Bricklayer). Tel Aviv: Am Oved, 1947.

———. *Huliyot* (Links). Tel Aviv: Am Oved, 1952.

———. *Ketanot* (Trifles). Tel Aviv: Hotsa'at Omanut, 1933.

———. *le-Et Atah* (For The Time Being). Tel Aviv: Am Oved, 1943.

———. *Mah she-Hayah* (What Has Been). Tel Aviv: Davar, 1939.

———. *me-Emesh* (From Yesterday). Tel Aviv: Am Am Oved, 1956.

———. *mi-Sham* (From There). Tel Aviv: Am Oved, 1946.

———. *Parshiyot* (Tales). Tel Aviv: Am Oved, 1951.

———. *Parshiyot* (Tales). Jerusalem: Mosad Bialik, 1968.

———. *Parshiyot Mukdamot* (Early Tales). Edited by Nurit Govrin and Avner Holtzman. Jerusalem: Mosad Bialik, 1988.

———. *Shavririm* (Sunbeams). Tel Aviv: Am Oved, 1949.

———. *Sipurim* (Stories). Tel Aviv: Davar, 1927.

———. *The Thorny Path and Other Stories*. Edited by Itzhak Hanokh. Translated by Joseph Shachter. Jerusalem: Israel Universities Press, 1969.

———. *Yalkut Sipurim* (Collected Stories). Edited by Rivka Gorfein. Tel Aviv: Yahdav, 1969.

Barthes, Roland. *Camera Lucida: Reflections on Photography*. Translated by Richard Howard. New York: Hill and Wang, 1981.

———. *S/Z*. Translated by Richard Miller. New York: Hill and Wang, 1974.

———. "To Write: An Intransitive Verb?" In *The Rustle of Language*, 11–21. New York: Hill and Wang, 1986.

Bartonov, S., ed. *M. Y. Berdischevsky and Y. H. Brenner: Correspondence, 5667–5681* (M. Y. Berdischevsky and Y. H. Brenner: Halifat Igrot, 1907–1921). Tel Aviv: ha-Kibuts ha-Meuhad, 1962.

Bauman, Zygmunt. "Allosemitism: Premodern, Modern, Postmodern." In *Modernity, Culture and "the Jew,"* edited by Bryan Cheyette and Laura Marcus. Stanford: Stanford Univ. Press, 1998.

Bendix, Regina. *In Search of Authenticity: The Formation of Folklore Studies*. Madison: Univ. of Wisconsin Press, 1997.

Benjamin, Walter. "The Work of Art in the Age of Mechanical Reproduction." In *Illuminations,* translated by Harry Zohn. New York: Schocken, 1968.

Ben Yehudah, Barukh. "Dvora Madrikhat Noar" (Dvora, a Youth Counselor). In *Agav Urkha: me-Izvonah, 'al Dvora Baron ve-Svivotah* (By the Way: From the Archives on Dvora Baron and Her Context), edited by Tziporah Aharonovitch. Israel: Poalim, 1960.

Berdischevsky, M. Y. "Urvah Parah" (A Raven Flies). In *Romanim* (Novellas). Jerusalem: Mosad Bialik, 1971.

———. "Without Hope." In *The Oxford Book of Hebrew Short Stories,* edited by Glenda Abramson. Oxford: Oxford Univ. Press, 1997.

Bergelson, David. 1909. *Arum Vaksal* (Around the Station: Stories). Warsaw: Ferlag Progres.

———. *The Stories of David Bergelson: Yiddish Short Fiction from Russia.* Translated by Golda Werman. Syracuse: Syracuse Univ. Press, 1996.

Berkowitz, Y. D. *Sipurim* (Stories). Cracow: Yosef Fisher, 1909.

Berlovich, Yaffa. "Rachel Morpurgo: ha-Teshukah el ha-Mavet, ha-Teshukah el ha-Shir; la-Tivah shel ha-Meshoreret ha-'Ivrit ha-Rishonah ba-'Et ha-Hadashah" (Rachel Morpurgo: The Desire for Death, the Desire for Poetry; Understanding the First Modern Hebrew Woman Poet in the Modern Period). In *Sadan: Studies in Hebrew Literature: Selected Essays on Women's Hebrew Poetry,* edited by Ziva Shamir, vol. 2. Tel Aviv: Tel Aviv Univ. Press, 1996.

Bialik, Chaim Nachman. "Agadat Shloshah ve-'Arba'ah" (The Legend of the Three and Four). In *Kol Kitve Chaim Nachman Bialik: be-Kerekh Ehad uve-Shnei Krakhim* (Collected Works of Chaim Nachman Bialik: In One Volume and in Two Volumes). Tel Aviv: Hotsa'at Va'ad ha-Yovel, 1932.

———. "Brawny Aryeh." In *Kol Kitve Chaim Nachman Bialik* (Collected Works of Chaim Nachman Bialik). Tel Aviv: Dvir, 1947.

———. "Hevle Lashon" (Language Pangs). In *Kol Kitve Chaim Nachman Bialik* (Collected Works of Chaim Nachman Bialik). Tel Aviv: Dvir, 1947.

———. *Kol Kitve Chaim Nachman Bialik* (Collected Works of Chaim Nachman Bialik). Tel Aviv: Dvir, 1947.

————. *Random Harvest: The Novellas of Bialik.* Translated by David Patterson and Ezra Spicehandler. Boulder: Westview Press, 1999.

Bordo, Susan. *Unbearable Weight: Feminism, Western Culture, and the Body.* Berkeley and Los Angeles: Univ. of California Press, 1993.

Bourdieu, Pierre. *Photography: A Middle-Brow Art.* Stanford: Stanford Univ. Press, 1990.

Boyarin, Daniel. *Unheroic Conduct: The Rise of Heterosexuality and the Invention of the Jewish Man.* Berkeley and Los Angeles: Univ. of California Press, 1997.

Boyarin, Daniel, and Jonathan Boyarin. "Diaspora: Generation and the Ground of Jewish Identity." *Critical Inquiry* 19 (summer 1993): 693–735.

Brenner, Batya. "I Become a Worker." In *The Plough Woman: Memoirs of the Pioneer Women of Palestinee,* edited by Rachel Katznelson-Shazar. New York: Herzl Press, 1975.

Brenner, Joseph Hayyim. "ba-Horef" (In Winter). In *Katavim* (Writings). Vol. 1. Israel: Hotsa'at ha-Kibutz ha-Meuhad, 1976.

————. *Breakdown and Bereavement: A Novel.* Translated by Hillel Halkin. Philadelphia: Jewish Publication Society, 1971.

————. "ha-Genre ha-Eretz Yisre'eli ve-Avizarotav" (The Eretz Yisrael Genre and Its Accouterments). In *Kol Kitve Y. H. Brenner* (Collected Works of Y. H. Brenner). Vol. 2. Israel: ha-Kibuts ha-Meuhad, 1960.

————. *Kol Kitve Y. H. Brenner* (Collected Works of Y. H. Brenner). Vols. 1–2. Israel: ha-Kibutz ha-Meuhad, 1960.

————. *me-Emek Akur* (From a Barren Valley). Warsaw: Toshiah, 1900.

————. "mi-Hirhure Sofer" (Musings of an Author). In *Kol Kitve Y. H. Brenner* (Collected Works of Y. H. Brenner). Vol. 2. Israel: ha-Kibuts ha-Meuhad, 1960.

————. "mi-Sadeh ha-Sifrut" (From the Literary Field). In *Kol Kitve Y. H. Brenner* (Collected Works of Y. H. Brenner). Vol. 2. Israel: ha-Kibuts ha-Meuhad, 1960.

Brinker, Menachem. *'Ad ha-Simtah ha-Teveryanit: Ma'amar 'al Sipur ve-Mahshavah bi-Yetsirat Brenner* (Narrative Art and Social Thought in Y. H. Brenner's Work). Tel Aviv: Am Oved, 1990.

Buber, Solomon, ed. *Midrash Tanhumah.* Vilna: 1885.

Cahan, Abraham. *The Rise of David Levinsky.* New York: Harper, 1966.

Chaver, Yael. *What Must Be Forgotten: The Survival of Yiddish in Zionist Palestine.* Syracuse: Syracuse Univ. Press, 2004.

Cheyette, Bryan, and Laura Marcus, eds. *Modernity, Culture and "the Jew."* Stanford: Stanford Univ. Press, 1998.

Cohen, Tova. "Betokh ha-Tarbut umi-Hutsah lah: 'Al Nikhus Sfat ha-Av ke-Derekh la-'Itsuv Intelectuali shel he-Ani ha-Nashi" (In the Culture and Outside the Culture: On the Acquisition of the Father's Language in the Construction of an Intellectual Authorial Voice for Women). In *Sadan: Studies in Hebrew Literature: Selected Essays on Women's Hebrew Poetry,* edited by Ziva Shamir, vol. 2. Tel Aviv: Tel Aviv Univ. Press, 1996.

Dauber, Jeremy. "A New Look at the *Tzenerene:* What Did It Take to Be an Uneducated Jew?" Rebecca and Joseph Meyerhoff Center for Jewish Studies at the Univ. of Maryland, Nov. 14, 2003.

Derrida, Jacques. "The Law of Genre." Translated by Avital Ronnell. *Glyph* 7 (1980): 176–201.

Dickinson, Emily. *The Poems of Emily Dickinson.* Edited by R. W. Franklin. Cambridge: Belknap Press of Harvard Univ. Press, 1999.

Dobroszycki, Lucjan, and Barbara Kirschenblatt Gimblett. *Image Before My Eyes: A Photographic History of Jewish Life in Poland, 1864–1939.* New York: Schocken, 1977.

Estraikh, Gennady, and Mikhail Krutikov, eds. *The Shtetl: Image and Reality.* Oxford: Legenda, 2000.

Ezrahi, Sidra DeKoven. *Booking Passage: Exile and Homecoming in the Modern Jewish Imagination.* Berkeley and Los Angeles: Univ. of California Press, 2000.

———. "When Exiles Return: Jerusalem as Topos of the Mind and Soil." In *Placeless Topographies: Jewish Perspectives on the Literature of Exile,* edited by Bernhard Greiner. Tübingen: Max Nieyamar Verlag, 2003.

Feiner, Shmuel. "ha-Ishah ha-Yehudiyah ha-Modernit: Mikrah Mivhan ba-Yahase ha-Haskalah veha-Modernah" (The Modern Jewish Woman: A Test Case in the Intersection of Modernity and the Enlightenment"). *Zion: A Quarterly for Research in Jewish History* (in Hebrew) 58, no. 4 (1993): 453–99.

————. "Towards a Historical Definition of the Haskalah." In *New Perspectives on the Haskalah,* edited by Shmuel Feiner and David Sorkin. London: Littman Library of Jewish Civilization, 2001.

Feiner, Shmuel, and David Sorkin, eds. *New Perspectives on the Haskalah.* London: Littman Library of Jewish Civilization, 2001.

Fishbein, Yael. "Tfilat ha-Yahid u-Tefilat ha-Tsibur" (Private Prayer and Public Prayer). *Davar,* Jan. 29, 1988.

Flaubert, Gustave. *Madame Bovary* (in Hebrew). Translated by Dvora Baron. Berlin: Shtibel, 1932.

Foner, Sarah Feige Meinkin. *Ahavat Yesharim o ha-Mishpahot ha-Murdafot: Sipur min ha-'Et ha-Hadashah* (The Love of the Righteous or the Pursued Families: A Modern Tale). Vilna: H. Katzenelenbogen, 1881.

————. *Beged Bogdim: Sipur mi-Yeme Shimon ha-Kohen* (The Garment of a Traitor: A Tale from the Days of Simon the Hight Priest). Warsaw: Druk Fun A Ginz, 1891.

————. *mi-Zikhronot Yeme Yalduti o Mar'eh ha-'Ir Dvinsk* (Memoirs of a Childhood or a Portrait of Dvinsk). Warsaw: bi-Defus ha-Tzefirah, 1903.

————. *A Woman's Voice: Sarah Foner, Hebrew Author of the Haskalah.* Translated by Morris Rosenthal. Wilbraham, Mass.: Dailey International Publishers, 2001.

Frankel, Jonah. *Darkhe ha-Agadah veha-Midrash* (The Ways of Legend and Midrash). Givatayim: Yad la-Talmud, 1991.

Frischmann, David. "Mendele Mokher Sforim." In *Kol Kitve David Frischmann* (Collected Works of David Frischmann). Vol. 6. Warsaw: Lilly Frischmann, 1931.

Gallagher, Catherine, and Stephen Greenblatt. *Practicing New Historicism.* Chicago: Univ. of Chicago Press, 2000.

Galton, Francis. "Composite Portraits." *Journal of the Anthropological Institute of Great Britain and Ireland* 8 (Apr. 19, 1878): 132.

Gates, Henry Louis, Jr. *The Signifying Monkey: A Theory of African-American Literary Criticism.* New York: Oxford Univ. Press, 1988.

Gil, M. "Sipure Dvora Baron" (The Stories of Dvora Baron). *Gilyonot* 9 (1941): 144–49.

Gilbert, Sandra, and Susan Gubar. *The Madwoman in the Attic: The*

Woman Writer and the Nineteenth-Century Literary Imagination. New Haven: Yale Univ. Press, 1979.

Gitlin, Moshe. "bi-Neurehah: mi-Zikhronot ben Ir" (In Her Youth: Memories of a Neighbor). In *Agav Urkha: me-Izvonah, 'al Dvora Baron ve-Svivotah* (By the Way: From the Archives on Dvora Baron and Her Context), edited by Tziporah Aharonovitch. Israel: Poalim, 1960.

Gluzman, Michael. *The Politics of Canonicity: Lines of Resistance in Modernist Hebrew Poetry.* Stanford: Stanford Univ. Press, 2003.

Goelman, Eliezer. "ha-Meavak Neged 'Ivrit ke-Safah Meduberet" (The Struggle against Hebrew as a Spoken Tongue). *Bitsaron* (in Hebrew) 10, nos. 45–48 (1991): 141–46.

Gordon, Y. L. *Kitve Yehudah Leib Gordon (Prozah)* (Collected Works of Yehudah Leib Gordon [Prose]). Tel Aviv: Dvir, 1950.

———. *Kitve Yehudah Leib Gordon (Shirah)* (Collected Works of Yehudah Leib Gordon [Poetry]). Tel Aviv: Dvir, 1928.

———. *Mikhtave Yehudah Leib Gordon* (Letters of Yehudah Leib Gordon). Edited by Yitzhak Yaakov Weisberg. Warsaw: Brothers Shuldberg Press, 1882.

———. *Tsror Igrot Yalag el Miryam Markel Mozesohn* (Collected Letters of Yalag to Miriam Markel Mosesohn). Edited by Avraham Yaari. Jerusalem: Azriel, 1937.

Gottlober, Avraham bar. Editorial. *ha-Boker Or* (Morning Light) (in Hebrew) 4 (1869): 1065.

———. Editorial. *ha-Boker Or* (Morning Light) (in Hebrew) 2 (1877): 155.

Govrin, Nurit. *Alienation and Regeneration.* Tel Aviv: Mod Books, 1989.

———. *Dvash mi-Sel'a: Mehkarim be-Sifrut Eretz Yisrael* (Honey from a Rock: Studies in Israeli Literature). Tel Aviv: Ministry of Defense, 1989.

———. *ha-Mahatsit ha-Rishonah: Dvora Baron, Hayehah va-Yetsiratah (1887–1923)* (The First Half: Dvora Baron, Her Life and Work [1887–1923]). Jerusalem: Mosad Bialik, 1988.

———. "Nashim be-'Itonot ha-'Ivrit: ha-Hathalot" (Women in Hebrew Journalism: The Beginnings). *Kesher* (in Hebrew) 28 (Nov. 2000): 8–20.

Grozinski, Shlomo. "Dvora Baron: he-Hayim ha-Mesuparim" (Dvora Baron: The Narrated Life). *la-Merhav* (In the Open) (Sept. 5, 1956).

Gusdorf, Georges. "Conditions and Limits of Autobiography." In *Autobiography: Essays, Theoretical and Critical,* edited by James Olney. Princeton: Princeton Univ. Press, 1980.

Haberman, A. M. "Nusah Kadum shel Makor 'Agadat Shloshah ve-Arba'ah' " (An Earlier Source for "The Legend of the Three and Four"). *Moznayim* 40, no. 2 (Jan. 1975): 88–91.

Halkin, Simon. *Mavo le-Sifrut ha-Ivrit: Reshimot lefi hartsaotav bi-Shnat 5712* (Introduction to Hebrew Fiction: Lecture Notes from 1952). Jerusalem: Mifal ha-Shichpul, 1957.

Hamburger, Kate. *The Logic of Literature.* Translated by Marilynn J. Rose. Bloomington: Indiana Univ. Press, 1973.

Harari, Yehudit. "Huryah. " In *she-Ani Adamah ve-Adam: Sipure Nashim 'ad Kom ha-Medinah* (Tender Rib: Stories by Women-Writers in Pre-State Israel), edited by Yaffa Berlovitz. Israel: ha-Sifriyah ha-Hadashah, 2003.

————. *Ishah ve-'Em be-Yisrael: mi-Tekufat ha-Tanakh 'ad Shnat ha-'Asor li-Medinat Yisrael* (Woman and Mother in Israel: From Biblical Times until the First Decade of the State of Israel). Tel Aviv: Masada, 1958.

Haraway, Donna. "The Persistence of Vision." In *Writing on the Body: Female Embodiment and Feminist Theory,* edited by Katie Conboy, Nadia Medina, and Sarah Stanbury. New York: Columbia Univ. Press, 1997.

Harshav, Benjamin. *Language in Time of Revolution.* Berkeley and Los Angeles: Univ. of California Press, 1993.

Hasak-Lowy, Todd. "Between Realism and Modernism: Brenner's Poetics of Fragmentation." *Hebrew Studies* 49 (2003): 41–64.

Heilbrun, Carolyn G. "Non-Autobiographies of 'Privileged' Women: England and America." In *Lifelines: Theorizing Women's Autobiography,* edited by Celeste Schenck and Ella Brodzki. Ithaca: Cornell Univ. Press, 1988.

Heinemann, Joseph. *Drashot ba-Tsibur bi-Tekufat ha-Talmud* (Public Sermons During the Period of the Talmud). Tel Aviv: Mosad Bialik, 1970.

————. "Mesirat ha-'Agadot Ba'al Peh" (The Oral Transmission of Legends). In *Agadot ve-Toldotehen* (Legends and Their Origins), edited by Joseph Heinemann. Jerusalem: Bet Hotsa'at Keter, 1974.

Hendel, Yehudit. *Small Change: A Collection of Stories.* Hanover, N.H.: Brandeis Univ. Press, 2003.

Heschel, Abraham Joshua. *The Earth Is the Lord's.* New York: Harper Torchbooks, 1966.

Hever, Hannan. *Producing the Modern Hebrew Canon: Nation Building and Minority Discourse.* New York: New York Univ. Press, 2002.

Hirsch, Marianne. *Family Frames: Photography, Narrative and Post-Memory.* Cambridge: Harvard Univ. Press, 1997.

James, Henry. *The Ambassadors.* Cambridge: Riverside Press, 1960.

Jelen, Sheila. "Writing from the Pulpit, Speaking from the Page: The Oral Voices of Modern Hebrew Fiction." Ph.D. diss., Univ. of California at Berkeley, 2001.

Kacyzne, Alter. *Poyln: Jewish Life in the Old Country.* Edited by Marek Web. New York: Metropolitan Books; YIVO Institute for Jewish Research, 1999.

Kaderi, M. Z. 1978. " 'Iyun be-Toldot ha-Lashon ha-'Ivrit ha-Modernit" (A Study of the Evolution of Modern Hebrew). *Bikoret u-Farshanut* 11–12 (1978): 5–17.

Kahana-Carmon, Amalya. "The Song of the Bats in Flight." In *Gender and Text in Mondern Hebrew and Yiddish Literature,* edited by Naomi Sokoloff, Anne Lapidus Lerner, and Anita Norich. New York: Jewish Theological Seminary, 1992.

Katsir, Yehudit. "Dvora Baron: Mahazeh bi-Shtei Ma'arakhot" (Dvora Baron: A Play in Two Acts). In *ha-Antologyah ha-Hadashah* (The New Anthology), edited by Menachem Peri, vol. 2. Bene Brak: ha-Sifriyah ha-Hadashah, 2000.

Katznelson-Shazar, Rachel. "Dvora Baron." In *Dvora Baron: Mivhar Ma'amare Bikoret 'al Yetsiratah* (Dvora Baron: A Selection of Essays on Her Work), edited by Ada Pagis. Tel Aviv: Am Oved, 1974.

————. "Language Insomnia" (Nedude Lashon). In *Al Admat ha-Ivrit* (On the Soil of Hebrew), 231–41. Tel Aviv: Am Oved, 1966.

Kauffman, Linda S. *Discourses of Desire: Gender, Genre, and Epistolary Fictions.* Ithaca: Cornell Univ. Press, 1986.

Keshet, Yeshurun. "'Al Dvora Baron" (On Dvora Baron). In *Dvora Baron: Mivhar Ma'amare Bikoret 'al Yetsiratah* (Dvora Baron: A Selection of Essays on Her Work), edited by Ada Pagis. Tel Aviv: Am Oved, 1974.

Klausner, Joseph. *Historyah shel ha-Sifrut ha-'Ivrit ha-Hadashah* (The History of Modern Hebrew Literature). Jerusalem: Ahiasaf, 1960.

Klirs, Tracy Guren, Faedra Lazar Weiss, and Barbary Selya, eds. *The Merit of Our Mothers: A Bilingual Anthology of Women's Prayers.* Translated by Tracy Guren Klirs, Ida Cohen Selavan, and Gella Schweid Fishman. Cincinatti: Hebrew Union College, 2005.

Kronfeld, Chana. *On the Margins of Modernism: Decentering Literary Dynamics.* Berkeley and Los Angeles: Univ. of California Press, 1996.

Krutikov, Mikhail. "Berdichev in Russian Jewish Literary Imagination: From Israel Aksenfeld to Friedrich Gorenshtein." In *The Shtetl: Image and Reality,* edited by Gennady Estraikh and Mikhail Krutikov. Oxford: Legenda, 2000.

Kuhn, Annette. *Family Secrets: Acts of Memory and Imagination.* New York: Verso, 2002.

Lahover, Fishel. *Toldot ha-Sifrut ha-'Ivrit ha-Hadashah* (The History of Modern Hebrew Literature). Tel Aviv: Dvir, 1947.

Larnac, Jean. *Histoire de la literature féminine.* Paris: Kre, 1929.

Lieblich, Amia. *Conversations with Dvora: An Experimental Biography of the First Modern Hebrew Woman Writer.* Edited by Chana Kronfeld and Naomi Seidman. Translated by Naomi Seidman. Berkeley and Los Angeles: Univ. of California Press, 1997.

———. *Rekamot: Sihotai im Dvora Baron* (Embroideries: My Conversations with Dvora Baron). Jerusalem: Schocken, 1991.

Lubin, Orly. "Zutot mi-Mitbaha shel Nehama: Leumiut Alternativit *ba-ha-Golim* shel Dvora Baron" (Tidbits from Nehama's Kitchen: Alternative Nationalism in Dvora Baron's *The Exiles*). *Teoriah u-Vikoret* (Theory and Criticism) 7 (1995): 159–75.

Lukacs, Georg. *Studies in European Realism.* New York: Grosset and Dunlap, 1964.

Lyotard, Jean Franáois. *Heidegger and "the Jews."* Translated by Andreas

Michel and Mark S. Roberts. Minneapolis: Univ. of Minnesota Press, 1990.

Maimon, Solomon. *Solomon Maimon: An Autobiography.* Edited by Moshe Hadas. New York: Schocken Books, 1967.

Marcus, Ivan. *Rituals of Childhood: Jewish Acculturation in Medieval Europe.* New Haven: Yale Univ. Press, 1996.

Mcquire, Scott. *Visions of Modernity: Representation, Memory, Time and Space in the Age of the Camera.* London: Sage Publications, 1998.

Miller, David Neal. "Transgressing the Bounds: On the Origins of Yiddish Literature." In *Origins of the Yiddish Language,* edited by Dovid Katz. Oxford: Pergamon Press, 1985.

Miller, Nancy K. "Women's Autobiography in France." In *Lifelines: Theorizing Women's Autobiography,* edited by Celeste Schenck and Ella Brodzki. Ithaca: Cornell Univ. Press, 1988.

Mintz, Alan. *"Banished from Their Father's Table": Loss of Faith and Hebrew Autobiography.* Bloomington: Indiana Univ. Press, 1989.

———. *Hurban: Responses to Catastrophe in Jewish Literature.* New York: Columbia Univ. Press, 1984.

Miron, Dan. *Bodedim be-Moadam: le-Diyuknah shel ha-Republikah ha-Sifrutit ha-Ivrit bi-Tehilat ha-Meah ha-Esrim* (When Loners Come Together: A Portrait of Hebrew Literature at the Turn of the Twentieth Century). Tel Aviv: Am Oved, 1987.

———. *Imahot Meyasdot, Ahayot Horgot: Al shte hathalot ba-Shirah ha-Erets Yisraelit ha-Modernit* (Founding Mothers, Adopted Sisters: Two Beginnings for Modern Palestinian-Jewish Poetry). Tel Aviv: ha-Kibutz ha-Meuhad, 1991.

———. *The Literary Image of the Shtetl and Other Studies of Modern Jewish Literary Imagination.* Syracuse: Syracuse Univ. Press, 2000.

———. *A Traveler Disguised: The Rise of Modern Yiddish Fiction in the Nineteenth Century.* Syracuse: Syracuse Univ. Press, 1996.

Moskona-Lerman, Billy. "Malka ba-Armon Shahor" (Queen in a Black Palace). *Weekend Maariv,* Feb. 22, 1988.

Neusner, Jacob. "The Oral Torah and Oral Tradition: Defining the Problematic." In *Method and Meaning in Ancient Judaism,* edited by Jacob Neusner. Missoula, Mont.: Scholars Press, 1979.

Nir, Yeshayahu. 1995. "Photographic Representation and Social Interaction: The Case of the Holy Land." *History of Photography* 19, no. 3 (1995): 185–99.

Novak, Daniel. 2004. "A Model Jew: 'Literary Photographs' and the Jewish Body in *Daniel Deronda.*" *Representations* 85 (winter 2004): 58–97.

Ogen, Yitzhak. "Dvora Baron." *Gilyonot* (in Hebrew) 15, no. 3 (1943): 147–50.

Olney, James. "Autobiography and the Cultural Moment." In *Autobiography: Essays, Theoretical and Critical,* edited by James Olney. Princeton: Princeton Univ. Press, 1980.

Olsen, Victoria. *From Life: Julia Margaret Cameron and Victorian Photography.* New York: Palgrave Macmillan, 2003.

Oren, Ruth. "Zionist Photography, 1910–1941: Constructing a Landscape." *History of Photography* 19, no. 3 (1995): 201–9.

Ostriker, Alicia. *Stealing the Language: The Emergence of Women's Poetry in America.* Boston: Beacon, 1986.

Ozick, Cynthia. "Notes Toward Finding the Right Question." In *On Being a Jewish Feminist,* edited by Susanna Heschel. New York: Schocken, 1983.

Pagis, Ada. *Dvora Baron: Mivhar Ma'amare Bikoret 'al Yetsiratah* (Dvora Baron: A Selection of Essays on Her Work). Tel Aviv: Hotsa-at Am Oved, 1974.

Parush, Iris. 1996. "Mabat Aher 'al 'Hayey ha-'Ivrit ha-Metah;' hav'arot ha-mekhuvanot bi-Leshon ha-'Ivrit be-Hevrah ha-Yehudit ha-Mizrah Iropit ba-Me'ah ha-19 ve-hashpa'atah 'al ha-Sifrut ha-'Ivrit ve-Kore'hah" (Another Look at the Life of Dead Hebrew: Deliberate Obstruction of the Hebrew Language in 19th Century Eastern European Jewish Society and Its Influence on Hebrew Literature and Its Readers). *Alpayim* 13 (1996): 106–65.

———. *Reading Jewish Women: Marginality and Modernization in Nineteenth-Century Easter European Jewish Society.* Translated by Saadya Sternberg. Hanover, N.H.: Brandeis Univ. Press, 2004.

———. *Reading Women: The Advantages of Marginality.* Tel Aviv: Am Oved, 2001.

Peli, Moshe. "Tehiyat ha-Lashon Hahelah ba-Haskalah: *ha-Measef,* Ktav ha-'et ha-'Ivri ha-Rishon, ke-Makhshir le-Hidush ha-Safah" (The Revival of Hebrew Began During the Enlightenment: *ha-Measef,* the First Hebrew Journal as a Tool of the Revival). *Leshonenu la-Am* 50, no. 2 (2000): 59–75.

Pinchuk, Ben Cion. "Jewish Discourse and the Shtetl." *Jewish History* 15 (2001): 169–79.

Pinles, S. Y. "Mah she-Hayah" (What Has Been). *Gilyonot* 1 (1939): 59–61.

Pinsker, Shachar. "Old Wine in New Flasks." Ph.D. diss., Univ. of California at Berkeley, 2001.

Raider, Mark A., and Miriam B. Raider-Roth, trans. and eds. *The Plough Woman: Records of the Pioneer Women of Palestine, a Critical Edition.* Hanover, N.H.: Brandeis Univ. Press, 2002.

Rakovsky, Puah. *My Life as a Radical Jewish Woman: Memoirs of a Zionist Feminist in Poland.* Edited by Paula E. Hyman. Translated by Barbara Harshav. Bloomington: Indiana Univ. Press, 2002.

Rattok, Lily. *ha-Kol he-Aher: Siporet Nashim 'Ivrit* (The Other Voice: Women's Fiction in Hebrew). Israel: ha-Sifriyah ha-Hadashah, 1994.

Renan, Ernest. "What Is a Nation?" In *Nation and Narration,* edited by Homi K. Bhabha. London: Routledge, 1990.

Robertson, Ritchie. "Historicizing Weininger: The 19th Century German Image of the Feminized Jew." In *Modernity, Culture and "the Jew,"* edited by Bryan Cheyette and Laura Marcus. Stanford: Stanford Univ. Press, 1998.

Rose, Gillian. *Judaism and Modernity: Philosophical Essays.* Oxford: Blackwell, 1993.

Rosenblum, Naomi. *A History of Women Photographers.* New York: Abbeville Press, 2000.

Roskies, David. "The Shtetl as Imagined Community." In *The Shtetl: Image and Reality,* edited by Gennady Estraikh and Mikhail Krutikov. Oxford: Legenda, 2000.

Roskies, Diane, and David Roskies. *The Shtetl Book.* New York: Ktav Publishing House, 1975.

Sadan, Dov. *'Al Sifrutenu* (On Our Literature). Jerusalem: Reuven Mass, 1950.

Sandler, Martin W. *Against the Odds: Women Pioneers in the First Hundred Years of Photography.* New York: Rizzoli, 2002.

Schenck, Celeste. "All of a Piece: Women's Poetry and Autobiography." In *Lifelines: Theorizing Women's Autobiography,* edited by Celeste Schenck and Ella Brodzki. Ithaca: Cornell Univ. Press, 1988.

Scholem, Gershom. *Von Berlin nach Jerusalem* (From Berlin to Jerusalem). Tel Aviv: Am Oved, 1982.

Seidman, Naomi. *A Marriage Made in Heaven: The Sexual Politics of Hebrew and Yiddish.* Vols. 1–2. Berkeley and Los Angeles: Univ. of California Press, 1997.

Shaked, Gershon. *ha-Siporet ha-Ivrit* (Hebrew Literature). Vol. 1, *ha-Golah* (The Exile). Israel: ha-Kibutz ha-Meuhad, 1977.

Shamir, Ziva, ed. *Sadan: Studies in Hebrew Literature: Selected Essays on Women's Hebrew Poetry.* Vol. 2. Tel Aviv: Tel Aviv Univ. Press, 1996.

Shapira, Anita. *Land and Power: The Zionist Resort to Force, 1881–1948.* Translated by William Templer. Oxford: Oxford Univ. Press, 1992.

———. *Yehudim Hadashim Yehudim Yeshanim* (New Jews Old Jews). Tel Aviv: Am Oved, 1997.

Shavit, Zohar. *Hayim ha-Sifrutiim be-Eretz Yisrael, 1910–1933* (Literary Life in the Land of Israel, 1910–1933). Tel Aviv: ha-Kibuts ha-Meuhad, 1982.

Shmeruk, Chone. "Di Mizrah-Europesheh Nusahaos fun der Tzenerene (1850–1786)" (The Eastern European Versions of the *Tzenerene* [1850–1786]). In *Max Weinreich, for His Seventieth Birthday: Studies in Jewish Languages, Literature and Society,* edited by Lucy S. Dawidowicz, Alexander Erlich, Rachel Erlich, and Joshua A. Fishman. The Hague: Morton and Kay, 1964.

———. *Sifrut Yiddish: Perakim le-Toldotehah* (Yiddish Literature: Chapters in Its Evolution). Tel Aviv: Porter Institute for Poetics and Semiotics, Tel Aviv Univ., 1978.

———. *Sifrut Yiddish ba-Polin: Mehkarim be-'Iyunim Histori'im* (Yiddish Literature in Poland: Studies and Historical Overviews). Jerusalem: Magnes, 1981.

Shohat, Azriel. "Yehasam shel Maskilim be-Rusyah el Lashon ha-'Ivrit" (The Relationship of Russian Enlighteners to the Hebrew Language). In *Sefer Avraham Even Shoshan: Studies in Language, Bible,*

Literature, and the Land of Israel (in Hebrew), edited by B. Z. Luria. Jerusalem: Kiryat Sefer, 1987.

Silver-Brody, Vivienne. *Documenters of the Dream: Pioneer Jewish Photographers in the Land of Israel, 1890–1933.* Philadelphia: Jewish Publication Society, 1998.

Silverman, Max. 1998. "Refiguring 'the Jew' in France." In *Modernity, Culture and "the Jew,"* edited by Bryan Cheyette and Laura Marcus. Stanford: Stanford Univ. Press, 1998.

Sivan, Reuven. *The Revival of the Hebrew Language.* Jerusalem: E. Rubinstein, 1980.

Soloveitchik, Haym. "Rupture and Reconstruction: The Transformation of American Orthodoxy." *Tradition* 28, no. 4 (1994): 64–130.

Sontag, Susan. *On Photography.* New York: Farrar, Strauss, and Giroux. 1974.

Stampfer, Shaul. "Gender Differentiation and Education of the Jewish Woman in Nineteenth-Century Eastern Europe." In *From Shtetl to Socialism: Studies from Polin,* edited by Anthony Polonsky. London: Littman Library of Jewish Civilization, 1993.

———. "Heder Study, Knowledge of Torah and the Maintenance of Social Stratification in Traditional East European Jewish Society." In *Studies in Jewish Education,* edited by Janet Aviad. 3d ed. Jerusalem: Magnes Press, 1988.

Steiner, George. "Our Homeland, the Text." *Salgamundi* 66 (winterspring 1985): 4–25.

Stern, David. *Parables in Midrash.* Cambridge: Harvard Univ. Press, 1991.

Stock, Brian. *Listening for the Text: On the Uses of the Past.* Baltimore: Johns Hopkins Univ. Press, 1990.

Stories Form [sic] *Women Writers of Israel.* New Delhi: Star Publications, 1995.

Sullivan, Constance, ed. *Women Photographers.* New York: Abrams, 1990.

Svirsky, Yosef. "Dapim Mitokh Pinkasai: Perakim mi-Tokh Sefer Zikhronotai mi-Yerushalayim" (Pages from My Notebooks: Chapters from My Jerusalem Memoirs). *Yeda Am* 33–34 (1967–1968): 108–16.

Uvasi, Y. "Dvora Baron." In *Masot u-Ma'marim* (Essays and Articles). New York: Ohel, 1947.

Weinreich, Max. "Ineveynikste Tsvey Shpra'khikeyt In Ashkenaz Biz Der Haskoloh: Faktn un Bagrifn" (Internal Bilinguialism in Ashkenaz until the Haskalah: Facts and Concepts). *Goldene Keyt* 35 (1959): 3–11.

Weissberg, Liliane. "Bodies in Pain: Reflections on the Berlin Jewish Salon." In *The German Jewish Dialogue Reconsidered: A Symposium in Honor of George L. Mosse,* edited by Klaus L. Berghahn. New York: Peter Lang, 1996.

Weissler, Chava. "For Women and for Men Who Are Like Women: The Construction of Gender in Yiddish Devotional Literature." *Journal of Feminist Studies in Religion* 5, no. 2 (1989): 7–24.

———. *Voices of the Matriarchs: Listening to the Prayers of Early Modern Jewish Women.* Boston: Beacon, 1998.

Werman, Golda. Introduction to *The Stories of David Bergelson: Yiddish Short Fiction from Russia,* by David Bergelson. Translated by Golda Werman. Syracuse: Syracuse Univ. Press, 1996.

Wersses, Shmuel. "Portrait of the Makil as a Young Man." In *New Perspectives on the Haskalah,* edited by Shmuel Feiner and David Sorkin. Oxford: Littman Library of Jewish Civilization, 2001.

Woolf, Virginia. *A Room of One's Own.* New York: Harcourt Brace and World, 1957.

Zarhi, Nurit. "Madame Bovary in Neveh Tzedek" (Madame Bovary bi-Neveh Tzedek). In *Oman ha-Masekhot* (The Mask Maker). Tel Aviv: Zmora Bitan, 1993.

Zborowski, Mark, and Elizabeth Herzog. *Life Is with People: The Culture of the Shtetl.* New York: Schocken, 1972.

Zemel, Carol. "Imaging the Shtetl: Diaspora Culture, Photography and Eastern European Jews." In *Diaspora and Visual Culture,* edited by Nicholos Mirzoeff. London: Routledge, 2000.

Zerubavel, Jacob. "Me-inyana de-Yomah" (Issues of the Day). *Ha-Achdut* 5, no. 36 (1914): col. 8.

Zierler, Wendy. *And Rachel Stole the Idols: The Emergence of Modern Hebrew Women's Writing.* Detroit: Wayne State Univ. Press, 2004.

Index

Italic page number denotes illustration.

New Criticism, xxviii
New Historical criticism, xxviii-xxix
"new Jew," 44
New Way *(ha-Mahalakh ha-Hadash)*
    movement, 55–56
Nister, Der, 195n. 16
Nomberg, H. D., 55
Nordau, Max, 44
"nusah" literary idiom, 54, 79, 82–83,
    100, 111

objectivity, 78
"Of Bygone Days" (Abramowitz), 79
Ogen, Yitzhak, 25, 32
Olney, James, xxv
Olsen, Victoria, 61
Only Yesterday (Agnon), 48
orality: "Abandoned Wife" blurring
    distinction between textuality and,
    91–92, 95; Baron's oral exposure to
    literary texts, xliii, 81, 83; Bialik on life
    for spoken languages, 109; as
    interwoven with textuality in Baron's
    vernacular literature, 98; midrashim
    seen as transcriptions of sermons, 85;
    and textuality as diachronic
    phenomena, 201n. 28; and textuality
    in Abramowitz's Hebrew writings,
    111, 204n. 28
Ozick, Cynthia, 102–3

Pagis, Ada, 179, 184
Pahenheim, Solomon, xxx
Palestine: as-if mimesis and
    construction of Hebrew-speaking
    society in, 33–34; Baron's stories set
    in, 47–50; Hebrew language as official
    language in, 114; Hebrew language

for stories about, 113; local mimesis
    of writers in, 57; photographs of to
    encourage migration, 52; Tel Aviv, xxi,
    34, 36; women Hebrew poets of
    1920s, 7; writers losing their way after
    coming to, 206n. 4. *See also* Yishuv
parables: in "Abandoned Wife," 87–90,
    92–95, 97–98; in Baron's literary
    universe, 120; in "Family," 97
Parshiyot (Tales) (Baron), xxii, 32, 81,
    175
Parush, Iris, 103
Paul, Saint, 3
Penny Books *(Sifre Agurah)*, 55, 56
Peretz, Y. L., 37, 121, 204n. 26, 206n. 42
Perl, Joseph, 36
photography: and Baron's mediational
    imperative, 57; Benjamin on, 69–70,
    76; democratizing potential of, 71–73;
    development of, 197n. 18; early
    women photographers, 61; exchanges
    between Eastern Europe and U.S.,
    51–52; Galton's "composite," 64;
    generic photographs, 67–68; in "In
    the Beginning," 52–53; as most
    mimetic of the arts, 33; negatives,
    60–62, 68–71, 73–74, 78, 197n. 18; of
    Palestine to encourage migration, 52;
    and realism, 62, 64, 70; from the
    shtetl, 62–67; in "The Thorny Path,"
    74–77; in "What Has Been," 60–62,
    68–71, 73–74, 78
Pinchuk, Ben Cion, 38, 39, 40–41
Pinles, S. Y., 25, 42, 196n. 23
Pinsker, Shachar, 179, 184, 200n. 26
Plato, 33
Plough Woman, The (Katznelson-
    Shazar), 116
ha-Poel ha-Tsair (The Young Laborer)
    (newspaper), xxi, xl, 130, 192n. 43

thick description, xxix
"Thorny Path, The" (Baron), 74–77
Thorny Path and Other Stories, The
 (Baron), 176
Three Stories (Baron), 176
tkhines, 101–2; in "Burying the Books"
 ("Genizah"), 100–101, 106, 107, 108,
 112–13, 119, 126; lowly status of, 107,
 202n. 15; variety of, 201n. 2
tlishut. See uprootedness
"Transformations" ("Gilgulim")
 (Baron), 117
transitional mimesis, 34, 35–36, 37, 53,
 54, 68, 76–78
Trifles (Ketanot) (Baron), xxii, 32,
 173–74
Tschernikhovsky, Saul, 7
Turniansky, Chava, 204n. 25
"Two Camps" (Berdischevsky), 38,
 39
Tzenerene, 102–4; in "Burying the
 Books" ("Genizah"), 100–101, 106–8,
 112–13, 126; as metacommentary,
 105; as middle ground between male
 and female textual worlds, 107;
 sources of, 202n. 12

uprootedness *(tlishut)*, xlii; in "As a
 Driven Leaf," 48; in Baron's work, xlii,
 24, 25–26, 27–28, 36, 43; in *The Exiles*,
 49; in Sender Ziv trilogy, 6, 31. *See
 also talush*
Uvasi, Y., 26, 32

Varnikovsky, Miriam, xli
vernacular, the, 79–98; Abramowitz's
 "nusah" idiom, 54, 79, 82–83, 100,
 111; vernacular imperative of

modern Hebrew renaissance,
 xliii, 79–80; vernacular mimesis,
 54
Vishniac, Roman, 69

Weinberger, Miriam, 179, 184–85
Weininger, Otto, 4
Weinreich, Max, 203n. 18
Weisel, Naftali Hertz, xxx
Weissler, Chava, 201n. 2, 202n. 15
Wersses, Shmuel, 10, 13
What Has Been (Baron), 32, 174
"What Has Been" (Baron): erudition of
 narrator in, 73–74; and the
 Holocaust, 43; narrator as literary
 mediator in, 28–29; narrator as
 photographic negative in, 60–62, 68,
 77–78; narrator becoming dominant
 voice in the story, 30–31; and
 transitional mimesis, 68–71
Wolf, Shana, xxxiii
women: abandoned woman as
 metaphor for exile, 41; advantages
 over men in traditional scholarly
 study, 103; in Baron's stories set in
 Palestine, 47–50; in Baron's treatment
 of the shtetl, xvii, xix, 32; Bible
 depicting female predicaments, 83;
 biblical narratives known by, 84; in
 classic shtetl narratives, 41–42; and
 democratizing potential of
 photography, 71–72; family purity
 laws for, xviii, 75, 199n. 40; and
 feminization of the "Jew," 4, 13–14;
 and Hebrew language, xxxiii–xxxviii,
 110; individual prayer of, 130–31;
 little chance of finding place in the
 Yishuv, 116–18; *tkhines* for, 101–2,
 107, 202n. 15; *Tzenerene* for, 102–4;